PLAYS OF THE YEAR SPECIAL

EDITED BY
J. C. TREWIN

ELIZABETH R

The Lion's Cub
John Hale

The Marriage Game
Rosemary Anne Sisson

Shadow in the Sun
Julian Mitchell

Horrible Conspiracies
Hugh Whitemore

The Enterprise of England
John Prebble

Sweet England's Pride
Ian Rodger

FREDERICK UNGAR PUBLISHING
COMPANY
NEW YORK

Published in 1972 by
PAUL ELEK LIMITED
54–58 Caledonian Road
London, N1 9RN

ISBN 0-8044-2885-9

Made and printed in Great Britain

CONTENTS

CONTENTS

LIST OF ILLUSTRATIONS

The above illustrations are reproduced by courtesy of the British Broadcasting Corporation.

INTRODUCTION

The six splendidly-organized television plays in this book follow the sequence on King Henry VIII and his wives. They tell the story of Elizabeth I, Queen of England and Ireland, King Henry's child by his second wife Anne Boleyn, to whom he was married secretly in January 1533. In September of that year the Princess Elizabeth was born. In November 1558, at the age of twenty-five, and upon the death of her elder half-sister, Mary I, she was proclaimed Queen: a Queen who inherited much of her mother's beauty. On 24 March 1603 she died at Richmond, aged sixty-nine. Her tomb is in Westminster Abbey.

A recital of historical facts can sound bare enough, chilling the drama of an intensely dramatic reign. But these plays of *Elizabeth R*, a royal progress in which six authors have shared, both animate history and clarify it. This is indeed, and excitingly, Gloriana's world.

No English monarch, with the exception of her father, has inspired so many writers: fittingly because she was a tireless patron of literature and of the developing stage. At the end of her reign the greatest of all dramatists, William Shakespeare, was at his zenith; previously he had spoken of Elizabeth, through the mouth of Oberon in *A Midsummer Night's Dream*, as 'the fair vestal throned by the west . . . the imperial votaress.' To use now the epithet 'Elizabethan' means a time of new discovery and new hope, a world expanding, an

A*

age—it has been said—of the sword and the madrigal. It was a cruel world also, desperate in its divisions and its angers. No monarch had to be more of a diplomatist than the imperious ruler who was called the Virgin Queen, and who rigidly put her country before herself.

She would live for us, if we knew nothing else about her, in three of her famous sayings. This for one:

I am your anointed Queen. I will never be by violence constrained to do anything. I thank God I am endued with such qualities that if I were turned out of the realm in my petticoat, I were able to live in any place in Christendom.

And this:

As for me, I see no great cause why I should either be fond to live or fear to die. I have had good experience of this world, and I know what it is to be a subject and what to be a sovereign. Good neighbours I have had, and I have met with bad; and in trust I have found treason.

Finally this, from the speech at Tilbury in 1588 after the news of the sailing of the Spanish Armada towards England (it can be found in *The Enterprise of England*, the fifth play in the series):

I know I have the body of a weak and feeble woman, but I have the heart and stomach of a king; and of a king of England too; and think foul scorn that Parma or Spain, or any prince of Europe, should dare to invade the borders of my realm.

There is the voice of the last of the great Tudors: a woman of redoubtable courage, used since girlhood to the perils and the responsibilities of her birth. She was (as the first play-title says) 'the lion's cub': 'Though I may not be a lion, I am a lion's cub and I have a lion's heart.' A haunted poem of our own century begins: 'Queen Bess was Harry's daughter.' From her father, says a historian, she took her 'dauntless courage and her amazing self-confidence. Her harsh manlike voice, her impetuous will, her pride, her furious outbursts of anger, came to her with her Tudor blood . . . But strangely in contrast stood the sensuous, self-indulgent nature she derived from Anne Boleyn'.

The actress, Glenda Jackson, proved in these television plays that she could bear the burden of a complex part as surely as Keith Michell who was the Henry of the earlier sequence. In six strongly dramatic texts we find Elizabeth in and before (the first scene is nine years before) the turmoil of history's most resplendent reign: we move from her daunting girlhood to those final years when winter had stolen at last upon the glory of the Tudor rose. To the end she was Elizabeth the Queen. 'Must!' she exclaimed to Cecil when he urged her to go to her bed. 'Is *must* a word to be addressed to princes?'

J. C. TREWIN

I am most grateful to my colleague, Mrs Judith Rayner, for her expert collaboration in the editing of this book.

Hampstead, London
1971

THE LION'S CUB

by
JOHN HALE

© *John Hale 1971*

The Lion's Cub was first shown on BBC television on February 17 1971, as the first play in a series entitled *Elizabeth R* with the following cast:

ELIZABETH I	*Glenda Jackson*
SIR WILLIAM CECIL	*Ronald Hines*
MARY TUDOR	*Daphne Slater*
KAT ASHLEY	*Rachel Kempson*
THOMAS CRANMER	*Bernard Hepton*
BISHOP GARDINER	*Basil Dignam*
PHILIP OF SPAIN	*Peter Jeffrey*
LADY TYRWHIT	*Nicolette Bernard*
SIR ROBERT TYRWHIT	*Stanley Lebor*
EDWARD VI	*Jason Kemp*
THOMAS SEYMOUR	*John Ronane*
JOHN PARRY	*Blake Butler*
ANTOINE DE NOAILLES	*Julian Holloway*
SENOR RENARD	*Brendan Barry*
SIR THOMAS WYATT	*Robert Garrett*
SIR HENRY BEDINGFIELD	*Alan Foss*
BRIDGES, LIEUTENANT OF THE TOWER	*Kevin Brennan*
THE EARL OF SUSSEX	*John Shrapnel*
JOHN DUDLEY, EARL OF WARWICK	*Philip Brack*
JOHN FOWLER	*Ian Barritt* (doubling Chaplain)
GUARD	*Richard Parry*
LADY JANE GREY	*Sarah Frampton*
GUILDFORD	*Robert Barry*
CATHERINE PARR	*Rosalie Crutchley*
GAOLER	*Ronald Mayer*
COURTIERS	*Dilys Marvin, Olive Mercer, Audrey Searle, Daphne Davey, Christine Cole, James Haswell, George Howse, Eden Fox, Paul Phillips, George Hancock*
YEOMEN	*Patrick Milner, Denis Balcombe, Geoff Witherick, Vic Taylor, George Romanov, Terry Sartin*
LIVERIED GUARDS	*Kedd Senton, Charles Finch, Barry Kennington, Frank Dunn*
MAIDS	*Margaret Lake, Ann Plenty, John Harsant*

Producer Roderick Graham
Director Claude Whatham
Designer Peter Seddon

CHARACTERS

ELIZABETH I

SIR WILLIAM CECIL

MARY TUDOR

KAT ASHLEY

THOMAS CRANMER

BISHOP GARDINER

PHILIP OF SPAIN

LADY TYRWHIT

SIR ROBERT TYRWHIT

EDWARD VI

THOMAS SEYMOUR

JOHN PARRY

ANTOINE DE NOAILLES

SENOR RENARD

SIR THOMAS WYATT

SIR HENRY BEDINGFIELD

BRIDGES, LIEUTENANT OF THE TOWER

THE EARL OF SUSSEX

JOHN DUDLEY, EARL OF WARWICK

JOHN FOWLER

GUARD

LADY JANE GREY

GUILDFORD

CATHERINE PARR

INTERIORS

A gallery at the palace
Ante-room
Royal bedroom
Elizabeth's bedroom
Corridor at Hatfield
Ante-chamber at Hatfield
The hall at Hatfield
Treasurer's room at Hatfield
Small cell in the Tower
Chapel
Elizabeth's apartment at Whitehall
Large cell at the Tower
Passageway in the Tower

EXTERIORS

A walled garden
Country road
Wyatt's capture
Elizabeth in a litter
Traitor's Gate

TIME

1549–1558

1

Interior, gallery, palace. Night. 1549.

Guards outside door of King's bedroom. Night. Freezing. 17 January 1549. Thomas Seymour, Lord High Admiral, brother of Protector Somerset, in company with John Fowler, Secretary to King Edward VI, move fast, confidently, along a gallery at the Palace of Westminster.

Interior, gallery. Night.

They reach a door. Seymour has a master key. He unlocks the door.

Interior, first ante-room. Night.

Seymour and Fowler enter a small ante-room. They move to another door and unlock it and enter.

Interior, second ante-room. Night.

Fowler moves quickly to a large press and begins to take out travelling clothes for the King. Seymour moves to the door of the royal bedroom.

Interior, royal bedroom. Night.

In the bedroom the curtains are drawn round the four-poster bed. The royal arms are prominent on the hangings. Seymour looks round to see how Fowler is succeeding with the selection of clothes. Then he walks quietly but with complete confidence to the bed. He draws the curtains and we see the King sleeping with a dog at his feet. The spaniel, which he has not seen, barks like a demented thing. Seymour falls back. He draws his sword.

Interior, second ante-room. Night.

In the ante-room Fowler has dropped the clothes in panic.

Interior, royal bedroom. Night.

Inside the bedroom we see Seymour stepping back. We see blood on the sword. There is a pause. The King, a cold, pale, solitary child of great intelligence, condemned to death by the inherited taint from his father's syphilis, gets from bed. He is coughing so that he can barely stand. He recovers. He forces himself to stand upright.

Interior, second ante-room. Night.

Fowler watches, horrified. Guards enter and take him.

Interior, royal bedroom. Night.

In the King's bedroom a circle of armed men forms round Seymour, who revolves slowly, sword in hand. A pause. A gap opens and the King moves through to face Seymour. Edward looks, apparently without emotion, at the intruders.

EDWARD : Why are you here, Uncle?

(*No reply.*)

And you, Master Fowler?

(*No reply. The head of the Dudley family, John Dudley,*

Earl of Warwick, future Duke of Northumberland, enters.)

DUDLEY: Your Majesty, are you harmed?

EDWARD: I am cold.

DUDLEY (*to guard*): How did they enter? Answer me.

SEYMOUR: Leave him. (*He drops the keys at Dudley's feet.*) I have a key to every door in the palace.

DUDLEY: Then you will be tried for it.

SEYMOUR: I have the trust of the King. I have it. Not the Council and not my brother, the Protector. I have it. *I am the friend and guardian of his Majesty.* (*He looks to Edward with confidence. Complete confidence.*)

EDWARD (*to the captain of the guard*): Take the dog and bury it.

SEYMOUR: I'll bring you another dog tomorrow. A litter to choose from, your Grace.

EDWARD: We believe this matter tends to treason. Arrest the Lord High Admiral and Master Fowler. Take them away.

(*Seymour is incredulous.*)

SEYMOUR: Your Majesty—

EDWARD: Go now.

(*Dudley takes Seymour out into the ante-room.*)

Interior, ante-room. Night.

The guards are coming through. The bedroom door is closed. Seymour and Dudley close together.

9

SEYMOUR: He's ill. That is the reason. His Majesty is ill.

DUDLEY: You have lost, my Lord.

(*Seymour is going from shock to panic.*)

SEYMOUR: I paid his debts.

DUDLEY: We shall investigate every source of money to your purse.

SEYMOUR: I told him how to be a true king.

DUDLEY: We shall investigate your dealings as Lord High Admiral.

SEYMOUR: I gave him my trust.

DUDLEY: We shall investigate your reason for attempting to abduct his Majesty.

SEYMOUR: I was his only friend.

DUDLEY: No, my Lord, he had another. And for many months she lived under your roof. We shall investigate your dealings with the Princess Elizabeth.

2

Interior, Elizabeth's bedroom. Day.

In her bedroom Elizabeth, the King's half-sister, jerks awake to the sound of voices in distress. The sound of feet marching, weapons clinking. The voices are those of her Treasurer Parry, and of her long-time nurse, mistress, confidante and loving friend, Kat Ashley. The sounds should be distorted, nightmarish and fading, as the Princess, at this point aged seventeen, wakes, gets out of bed. She should appear very solitary in the chamber.

ELIZABETH: Kat! Kat Ashley.

Interior, corridor (Hatfield). Day.

Kat Ashley and Parry are hurried down corridor.

Interior, Elizabeth's bedroom. Day.

Elizabeth gets out of bed and goes to door.

Interior, ante-chamber. Day.

Elizabeth enters and goes to door.

Interior, hall. Day.

Elizabeth walks along hall.

ELIZABETH: Kat Ashley!

Interior, corridor with stairs. Day.

Elizabeth comes down stairs and moves forward to camera.

ELIZABETH: Kat Ashley!

Interior, corridor with door. Day.

Elizabeth enters and stops at door.

ELIZABETH: Kat Ashley!

Interior, hall outside Treasurer's room. Day.

Elizabeth looking at door. She turns and runs to Treasurer's room and enters.

11

3

Interior, Treasurer's room. Day.

The room has been ransacked. On a table are the account books, all open. Sir Robert Tyrwhit bows correctly but deliberately says nothing. He is the kind of man who later on would have served Cromwell extremely well.

ELIZABETH: Sir Robert Tyrwhit.

TYRWHIT: Your Grace.

ELIZABETH: Where are my people?

TYRWHIT: I am sent by the Council by order of the King.

(Elizabeth has grown up with four step-mothers. Her mother was executed, and her most loving step-mother, Howard, was also executed. Her father had her disinherited and then reinstated. Her sister is a fervent Catholic with an undying hatred of her mother and, in a sense, of her too. Her brother is a strange, cold and remote child, governed by a council jostling for personal power and Elizabeth is both afraid and has a guilty secret which could finish her. Nothing that she says in public or to a stranger is uncalculated, and she is only indiscreet under great stress. She, immediately, is in command of herself.)

ELIZABETH: I pray that his Majesty is well.

TYRWHIT: He is well.

ELIZABETH: I long to see him. I long to come to Court.

TYRWHIT: Your Mistress Ashley and your Treasurer, Parry are arrested.

(*Elizabeth immediately bursts into tears.*)

ELIZABETH: No! No! What have they done?

TYRWHIT: The rest of your household are forbidden your presence during the time I am here to question you.

ELIZABETH (*outburst*): I will not be questioned. I am Elizabeth.

TYRWHIT: You are but a subject, lady. I tell you plainly when there is a question of treason you are as any other subject and you will answer.

ELIZABETH: What treason?

TYRWHIT: You will not question, your Grace. You will answer.

ELIZABETH: So I will, Master Tyrwhit, because anything that threatens my loved brother, his Majesty, threatens every loyal subject.

TYRWHIT: Thomas Seymour, the Lord High Admiral, is in the Tower.

(*Elizabeth is terrified.*)

I see you are moved by this news.

ELIZABETH: He was my guardian and my friend. He and my dear step-mother, Catherine.

TYRWHIT: She is dead, lady. But you are alive and young and a great prize—and the Admiral has proposed marriage to you.

ELIZABETH: No.

TYRWHIT: You agreed to marry him.

13

ELIZABETH: No.

TYRWHIT: It is treason for any subject to attempt marriage in secret to an heir to the throne.

ELIZABETH: All the world knows that.

TYRWHIT: And it is forbidden you to attempt marriage in the lifetime of his Majesty without the permission of the Council.

ELIZABETH: I will never marry. Never. Never. Never.

TYRWHIT: You were misled. You were flattered. The Admiral is handsome. Even his Majesty misplaced his trust in the Admiral. The Council will protect you from your youth and inexperience—confess your dealings fully—the blame will be taken by Mistress Ashley and Thomas Parry who worked in the interests of Seymour.

ELIZABETH: They are my true and loyal servants.

TYRWHIT: When we came to arrest Parry, your loyal servant, he took his chain of office from his neck and threw it down. Here it is. And he was distraught as any guilty man would be, and he said: 'I would to God I had never had dealings with the Admiral.'

ELIZABETH: Tell the Council I have done nothing wrong.

TYRWHIT: It is generally believed that you are with child by Seymour.

ELIZABETH: I will not have such vile and filthy rumours spoken.

TYRWHIT: It is spoken.

ELIZABETH: I will not have my honour impugned.

TYRWHIT: Then confess.

14

ELIZABETH: I will not have the people taught to think ill of me while I am kept here helpless without servants. Tell the Council—

TYRWHIT: You may write to them.

ELIZABETH: They shall deny it by proclamation, or let them bring me to Court where all men can see that I am not with child. Let me face my accusers.

TYRWHIT: You have a guilty look and a guilty manner.

ELIZABETH: It is anger and shame to hear such monstrous charges.

TYRWHIT: No subject can love the King and have Seymour as a friend.

ELIZABETH: I have not seen the Admiral since he was my guardian.

TYRWHIT (*the anger is genuine*): He planned to marry the King to Lady Jane Grey, whose wardship he bought for two thousand pounds. He came by night to take the King.

ELIZABETH: I know nothing of these matters.

TYRWHIT: He planned two marriages, his Majesty to Lady Jane, and the Admiral himself to you. Thus he would hold England in his hands. His chaplain was waiting to perform the ceremonies in his apartments that night.

ELIZABETH: Do you believe me such a fool that I would act without the consent of the good Protector and the Council in any question, no matter how small, that would bear upon the succession?

TYRWHIT: The penalty for treason for a woman is decapitation or burning. (*Deliberately.*) Remember the death of your mother, your Grace.

15

(It is as if Elizabeth had been struck. She nearly faints. At no time in her life is it recorded that she ever spoke of her mother, certainly not by name.)

ELIZABETH *(gasping)*: You are here not to trap the Admiral, but to destroy me. If you have proof of the Admiral's treason, then you need nothing from me.

TYRWHIT: The Council will decide.

ELIZABETH: By law you may condemn him now.

(She turns and runs from the room.)

4

Interior, corridor. Day.

Elizabeth running. She stops, panting.

Exterior, walled garden. Day.

A small, handsome, walled garden in summer. Kat Ashley is approaching her, the camera, with flowers. Kat Ashley is suggestive, and gossipy, full of old wives' tales and warm hearted and randy and silly, and the only friend that Elizabeth has had or has in the world. In this scene Elizabeth is the camera.

ASHLEY: But I tell you, if he could have had you, my Lady, he would not have married the Queen Dowager.

(Elizabeth out of view laughs at her and starts to turn away. Ashley, her face close to Elizabeth's and the tone softer:)

ASHLEY: Don't blush, don't blush. It is true. He spoke of it himself. He asked the Council and his brother, the Protector. He is a fine man and he would die for you.

16

(In the background a wedding party is approaching. Seymour, Catherine the Dowager Queen, now his wife, their attendants and in particular, Lady Tyrwhit who carries the train of the Queen Dowager's dress. Establish her.)

He's a fine man in bed and out.

(She turns and runs to present the flowers to Catherine, the Dowager Queen. Elizabeth follows and as Catherine takes the flowers, smiling, Seymour turns for a moment to look at Elizabeth. It is a very calculating look.)

Interior, Elizabeth's bedroom. Night.

Inside the bed curtains of Elizabeth's bed. The curtains are suddenly ripped open. Seymour—beard and glittering eye and sensual lips and shining teeth, and all the rest of it as seen from the point of view of an excited, frightened, and that complex of sexual emotions of early puberty—Seymour looking down at the girl's face, the camera, on the pillow—Seymour leaning in— Seymour dressed only in his nightgown, bare legs and feet because it's as farcical as it is sexual. Seymour putting a hand on Elizabeth.

SEYMOUR: Up, up, my Lady. You are lazy lying abed. Come let me help you.

(He starts to tickle her. She is giggling and wriggling. Suddenly Ashley is there in the background, eighty per cent shocked and twenty per cent titillated, almost hauling him off her charge.)

ASHLEY: My Lord, my Lord. This is wrong. Go at once.

SEYMOUR: Wrong? To get the child from bed.

ASHLEY: The princess is *fourteen*, Lord Admiral. If

17

anything goes amiss I shall bear the blame. Leave us for shame.

SEYMOUR (*blustering and going*): I'm her guardian by God's wounds and I'll do as I choose.

ASHLEY: Then I will speak with the Queen, your wife.

SEYMOUR: Do so. I shall speak to the Council of you, mistress.

(*He goes. Ashley turns. Elizabeth is giggling. Ashley starts to laugh.*

Interior, hall. Day.

ELIZABETH: How could I help it?

Exterior, walled garden. Day.

In another Season. At any rate the clothes of Seymour and Catherine are different from their wedding clothes that we saw last. They are chasing Elizabeth, the camera, it seems like ordinary tag, but suddenly Seymour has her in his arms. Catherine, nearby, runs to hold her. Seymour steps clear and draws his dagger, and the phallic significance may be made clear because next as Elizabeth screams and giggles and Catherine laughs, Seymour cuts Elizabeth's gown to pieces in an act of symbolic rape made more kinky by the aid of his wife. Elizabeth breaks free and runs, almost bowling over Ashley. Ashley is very troubled.

ASHLEY: My child, my child. Your gown is cut to pieces.

ELIZABETH (*defiant*): We were wrestling. It was a game.

ASHLEY: It is the mourning dress for your father, the King.

ELIZABETH: But the Queen held me. It was only a game.

(*Her voice is now near to tears.*)

ASHLEY: It was wrong.

ELIZABETH (*weeping and angry*): How could I help it?

Interior, section three. Day.

Elizabeth is walking slowly.

TYRWHIT (*voice over, loud*): Treason, madam.

ASHLEY (*voice over, frightened*): My lady, you are evilly spoken of.

ELIZABETH: What harm is there in flattery.

Exterior, Seymour in garden. Day.

Seymour kneeling to Elizabeth among trees. He has hold of both her hands. He kisses them in turn and then looks up adoringly at her, the camera.

SEYMOUR: Your beauty and your many excellent qualities both of mind and person have bewitched me. I am no longer master of myself. I have so much respect for you my Princess that I dare not tell you of my hopes.

Catherine, heavily pregnant, comes into the background of the shot. Shock cut to:

Interior, Ashley in Elizabeth's bedroom. Day.

Her face close.

ASHLEY (*almost whispering*): We are banished out of the

19

house, what has happened? Lady, answer me, what has happened?

Interior, corridor door. Day.

Elizabeth in corridor. She enters.

Interior, ante-chamber. Day.

ELIZABETH: Poor Queen. All affection is false.

Interior, Catherine's bedroom. Day.

Catherine dying in her childbed. Elizabeth, the camera, sees in turn the baby in the nurse's arms, the solemn Admiral kneeling at his wife's bedside and a little in the background, Lady Tyrwhit. Catherine has suffered terribly bearing the child some weeks before. She has a fever, and she knows in the deepest sense that she has been betrayed.

CATHERINE: Those I have loved laugh at my grief. The more I have loved and trusted them the more they mock me. They mock me.

SEYMOUR: Sweetheart, not I my dear wife.

CATHERINE: You taunted me. You wished me dead.

SEYMOUR: By God's precious soul I deny it.

(Catherine turns towards Elizabeth, the camera.)

CATHERINE: And you lady? And you?

(Lady Tyrwhit comes into focus to comfort the Queen and look hard at Elizabeth.)

5

Interior, Elizabeth's bedroom. Day.

Elizabeth entering her bedroom at Hatfield and there four-square is Lady Tyrwhit.

ELIZABETH: Lady Tyrwhit.

LADY TYRWHIT: I am appointed by the Council to be your new mistress.

ELIZABETH: I will have no mistress other than Mistress Ashley; touch nothing of mine. (*She goes.*)

Interior, Elizabeth's ante-room. Day.

LADY TYRWHIT: I like it no better than you, your Grace. I loved the late, sweet Catherine as you did not.

ELIZABETH: That is a lie.

LADY TYRWHIT: I am ordered here, and here I stay.

ELIZABETH: I know why you are here, madam. I have just spoken with your husband. I am innocent and I am alone and kept from the loving company of my sweet brother, the King—

(*Lady Tyrwhit is not having that.*)

LADY TYRWHIT: His Majesty is more interested in what your servants will say than in words of yours.

ELIZABETH: They have done nothing.

LADY TYRWHIT: Then they need fear nothing.

ELIZABETH: Where are they taken?

(*Lady Tyrwhit does not reply.*)

Where are they kept?

ELIZABETH R

LADY TYRWHIT: The Tower.

(*Elizabeth begins to cry.*)

ELIZABETH: Have they made any confession? Have my servants made any confession?

6

Interior, small cell. Day.

Kat Ashley sits shivering in a vile cellar in the Tower. The cell door opens. Parry, dishevelled but unhurt, enters. He is deeply ashamed. Behind him enters Dudley carrying Parry's confession. Behind him a gaoler enters with paper, ink and quills and lays them on the cell table. Kat Ashley rises. Dudley places Parry's confession on table. She begins to read. She does not have to read much.

ASHLEY: The first occasion that I did take of talking of the marriage between the Lord Admiral and Lady Elizabeth was about fourteen days before Christmas last ...

(*Ashley lowers the confession.*)

You wretched man.

PARRY: They showed me the rack.

ASHLEY: You swore you would say nothing if horses pulled you apart.

PARRY: They showed me the instruments.

(*The table is now laid with writing materials.*)

DUDLEY: Mistress, you must write all you know of the dealings between her Grace and the Lord Admiral.

22

(Ashley does not move.)

PARRY: After confession there is mercy.

(Ashley sits to begin. Dudley takes the confession from her or from where it is lying. Push in on it.)

7

Interior, ante-room. Schoolroom. (Hatfield). Night.

Pull back from the confession into a high shot to show Elizabeth sitting alone and desolate in the small ante-room at Hatfield which adjoins her bedroom. This is her schoolroom for the moment. The Parry confession is in her hand, the Ashley confession on the floor beside her. It is night. The door opens softly. William Cecil, aged twenty-seven at this time, enters quickly and locks the door. Elizabeth rises.

ELIZABETH *(desperate)*: They gave me until morning to reply, Master Cecil. Why have you come now?

CECIL: Speak softly. They are sleeping. I have come to advise you.

(At once she is alert.)

ELIZABETH: You were ever my friend, but you serve them—why should I trust you?

(Cecil ignores this and speaks with complete authority indicating the two confessions as he refers to them.)

CECIL: By morning you must write your confession. There is very little time. I have come here to tell you the law.

(She attempts to interrupt him.)

Listen to me. Make no interruption. The Parry confession is treason only if you used the man as your

23

messenger to the Admiral and only then if the object of your message was to arrange your marriage. The Ashley confession is treason if you admit that from the beginning even during the life of the late Queen it was your plan to marry the Admiral, and he to marry you. Both of these confessions are treason if it was your intention to take any action against, or without the permission of the Council. Hold to that.

ELIZABETH: So must I admit all that happened in the household of the Admiral?

(*Slight pause.*)

CECIL (*measured*): How could an innocent child prevent the attention of her guardian when even the Queen took part in the earling morning romps?

ELIZABETH: I will not betray my servants to save myself.

CECIL: No! Show them to be the fools they are. Gossiping fools; but ensure your own innocence. If you are innocent, they are innocent.

ELIZABETH: And the Admiral?

CECIL: Nothing can save him.

ELIZABETH: Poor Thomas.

CECIL: And I believe his brother, the Protector, will not be long after him.

ELIZABETH: And then?

CECIL: I shall be secretary to a new master.

ELIZABETH: Why do you risk yourself for me?

CECIL: I risk myself for the proper order of the realm.

ELIZABETH: My brother is a sickly king and the proper order is that after him comes Mary who would put her head on the block before she denied the Pope and the old religion.

CECIL: Whatever qualms or scruples may touch my mind I serve the proper order and the good of this land.

ELIZABETH: To Mary you and your friends are heretics. Will you swallow your conscience with the Mass, Master Secretary.

CECIL: I will do what I must; speak softly, and wait for better times.

ELIZABETH: So will we all save the Admiral who will be dead.

CECIL: I will do what I can to save you from harm, your Grace, for after Mary you will reign. That is the proper order.

ELIZABETH: I have trusted no man since the day when I was eight and the Queen Catherine Howard ran screaming along the galleries of the palace to plead with great Henry. The guards took her and screaming still she was dragged away. On every hand men had betrayed her; and one before her. First there is trust, then there is passion, then death.

CECIL: I am a lawyer. I have told you the law in this matter. Trust that. Now sit, your Grace, and write the document which I shall deliver tomorrow.

8

Interior, Treasurer's room. Day.

Tyrwhit, angry, tired and baulked, hits the document in the beautiful Italian hand which lies before him. Beside it are the other two confessions.

TYRWHIT: It is a sign of guilt that you will now speak and before you denied everything.

ELIZABETH: I did not understand, Master Tyrwhit, that you wanted servant's gossip concerning the Admiral. You spoke of treason and I know nothing of treason.

TYRWHIT (*indicating the documents*): In every line— your servants speak of marriage.

ELIZABETH: My step-father, the Admiral, is a foolish strutting man and the messages of marriage and all such stuff caused us laughter. Is it treason to mock a fool?

TYRWHIT: When I showed you their confessions yesterday, you were in terror.

ELIZABETH: That is true.

TYRWHIT: Tell the Council that, Master Cecil.

ELIZABETH: I was in terror that my dear mistress and foolish Parry, who can barely keep his accounts in good order, had been tortured for my sake.

TYRWHIT: That is clever.

ELIZABETH: Their writing was wild. The Tower is a fearsome place, Sir Robert; my terror was for them.

TYRWHIT: I do not believe your put on innocence, madam.

ELIZABETH: Can you see into my soul?

TYRWHIT (*shaken*): No, madam.

ELIZABETH: Master Cecil, knowing myself innocent, I humbly beg the Council to release my servants, for if I am innocent they cannot be guilty.

9

Interior, royal bedroom. Day.

The King's eyebrows have gone and patches of his hair. He has supernatural courage derived from the fanatical religious faith. Cranmer is beside him, Dudley nearby and other members used as interesting human furniture. Cecil is discreetly placed. Old Cranmer is at the height of his power and enjoying it. He is presenting the King with the new Prayer Book. Behind him a clerk carries the draft of the Forty-Two Articles. Cranmer and Dudley dislike each other.

CRANMER: My Liege, it is my joy to bring you the first printing of the new Prayer Book.

(As Edward opens it, Dudley speaks softly and angrily to Cranmer:)

DUDLEY *(very close to Cranmer)*: There are other matters—

CRANMER: God comes first in all things, my Lord—

DUDLEY *(turning to Cecil)*: Where is the Lord Protector?

CECIL: Diplomatically ill.

DUDLEY: Has he abandoned his brother?

(Cecil nods. Dudley turns towards the King to take advantage.)

With your permission, your Majesty.

(Cranmer cuts in and they wrangle across the bed, ignoring Edward, until he suddenly speaks.)

CRANMER: His Majesty may now consider and dispute with me—

DUDLEY: The charge of treason requires that his Majesty—

27

CRANMER: His Majesty is tired by temporal—

DUDLEY: If the Admiral is to be condemned—

CRANMER: The reading of the articles—

(*The King has been watching them.*)

EDWARD (*suddenly*): Does he repent?

CRANMER: Repent?

EDWARD (*impatiently*): My uncle, the Admiral. Does he repent?

DUDLEY: He does not repent.

EDWARD: Then he must die.

(*Pause. Not shock exactly, but the child back in his Prayer book turning a page and pleased with what he reads gives them pause.*)

CECIL: Your Majesty, the evidence from Hatfield is that Elizabeth, her Grace, has been slandered and is innocent.

EDWARD: Does she love me?

CECIL: She loves you more than her life.

EDWARD: She writes most lovingly. Her letters comfort me.

10

Interior, ante-room. Day.

Elizabeth at her desk in her schoolroom is writing. Translating. Books are open by her. Today she is the model scholar. Lady Tyrwhit, who wishes herself any-

where but here and is implacably biased against her charge, torments her.

LADY TYRWHIT: All the houses and property of the Lord Admiral are sold one by one.

(*No reply.*)

The servants of the Admiral are turned out to shift for themselves.

(*No reply.*)

His goods are confiscated.

(*No reply.*)

And he is condemned.

ELIZABETH (*flaring up*): But not yet dead.

LADY TYRWHIT: Nothing can save him.

(*Cecil enters, travel-stained.*)

CECIL: Your Grace! Madam!

ELIZABETH: Master Cecil.

CECIL: Your servants are freed.

(*Elizabeth cannot speak.*)

A proclamation is made clearing your good name.

(*He unrolls it and she reads it, eagerly. He glances at Lady Tyrwhit. Elizabeth, excited and happy, still reading the proclamation.*)

ELIZABETH: When do they return? When shall I see my dear Kat?

29

CECIL: That is forbidden.

(*She looks at him.*)

You will be safer here. Today a traitor died defying the King's Majesty and the King's Council.

Interior, Elizabeth's bedroom.

Above Elizabeth, the camera, in the bed at Chelsea, the head and shoulders of the Admiral.

SEYMOUR: My love. My love.

(*Cut. An axe swings against sky.*)

Interior, ante-room. Day.

ELIZABETH: This day died a man of much wit and very little judgment.

(*Sir Robert Tyrwhit is in the doorway, where he has been waiting for her reaction. He salutes her courage with a tight smile. Cecil moves to her.*)

CECIL (*without expression*): Well said, your Grace.

(*Elizabeth turns from them into her bedroom.*)

11

Interior, royal bedroom. Day.

Inside the King's bedroom as the King in his night-gown, moves gasping back to his bed. He is in extremis, lungs nearly gone. As he lies there gasping the lightning flashes outside the window and as it does, cut to the group who stand in shadow at the far end of the King's bedchamber. Another flash lights them—Dudley, now Duke of Northumberland, richly dressed and certain of victory, in front of him, also facing the bed, are the two innocent sixteen-year-olds, Northumberland's son Guildford and the Lady Jane Grey. This frozen group, Northumberland with his predatory hands on their shoulders and his two dupes with tears running down their cheeks, hear the King gasp out his last prayer.

EDWARD: Lord, thou knowest how happy I shall be, may I live with thee for ever. Yet would I might live and be well for Thy elects' sake.

Exterior, country road. Day.

(Cecil riding.)

12

Interior, chapel. Day.

Mary has just risen from prayer and turned, as Cecil, filthy from travel, wet from rain, comes through the chapel door. A frightened looking servant closes the door and the thunder rolls. Cecil kneels and bows his head very low then he takes her hand and kisses it. It might be a very touching scene until she speaks.

MARY: I see that my brother is dead and I am now Queen. No other reason would bring you on your knees before me, Master Cecil. And I never doubted that you would be the first to turn his coat and come running to me.

CECIL: Madam, your Grace, I have news which I must . . .

MARY: I have known you for an enemy these many years.

31

CECIL: It is most urgent and necessary.

MARY: You are my enemy in religion and in statecraft.

CECIL: Forgive me, your Grace, but I must tell you . . .

MARY: *But* I will not persecute you for it.

CECIL: Madam, the Act of Succession has been altered. Northumberland has married his youngest son to the Lady Jane Grey and she will be proclaimed the Queen.

MARY: Northumberland?

CECIL: Yes.

MARY: Your master?

CECIL: No more.

MARY: Who dubbed you Sir William Cecil and to whom you owe all allegiance?

CECIL: Madam, you are disinherited and named bastard.

MARY: Again!

CECIL: As is the Princess Elizabeth.

MARY: Justly so. She is the daughter of a whore.

CECIL (*pause*): No, not justly so.

MARY: You serve her. That is why you are here. You serve Elizabeth. Trap me, discredit Northumberland, and she will reign to the joy of all heretics. That is your plan.

CECIL: Your Grace, I swear that if you take the bait and go to London, believing that you will be proclaimed Queen, you will be welcomed into the Tower and never again leave it.

MARY: If I reign you and your friends will have no joy of it. I will bring this land back to the true church. Your news is false. You would never risk yourself for me. You are the most cunning man in the Kingdom.

CECIL (*wearily*): Madam, I could be at Dover. I could be clear away, your Grace. I care for my skin as much as the next man and as you say I have no taste for the old religion, but I will not see the right order overthrown, and the people betrayed. You are the next rightful Queen.

(*Pause. She believes him.*)

MARY: Is the King dead?

CECIL: Without doubt.

MARY: God be praised.

CECIL: Ride to the eastern counties. Proclaim yourself sovereign. Go now, your Grace.

(*Mary puts out her hand. Cecil kneels and kisses it. Mary walks out of the chapel and as the door swings behind her cut to:*)

13

Interior, small cell. Day.

A hand shooting a bolt. Go up sharply and see framed in the barred spy window of the thick cell door the Duke of Northumberland, his fine clothes dishevelled and torn, standing in chains.

Interior, small cell. Day.

As before. Go up to see Cranmer, the old Archbishop.

*He is degraded because his fine robes have been taken
from him and he is in an old gown and an old square
hat.*

Interior, small cell. Day.

*As before and show the young Lord Guildford who,
as we see, turns to beat on the cell wall.*

Interior, small cell. Day.

*Lady Jane Grey, stock still in her foul cell with dirty
straw on the floor and as she puts her hands to her
throat . . .*

14

Interior, gallery. Day.

*Close shot of a gold crown being placed on the head
of the wearer by a pair of hands, both of which have
fine jewelled rings. During the preceding sequence from
the moment that Cecil kneels to Mary to the moment
that we see Jane Grey, drums roll, increasing in volume
and tempo and coming to a climax with Jane Grey
in her cell. Then on the cut to the crown there is the
first of a series of triumphant fanfares. Pull to show
that the wearer of the crown is Elizabeth, now eighteen,
dressed simply, but richly, fresh from the coronation,
and the ringed hands are those of Antoine de Noailles
the first of many men to understand that Elizabeth was
best approached and intrigued by flattery which com-
bined boldness with sexual suggestion close under the
surface, but never gross or too close to the mark. De
Noailles is the French ambassador.*

ELIZABETH: It caused my head to ache. I am unfamiliar
with crowns.

34

NOAILLES (*as Mary at the far end enters the gallery with her party*): Your Grace will have a more comfortable crown in due time.

(*Both look along the gallery at Whitehall, seen by us in daylight for the first time with the sun pouring in the windows on one side making the golden points of the halberds glitter.*)

ELIZABETH: Will that please the French King, Monsieur de Noailles?

NOAILLES: All the bells in all the cathedrals in France will ring with joy on that day.

(*Mary passes and moves down the long gallery. She stops to speak to a courtier. She moves into the small gallery and stops at an arch.*)

ALL: God save the Queen Mary.

MARY: I thank you my good people.

Interior, gallery. Day.

(*Elizabeth and De Noailles.*)

ELIZABETH: Do they ring today for my dear sister?

NOAILLES: No, your Grace, because your dear sister is half Spanish and as you see the Imperial Ambassador is already her dearest friend.

ELIZABETH: Must we choose then? Must the English Queen choose either France or Spain as a friend? Is it one or the other?

NOAILLES: It would take a genius to have us both, your Grace.

35

ELIZABETH: And you have chosen me because Señor Renard has my sister in his hand.

NOAILLES: Who would not choose to be the friend of the youngest and most beautiful princess in the whole of Europe.

ELIZABETH: Your master, the French King. He has already chosen the young Scottish Queen and he has her safe in France.

NOAILLES: Your Grace, that lady is a child and will be content to rule France when her time comes.

(*Elizabeth taps him lightly on the cheek.*)

ELIZABETH: Well put. And when you write your secret letters to France, tell his Majesty, we must all be content with our lot and thank God for it.

(*The fanfares end and the whole company salute the new Queen.*)

ALL: God save the Queen Mary.

MARY: I thank you my good people.

(*She has reached the centre of the gallery. Elizabeth now moves to her and with her instinct for the best effect, prostrates herself at Mary's feet. How hard it is to forget Boleyn and all the bitter years that followed, but in this moment Mary does put it all aside. She reaches with both hands and brings Elizabeth to her feet.*)

I am your loving sister and Queen. We have come through many perils. Will you serve me truly?

ELIZABETH: With all my heart.

(*Mary impulsively kisses her. The people applaud.*)

*Present are Kat Ashley, Parry, Gardiner, the now age-
ing Bishop who crowned Mary and is also her Lord
Chancellor, Cecil and in the background the ladies-in-
waiting and the lords with the regalia. At this moment
of unlikely and spontaneous accord Sir Thomas Wyatt
is seen to rise and shout.)*

WYATT: God save the Princess Elizabeth!

*(There is a great shout from the halberdiers, courtiers
and so on. Mary is shocked and looks sharply around.)*

MARY: Who is that gentleman?

GARDINER: Sir Thomas Wyatt.

MARY: Send him from the Court.

*(Her mood has changed. Her suspicions, well-enough
founded for thirty years that she is threatened, are back.
She turns on Elizabeth.)*

We will talk privately.

*(She hurries to the door to the ante-chamber and enters.
Elizabeth follows.)*

RENARD *(quietly to Gardiner)*: There will be no peace
until Elizabeth is banished.

GARDINER *(quietly)*: Or executed.

RENARD: She is clever and the people love her.

GARDINER: She has a spirit full of incantation. Her
mother, Bullen, was a whore and a witch and to my
eternal shame I had some dealings in the divorce. Now
in my old age I repent and would do all I can to make
amends. When I look at them together I see Catherine
of blessed memory and I see the witch, Bullen, torment-
ing her to the grave.

WYATT: God save Princess Elizabeth!

15

Interior, ante-room. Day.

The sisters are alone in the ante-room to the bed-chamber.

MARY: Why am I hated?

ELIZABETH: You are loved.

MARY: I am merciful. I have spared the Lady Jane Grey and her lord. I will spare Cranmer if he recants. I condemned Northumberland with regret.

ELIZABETH: The people support you. The people ousted Northumberland for you.

MARY: The people are glad I am old enough to die in time for you to be Queen.

ELIZABETH: I am your devoted servant, sister. I want nothing.

MARY: Then you will obey me?

ELIZABETH: With all my heart.

MARY: I have ordered the celebration of a requiem mass to the memory of our brother, the late King.

(*Elizabeth is silent.*)

Will you go with me?

ELIZABETH: Sister, I was taught to serve God first and then the King.

MARY: Sister, I have been in peril under two kings. I know the shifts to make. You cannot deceive me with clever words.

ELIZABETH: Let me leave the court, your Grace.

MARY: No. You will give a focus to my enemies.

MARY (*cutting in*): In the true religion?

ELIZABETH: I was brought up another way. I beg you to leave the use of my conscience to myself.

MARY: A private man may have the use of his conscience, but my sister may not to give heart to every heretic in the realm.

ELIZABETH: Your Majesty, in the reign of our late brother you were summoned before the council in order to deny your beliefs. You defied the Council but you were not punished. You had the use of your conscience.

MARY: But mine is the true faith. I would gladly have died for it.

Will you die for the Lutheran heresy, or the abominations of Calvin and his brothers in Christ?

Or is it that you fear the people will not love you if you return to the true church?

(*Elizabeth is silent, and Mary, who is sadly unbalanced by her years of suffering and fear and solitude begins to go over the edge.*)

Or is it that you hate me?

(*Elizabeth is terrified but she does not reply.*)

Does your conscience trouble you?

ELIZABETH (*kneels*): I am at your mercy. I have opened my heart to you. I rode with you joyfully to confront the rebels and traitors who tried to steal your crown.

MARY: I am unloved yet I loved and befriended you as a child. Did I not? Answer me.

ELIZABETH: Yes, madam.

MARY: Did I not help you with your learning? Play with you? Ease your pains when you were sick?

ELIZABETH: Sister you did, to my comfort and joy.

MARY: But you defy me. You look at me with the eyes of your mother, who said of my mother, 'She will be my death, or I will be hers!' And when my mother lay dead and they took the heart from her body, they found at the heart's centre, a black and terrible core.

ELIZABETH: Madam, madam, I beg you. Sister, I beg you let the past be buried.

MARY: No water could wash away the blackness of the thing that had stopped my mother's heart, and it came there by foul practices of witchcraft.

ELIZABETH: God forbid that should be true.

(*She is shivering. Mary's mood changes.*)

MARY: It gives me no pleasure to see you fearful and trembling.

ELIZABETH: It is not fear. The service was long. My head is painful.

MARY: Will you hear mass? Answer me honestly.

ELIZABETH: I cannot without belief.

MARY: Belief will come. Try.

(*Elizabeth is silent.*)

Leave me.

(*It is as if she has struck Elizabeth.*)

ELIZABETH: Sister, do not cast me away.

MARY: You must choose.

ELIZABETH: I have many enemies. They will speak ill of me.

MARY: Leave me.

(*Elizabeth turns to go.*)

(*As the door closes.*) Do you wish me dead? (*And she means 'I wish you dead'.*)

16

Interior, Elizabeth's apartment. Day. (Whitehall.)

Elizabeth sits in her own apartment in the palace of Whitehall playing the virginals. In the background sits Ashley sewing. De Noailles stands somewhere near and as the scene begins (played at first very lightly, almost flirtatiously), he moves to turn the handwritten sheet of music.

NOAILLES: It seems true that the Queen is angry with you, your Grace.

ELIZABETH: The Queen is my loving sister, your Excellency.

NOAILLES: But you are quite isolated here in your apartments. The young men of the court dare not visit you.

ELIZABETH: Parliament guided by the Lord Chancellor has annulled the great divorce. I am once more the bastard Elizabeth and therefore solitary.

NOAILLES: Ah! Now I see. I had expected you to talk of the marriage, but being solitary you will not have heard.

ELIZABETH: The marriage?

NOAILLES: Her Majesty is to marry.

(*Elizabeth stops playing.*)

ELIZABETH: She no longer wears black. The court is full of colour. Of course.

(*De Noailles is enjoying himself.*)

NOAILLES: Philip of Spain—and she talks of children.

(*Elizabeth is almost in a panic.*)

ELIZABETH: Children? The doctors, her doctors, what do they say? She is too old for children. Do they say that?

NOAILLES: My spies tell me—

ELIZABETH: Yes?

NOAILLES: That she has good hopes of children.

ELIZABETH: I must see her. I must talk to her.

NOAILLES: She will not see you, your Grace.

ELIZABETH: The good citizens in Parliament will never change the act of succession, only treason can displace a prince.

NOAILLES: Or a male child for a queen.

17

Interior, gallery. Day.

The Queen and her ladies gaily dressed and laughing and chattering in company with Renard and Gardiner and a chaplain are crossing the gallery coming from mass, when Elizabeth suddenly runs from a corner and kneels weeping in the path of the Queen.

ELIZABETH: Your Majesty.

MARY: Lady.

ELIZABETH: I beg you to grant me the favour of books and teachers. I have been brought up in errors and I am deeply penitent.

MARY: What errors?

ELIZABETH: When I cannot sleep at night I hear your voice saying 'Mine is the true faith and I would gladly die for it'.

MARY: This has never been a secret, sister!

ELIZABETH: If my loved and revered sister, the Queen, would die for her faith—if she has been brought safe through all her perils by her true faith, then I, Elizabeth, must be in error and I long to learn the truth.

(Mary is genuinely moved by this.)

MARY: Is it true?

ELIZABETH: Grant me instruction, your Majesty. Help me to serve God as you would have me do.

(Show the disbelief in the faces of Renard and Gardiner.)

MARY: I have prayed for you. I am happy.

(*Impulsively she gives Elizabeth her rosary of white coral and as Elizabeth takes it and kisses it the ladies-in-waiting are delighted.*)

(*To the priest.*) Go with Princess Elizabeth. Instruct her. Let her attend her first mass on the nativity of the Virgin Mary. (*She turns to the company.*) My Lords, this lady and I are the daughters of that king who made himself the only supreme head in earth of the Church of England. The words of the Act are burned in my heart, for in my time of greatest peril I bowed to them. 'The King has power to repress, redress, reform, correct, restrain and amend all errors, heresies, abuses, offences, contempts and enormousies in matters of religion.'

(*Pause.*)

Note well what has happened. That King is dead. I will not have the title of supreme head of the Church of England. I adhere to the true Church and now God has guided my sister to that haven. With God's help it is I who will amend all errors in this land.

(*The company cross themselves and murmur 'God be praised'.*)

But with mercy, with loving kindness, the Pope shall forgive us.

(*Mary is gloriously happy for the moment.*)

ELIZABETH: I thank you with all my heart.

MARY: Be faithful.

(*Mary goes off with the whole company except the priest. Pull to a long shot showing the Princess and the priest in the gallery alone. The priest opens his Bible He moves to Elizabeth. They begin to talk solemnly together as he instructs her earnestly in the doctrine of transubstantiation. Cut to Noailles and Wyatt big in the foreground and Elizabeth and the priest framed in the background.)*

NOAILLES: How clever she is.

WYATT: She must be made queen before Mary delivers us all to the Spanish papist.

NOAILLES: Amen to that.

WYATT: But she must leave the Court. She must be safe in the country when we act.

NOAILLES: I will talk to her.

WYATT: Take this letter.

(We must see the letter and the seal. As De Noailles turns to go, Wyatt puts a hand on his arm.)

If you betray her the Spaniards will rule here.

(De Noailles smiles.)

NOAILLES: Sir Thomas, no man can detest the Protestant heresy more than I but the thought of France surrounded by the power of Spain in England, in the Netherlands, in Spain itself, and controlling the Channel, is enough to keep me faithful unto death.

18

Interior, royal bedroom. Day.

A copy of the portrait by Titian of Philip of Spain in armour, aged twenty-four and looking a good catch indeed for a sad and ageing English queen. The portrait is on an easel in the Queen's private apartment, and Mary is sitting before it stricken with grief and doubts.

Interior, ante-chamber. Day.

Guards let Renard through.

Interior, ante-chamber. Day.

Renard enters ante-chamber.

Interior, royal bedroom. Day.

Renard comes hurrying into the room, literally out of breath. He bows. He is as near to panic as it is possible for a Spanish grandee to be.

RENARD: Your Majesty I came at once—is it rebellion?

MARY: Terrible rumours.

RENARD: An uprising, the heretics?

MARY: The Prince of Spain.

RENARD: The Prince? Oh, madam, be calm, the Prince is in perfect health.

MARY: He has broken my heart.

(Renard is totally at a loss.)

RENARD: Your Grace?

MARY: He has mistresses. He has bastards. I believed him pure.

(Renard almost laughs. He becomes very, very solemn to hide his feelings.)

RENARD: He is as chaste as ice.

MARY: How can I marry such a man? Even when his wife was alive I am told he . . .

(*And she can't go on.*)

RENARD: Madam you must not believe lying rumours.

(*Mary may be heartbroken, which she genuinely is, but she has not lost her other wits.*)

MARY (*very sharp*): Or lying servants defending their masters.

RENARD: Your Majesty may take my life if you find him other than I have told you.

MARY: Is it true? All that you have told me?

RENARD: This picture does not lie. He is as wise as he is handsome, brave in war, faithful in love—and in religion the Pope's elect of all the Princes in Christendom.

MARY: I long for him.

(*Renard puts the goad in.*)

RENARD (*sadly*): I must say it. Your Grace, he may not come here.

MARY: Why, why?

RENARD: For his safety's sake. Until the plots and treason of the friends of Madam Elizabeth have been unmasked.

MARY: Elizabeth? She is loyal. She has embraced the true church.

RENARD: She mocks the mass. She stoops and bends and moans and her ladies rub her back and stomach even at the moment of the elevation of the host.

47

MARY: I believed her ill as she often is.

RENARD: In her apartment afterwards she laughs and jests with the French ambassador.

(*Pause.*)

MARY: Are your spies reliable?

RENARD: Yes.

MARY: Does she mock me?

RENARD: Yes.

MARY: She has betrayed me?

RENARD: Yes.

MARY: How shall I act to bring her down and bring your master safe to this court?

RENARD: First let her go from court which she longs to do.

MARY: No. I will have her under my eye.

RENARD: Send spies with her, keep up all appearances of friendship.

MARY: Are there many who will rise against me for her sake?

RENARD (*rubbing it in hard*): She is much loved by the people.

MARY: It is true.

RENARD: She is tainted with heresy.

MARY: It is true.

48

RENARD: And she is young.

MARY: Leave me.

(*Renard bows out. Mary in great misery goes to the portrait of Philip and touches the face gently with her fingers.*)

Young, young.

(*She picks up a mirror and looks at her face. She can hardly bear to look.*)

She is *young*. Oh God, oh God, all my youth has gone.

19

Interior, gallery. Day.

De Noailles and Wyatt are big in the foreground. In the background is the gallery and where last time we saw Elizabeth with the priest, Mary and Elizabeth meet to say farewell. In the background also are Renard, Gardiner, the ladies-in-waiting to the Queen, members of Elizabeth's household including Parry and Ashley. Cut close to the sisters for a scene of mutual and moving hypocrisy.

ELIZABETH: Hear nothing ill of me, dear sister.

MARY: I will hear only the truth of you.

ELIZABETH: Send me as you promised the copes and chasubles and all that is needful so that I may celebrate mass each day.

(*They embrace. Cut to de Noailles and Wyatt.*)

WYATT: We shall see her queen within the month.

NOAILLES (*pleasantly*): Or you will be dead.

MARY: God be with you, my dear sister.

WYATT: The whole country will rise with me.

NOAILLES (*ironically*): God be with you.

(*Cut to Renard and Gardiner as Elizabeth and some of her household begin to move towards the door. Renard smiling towards Elizabeth.*)

RENARD: The rebels will swarm round her.

GARDINER: It is a great risk.

RENARD: Only treason will do to remove Madam Elizabeth from the line of succession, and treason we must have.

(*Cut to Elizabeth smiling and turning to wave. Voices shout.*)

VOICES: Long live the Princess Elizabeth.

(*Cut close to Mary, tormented by it all. Suddenly Mary makes her last effort of love out of hatred.*)

MARY: Be faithful.

Exterior, road. Day.

Elizabeth riding at the head of her household along a narrow country lane, tree lined or with high banks. Suddenly she looks up at the morning sky and laughs out loud.

ELIZABETH (*shout*): Free! Free! Free!

(*She puts spurs to her horse and gallops leaving the*

rest of the household behind. Come down to show the galloping legs of the horse. Bring in the sounds of conflict and war.)

Exterior, Wyatt's capture.

A banner, tattered, caught in the branches of a tree. Pan down the banner and the banner pole. Come to the trampled earth where horses have circled and men have fought. See a sword gripped tight in a hand. Go up the arm and see that the arm is severed. Further on the rest of the dead soldier lying there crumpled. Horses hooves have trampled the mud. Move to a cannon, broken-wheeled and tipped over and just beyond see a raven strut upon a corpse, as it pecks cut to: The legs of a horse being pulled cruelly round in a tight circle. Move up to the jaw breaker bit, the foam at the mouth, the rolling eyes. Then cut from the horse's head to the head of the rider. Wyatt, dirty and panting, trapped in a clearing in the wood.

20

Interior, large cell. Day.

Close, Gardiner, in a long, low-vaulted chamber in the Tower. Cut again and show Wyatt, dirty and in chains standing before him. Gardiner knows Wyatt. They were both in favour in the court of Henry VIII.

GARDINER (*gently*): You would have done better to have fallen on your sword than be taken, Thomas.

(Wyatt is terrified now he is caught. He is confused and stupid.)

Nothing can save you.

WYATT: I repent my action. I repent.

51

GARDINER: You will die the vile death of a traitor.

WYATT: My Lord, beg the Queen for mercy for me. Help me.

GARDINER: Thomas, you have rebelled against your lawful sovereign.

WYATT: Against the Spanish marriage, that is all.

GARDINER: That is not all.

(*Silence.*)

You may die cleanly by the axe if you confess.

WYATT: Confess?

GARDINER: The rebellion was to crown the Princess Elizabeth.

WYATT: I cannot say it.

GARDINER: And the Princess knew of it and approved of it.

21

Interior, ante-room/schoolroom. Day.

A door opening on the work room of Elizabeth at Hatfield, where in the middle of the room she is sitting and playing chess with Ashley. Both of them look towards the door. Elizabeth rises slowly. Ashley rises and backs away. Cut to the reverse shot. A nobleman at the door (Sussex). Behind him the escort of soldiers. Cut to the reverse shot. Elizabeth faints to the floor. Into the shot come the three men and their boots and spurs. Frame the stricken Elizabeth.

Exterior, Elizabeth in a litter.

Look up while tracking at heads on pikes against the sky to the right. Look down at the sick Elizabeth in a litter moving along, surrounded by an escort more heard than seen. Look up while tracking at heads on pikes to the left against the sky. Look down at Elizabeth in the litter. She turns from the dreadful sight and is sick over the side of the moving litter.

22

Interior, Elizabeth's apartment (Whitehall). Day.

The door of Elizabeth's room in the palace. It opens. A table has been set up. Gardiner sits in the high-back chair behind it. A wide shot shows the sick Elizabeth, pale and dressed in white and her three captors. Gardiner rises. He bows slightly.

GARDINER: Your Grace.

ELIZABETH: My lord.

GARDINER: Please be seated.

ELIZABETH: I demand to see the Queen.

GARDINER: The Queen will not see you.

ELIZABETH: Why am I here?

GARDINER: I am old, and cannot stand long without pain but stand I must until you sit, lady.

(As she sits, he waves the three gentlemen away. His manner is that of a wise and humane old man, friendly, and caring for Elizabeth's welfare you might think.)

I was in the Tower five years in your brother's reign.

(*She is silent.*)

My joints swelled with the cold winds that blow in from the river from the east. I have never recovered from that time.

(*She is silent.*)

You are ill, I am told.

(*She is silent.*)

Yes, I see you are. You would suffer greatly from the east wind, and from the doubts and fears that crowd the spirit as day drags into day.

(*She is silent.*)

(*The same tone.*) The Lady Jane Grey was executed eight days ago.

ELIZABETH (*shocked*): She was pardoned.

GARDINER: True. But her father, who was also pardoned, chose to follow the traitor Wyatt. Traitors are not pardoned twice. Both are dead.

(*She is silent.*)

The rebellion has quite changed the Queen. Her blood is up. If you wish to live you must confess and place yourself upon the mercy of her Majesty.

ELIZABETH: I pray God that I may die the shamefullest death that any died, if I have any part in the treason against the rightful Queen, my dear sister.

GARDINER: The Queen will pardon you.

ELIZABETH: I have done nothing.

GARDINER (*suddenly very stern*): You have caused

rebellion, noble blood has been shed for you, in battle and on the block. Beg for mercy while there is time.

ELIZABETH: I am innocent. To beg for mercy is to confess guilt. I will not beg, and I do not confess.

(*Gardiner glances towards the door.*)

If I am guilty, let me see your proof, my Lord.

GARDINER: We have proof and you must confess.

Interior, ante-room. Day.

In the small ante-room on the other side of that door, Mary is there.

ELIZABETH (*voice over*): If I am guilty let me see your proof, my Lord.

(*Mary quietly closes the door. She turns to Renard. It is a small chamber.*)

MARY: She will never confess, but she shall not inherit. I swear to you that she will not inherit. I will bear a son. I will bear Philip a son.

RENARD: Your Grace, the precious person of Philip cannot be entrusted to you while the dangerous traitor, Elizabeth, is alive.

MARY: But the rebellion is over. God has delivered my enemies into my hands. It is safe for him to come as you promised.

RENARD: Not while Elizabeth lives.

(*Slight pause.*)

MARY: He shall come. I love him. He shall come to me.

RENARD (*delightedly*): Ha!

55

Interior, Elizabeth's apartment. Day.

Elizabeth is on her feet in the other room.

ELIZABETH: No.

GARDINER: If you will not answer, her Majesty will have you in the Tower.

ELIZABETH: I shall stand condemned without trial. People will say 'She must be guilty for she is shut up in the Tower with other traitors'.

GARDINER: It is the Queen's pleasure.

ELIZABETH: I have heard in my time of many cast away for the want of coming to the presence of their princes. This is your doing, my Lord.

GARDINER: The Queen will have it.

ELIZABETH: If Thomas Seymour could have come to his brother, the Protector, he would not have been condemned. I know it. Let me come to my sister. Let me talk to her.

GARDINER: There is no remedy but your confession.

ELIZABETH: Then I beg you to let me write to her.

GARDINER: Tomorrow is Palm Sunday. Each good citizen will keep the church and carry his palm. In that quiet time you will go by boat to the Tower. You have the night to think on it.

(*She is quite still as he goes out.*)

Exterior, Traitor's Gate. Day.

To the steps outside Traitor's Gate. In the foreground the bow of a barge. It is pouring with rain. There is the sound of water lapping on the steps, and a very curious tableaux. Elizabeth without a cloak, is sitting on a stone projection outside the gate. The portcullis is up and the guards are lined up. Near to Elizabeth, completely at a loss, is one of the gentlemen who have been her captors. This gentleman is Sussex. Ashley at the moment unseen off camera is 'in' the boat.

SUSSEX: Madam, you had best come out of the rain.

ELIZABETH: Better sit here than a worse place.

(Sussex dare not touch her.)

SUSSEX: Madam, you must enter.

ELIZABETH *(playing to the assembled guards)*: I am as true a subject being prisoner as ever landed at these stairs. I speak it before God, having no other friend but God alone.

SUSSEX: Madam, you will be ill if you sit longer.

(Elizabeth, moving from a sitting position to a kneeling position, the rain pouring down on her, she speaks very loudly:)

ELIZABETH: I pray that God may confound me eternally if I ever, by any means, was privy to the treachery of Sir Thomas Wyatt or any that rebelled with him against the Queen's lawful majesty.

(The guards are very affected by this, and first one and then another removes his hat and kneels until all are kneeling and then one shouts:)

GUARD: God preserve your Grace.

(At this point, the Lieutenant of the Tower, Bridges, appears. He is dismayed and angry. He strides to the guards and would kick them to their feet.)

BRIDGES: Up, up. Stand up. Move. Get up.

(*Elizabeth, seizing the opportunity, stands up and speaks sharply to Sussex:*)

ELIZABETH: Why are these poor fellows kept here in the rain?

BRIDGES (*very angry*): It is the rule, your Grace, when any prisoner is landed here.

ELIZABETH: Is it so? Then I beseech that they are dismissed or do you fear that this one poor woman prisoner has not enough guards already?

BRIDGES (*sufficiently angry to try force*): If your Grace does not come in then you shall be made to.

ELIZABETH: Dismiss your men.

BRIDGES (*to the men*): Go. Go all of you.

(*The guards start to go and Bridges moves towards Elizabeth, determined to bring her into the Tower. Sussex confronts him.*)

SUSSEX (*quiet and firm*): My Lord Lieutenant, let us take heed and do no more than our commission. Let us remember that the lady is the daughter of the King. That she may come to judge us one day. If we are just we have nothing to fear.

(*Bridges hesitates. Then he suddenly takes off his cloak and makes to put it round Elizabeth, hoping to cover, as it were, his gaffe. She immediately dashes the cloak away from her very violently, and it falls to the soaking ground. She then sits again.*)

ELIZABETH: I will not be put into that cruel and doleful place. I will not enter by Traitor's Gate.

(*There is a wailing, and Ashley comes crying from the boat and attempts to get to the crouched and soaking*) *and shivering figure of Elizabeth. Like so many occasions in life that are potentially tragic, there is a fair element of farce. Ashley is held back by the guardians of Elizabeth. Bridges turns away in anger. Sussex is baffled.)*

ASHLEY: Your Grace, my child, you will be ill. You will die if you stay out here. Oh! Oh! Oh!

(And she begins to wail. Elizabeth suddenly straightens up, rises and goes to Ashley.)

ELIZABETH: Stop howling. Stop at once. It is your business to comfort me. Not howl and talk of death and illness. Come you stupid woman. Have you my book?

(Ashley produces her book.)

There. There. Now open it. Have faith. Now we will go in. Walk with me. We will go in together.

(Elizabeth and Ashley walk solemnly under the gate, saying alternate lines of the Magnificat:)

My soul doth magnify the Lord and my spirit hath rejoiced in God my Saviour
For he hath regarded the lowliness of his handmaiden.
For behold from henceforth all generations shall call me blessed
For he that is mighty hath magnified me and holy is his name
And his mercy is on them that fear him throughout all generations. *etc. etc.*

23

Interior, large cell. Day.

Elizabeth and Ashley are in the vaulted chamber last used for Gardiner to interrogate Wyatt. The floor is covered with rushes. There are two beds, a table and chairs. Open close on Elizabeth at the barred window. Rain drips steadily across it outside. She turns to Ashley. Her spirits are very low.

ELIZABETH: Lady Jane Grey's scaffold is left standing.

ASHLEY: It is to strike fear into the prisoners. I am not so fearful this time as last.

ELIZABETH: It does strike fear.

(*Ashley suddenly turns to the door and hammers on it. When she speaks she is making up for earlier tears. A guard opens the cell door.*)

ASHLEY: We need food. Hot food and wine. And fresh clothes for my mistress. Tell his Excellency that the Princess Elizabeth must be warm and well fed or he will answer for it.

ELIZABETH: Kat!

ASHLEY: Don't stand gaping.

ELIZABETH: Kat!

ASHLEY: Go.

ELIZABETH: Stay. Kat, you are too shrill.

(*She turns her irresistible charm on the poor fellow.*)

Good fellow, it will help to bear this grim place if my servants may bring me warm clothes and good wine here. Speak to your captain for me and I will not forget you.

(*The guard drops to one knee. Kisses the hem of her dress and then runs, slamming the door. Elizabeth is less afraid for a moment.*)

Surely the people will not let her kill me.

ASHLEY: The people are in great confusion. They hate a traitor; and they hate the Spanish marriage. They won't see the rightful Queen put down; but they won't bow their necks to the foreigner. And as for religion, God help us, they would be Jews or Turks as long as they are left in peace.

ELIZABETH: They will hate me, if they believe me a traitor.

ASHLEY: The people will never hate you, your Grace.

ELIZABETH (*seeing in her mind's eye her mother in this place*): If it comes to it I will beg her to send to France for an executioner who uses a sword. She could not deny me that. There is a precedent.

24

Interior, passage-way in Tower. Day.

The door of the cell opens, and Elizabeth in a different costume, is brought out into the passage-way. Gardiner is behind her. Sussex and Bridges are there. Guards with torches. The door is closed on Ashley. Elizabeth, Gardiner etc. move out of shot as we push in on the grille in the cell door where Ashley has her face pressed.

25

Interior, small cell. Day.

To a grille in Cranmer's cell with the torchlight flickering as it approaches. A guard throws open the door and the old Archbishop, very painfully, drags himself to his feet. Gardiner brings Elizabeth into the cell. Cranmer slowly recognizes her and tries to kneel. She stops him and holds one of his hands in both of hers.

CRANMER: Your Grace.

ELIZABETH: Godfather, I am sad to see you in this place.

CRANMER (*wryly*): Bishop Gardiner will tell you it's a fair exchange. He was here during the late reign.

GARDINER: This lady, Elizabeth, your god-daughter, stands in as great a peril as the lady you married to her father.

CRANMER: Through you Bishop? Is it through you? Are you buying your place in heaven with the deaths of those you once supported?

GARDINER: She does not understand that the Queen is implacable. The Queen will have either dead traitors or those who truly confess and repent and recant.

CRANMER: I believe this lady understands very well.

GARDINER: Madam, before you is the great Archbishop who pronounced the divorce and stood as the right hand of King Henry, your father. The great Archbishop who devised the prayer books of Edward, your brother. Look well at him. He is degraded from all offices. The divorce is revoked. The prayer books are gone and the mass is returned. What hope have you, if this man is so cast down?

(*Elizabeth is trembling and Cranmer finds it hard to stand.*)

CRANMER: Forgive me. (*He sits down. Still wry.*) It is the east wind. It is most cruel to the joints of an old man. You felt it in your time, did you not, Gardiner?

GARDINER: It is the duty of a godfather to guide with wisdom. Guide this lady from her folly of defiance and silence.

CRANMER: Are you innocent, Elizabeth?

62

ELIZABETH: I am innocent.

CRANMER: Then God be with you.

(*Gardiner looks from one to the other. Elizabeth turns and walks out of the cell. Gardiner follows and Cranmer is painfully kneeling to pray when the cell door closes on him.*)

26

Interior, large cell. Day.

The door to Elizabeth's cell is open. The torchlight flickers round the entrance, but the cell is shadowed by the further end. Elizabeth enters. There is a vague figure in the background. Gardiner, Bridges and Sussex come in with guards and the torchlight shows Wyatt standing in chains. Elizabeth is shocked by the sight of this wild figure. She does not know Wyatt by sight. Wyatt suddenly rushes forward, and she shrinks back. He throws himself on his knees before her.

WYATT: Your Grace.

(*Elizabeth turns to Gardiner.*)

ELIZABETH: Who is this?

GARDINER: Sir Thomas Wyatt.

ELIZABETH (*backs away*): The foul traitor.

GARDINER: Your devoted follower.

ELIZABETH: I know nothing of this fellow.

GARDINER: Sir Thomas?

WYATT: Lady, it was for you that we rebelled against

the lawful queen. I wrote to you. You had a letter from me.

(*Gardiner producing the letter we last saw being passed to de Noailles.*)

GARDINER: This is the letter.

(*Elizabeth is on the edge of panic she instinctively turns to Sussex whom she knows to be susceptible. Sussex is very affected by her youth and fear and brave stand. At this moment she is an intensely romantic figure.*)

ELIZABETH: My Lord, I am alone. I have no council. No friend. My enemies wish me dead. I am innocent. I love my sister with all my heart.

SUSSEX: Lady, you shall be fairly heard I promise you. I will speak to the Council if anything untoward is done here.

GARDINER: You do not deny the letter.

ELIZABETH: Where is my reply, Bishop?

GARDINER: Sir Thomas will testify you were privy to the rebellion.

ELIZABETH: Then bring me to trial. And bring him to testify. See what he will say when he has taken the oath and faces the people.

(*Gardiner looks at Wyatt. Wyatt is wavering.*)

ELIZABETH: Either bring me to trial or declare me innocent.

(*Suddenly Sussex intervenes.*)

SUSSEX: I am deeply troubled to see her Grace so tormented.

(*Gardiner loses his temper as he turns on the guards and indicates Wyatt.*)

GARDINER: Out. Out. Take him out. Take him out of my sight.

(*The door closes. A torch in a wall fitting lights her face, she falls to her knees.*)

ELIZABETH: I will survive.

27

Interior, ante-room. Day.

Gardiner comes striding into the ante-room to the Queen's bedroom at Whitehall and is stopped short by armed guards.

GARDINER: What in God's name?

RENARD (*voice off*): Her Majesty will see no one.

GARDINER: I am the Lord Chancellor. Let me pass.

RENARD: Save her confessor.

GARDINER (*turning to him*): Confessor?

RENARD: And her doctors.

(*Gardiner understands at once and is extremely agitated.*)

GARDINER: How long?

RENARD: Since midnight.

GARDINER: Will she die?

(*They stop.*)

RENARD: The doctors think it possible. She despairs. She says her prince has denied her and all men love and protect her sister.

GARDINER: Ah. Then you must see that her prince comes to her, your Excellency, and without delay.

RENARD: Agreed.

GARDINER: Write urgently to Madrid. Give a copy to her confessor and then her Majesty will know that it is not a trick.

RENARD: But the Princess Elizabeth?

(*Gardiner makes his decision in that moment. Forgetting Renard he turns his back on him and hurries out leaving Renard gaping at this breach of behaviour.*)

28

Interior, large cell. Day.

Marching feet approach. Elizabeth rises from table crosses to fire and sits. We see the turn of the key. See the door swing open slowly. Ashley and Elizabeth have been eating. It is early in the morning. Ashley rises. Elizabeth sits still, trembling. Bridges enters followed by the Chaplain who has with him all that is necessary to say Mass. Elizabeth looks from one to the other. Bridges bows formally. In his hand is a document with a seal hanging from it.

ELIZABETH: Is it death?

BRIDGES: You must prepare yourself. Your chaplain will hear your confession and write your last wishes. These will be witnessed by your servant, Mistress Ashley.

ELIZABETH: Is it now?

BRIDGES: Within the hour.

ELIZABETH: Let me write to the Queen.

BRIDGES: I dare not, madam.

ELIZABETH: A few words only. My chaplain could deliver them.

BRIDGES: The Queen is ill, your Grace. She will see no one.

(*Elizabeth is startled by this.*)

ELIZABETH: Ill?

BRIDGES: Yes.

ELIZABETH: Good Lieutenant, I have had no trial.

BRIDGES: Prepare yourself, your Grace, for there is no appeal.

ELIZABETH (*she is desperate for anything to prolong the moment*): Is that the warrant?

BRIDGES: It is, my Lady.

ELIZABETH: Then give it to me.

BRIDGES: I may not.

ASHLEY (*suddenly*): May not? May not show the heir to the throne the warrant that concerns her? By God's death you may. Or is it a conspiracy? Are you part of a conspiracy, sir?

BRIDGES: No conspiracy. Here is the seal.

(*He hands the document to Elizabeth who makes herself read it. Then it dawns on her.*)

67

ELIZABETH: Have you read this document?

BRIDGES: I have.

ELIZABETH: Then where is the signature of my sister, the Queen.

BRIDGES: As she is ill the Lord Chancellor has signed for her Majesty.

ELIZABETH: Have you proof?

BRIDGES: The Lord Chancellor himself gave me the warrant.

ELIZABETH: Will you execute me when the Queen is ill and may die and I am the next heir. Will you take such a terrible action?

(*Bridges is uneasy.*)

Execute me and the Lord Chancellor will deny all knowledge of the warrant. You will die for it.

BRIDGES: He is head of the Council, he is the first man in the land. I cannot deny him.

ELIZABETH: Good sir, if you value your life go not to the first man but to the first woman in this kingdom. See if she has condemned her sister to die without proof or without trial.

(*Bridges suddenly takes back the warrant.*)

BRIDGES: I will do as you say. (*To the priest.*) Come. You shall be my witness.

(*The door closes behind them. Elizabeth moves for the first time in the scene. She rises. She stretches like a cat. She suddenly dances wildly round the dungeon. She begins to laugh. Ashley is shocked.*)

ASHLEY: Stop. Stop. Are you mad? You will be heard.

ELIZABETH: I have won. I have won.

ASHLEY: Be silent for God's sake.

(Elizabeth embraces her and puts her mouth to her ear.)

ELIZABETH: Kat, Kat, don't you see. They've tried to kill me unlawfully because they have despaired of bringing me to trial. They know the law will not condemn me.

ASHLEY: But she will sign the warrant now. She was too ill to sign earlier.

ELIZABETH: Well or ill she dare not. Gardiner signed and failed. She dare not be seen by all the world to be her sister's murderer.

ASHLEY: Are you sure, my Lady? I know how clever you are but are you sure?

ELIZABETH: All that is left to them is the assassin. Of that I am sure.

ASHLEY: God help us both.

29

Interior, large cell. Day.

Two guards are boarding up the window of the cell. The cell door is open. From outside Elizabeth with another guard approach and enter. Elizabeth carries flowers. She is shocked by what she sees. The first two finish and move out without speaking. The third sees them out and is about to lock the cell door. He is the guard whom Elizabeth charmed on the first day.

ELIZABETH: Where is mistress Ashley?

GUARD: I know not.

(*Outside the drums start to roll.*)

ELIZABETH: What is happening?

GUARD: I know not, your Grace.

ELIZABETH: Come, be open with me—I will not betray you.

GUARD (*quick and quiet*): Sir Thomas Wyatt goes to the block out there. You are not to see or hear.

ELIZABETH: And Mistress Ashley?

GUARD: She is shut away in another place and she may not . . .

(*He stops as armed feet come marching and into the doorway comes Sir Henry Bedingfield, who has the look of a villain and the soul of a timid civil servant. With him are armed men in livery.*)

ELIZABETH: What is this?

BEDINGFIELD: Your escort, your Grace.

(*The drums reach their climax and in the dead silence Elizabeth's head turns sharply for a moment towards the boarded window.*)

ELIZABETH: Where is the Lieutenant of the Tower?

BEDINGFIELD: He is replaced for failing in his duty.

ELIZABETH: And you? What are you? Do you come to take me for a lamb to the slaughter?

(*Bedingfield is shocked.*)

70

BEDINGFIELD (*producing his warrant from Mary which is seen again later in a much thumbed condition—now fresh and new and sealed*): I, Sir Henry Bedingfield am commanded by her most gracious Majesty to keep you close confined until such times as you confess your practices against her.

(*Elizabeth plays to the guard.*)

ELIZABETH: Close confined! I am already close confined. Where do you take me? To Pomfret Castle where there were other murders in the past?

BEDINGFIELD (*to the guard*): Out.

(*As the guard obeys Elizabeth takes a step and gives him the flowers.*)

ELIZABETH: Remember me?

(*He is too frightened to kiss her hand. He goes.*)

ELIZABETH: You have not answered.

BEDINGFIELD: My orders are that you be moved in secret from this place.

ELIZABETH: In secret. Then you shall drag me, Master Bedingfield, for I will not go willingly to my death, I am innocent.

(*Suddenly there is a distant sound of bells pealing.*)

BEDINGFIELD: Madam, I am a true knight and no man shall harm you.

ELIZABETH (*sitting on the floor*): Then why in secret?

BEDINGFIELD: The Prince of Spain has come this day and meets the Queen's Majesty. There must be no disturbance in this happy time. You are to be far from London. You must be shut away.

71

(*Cannon sound.*)

BEDINGFIELD: Come. Rise up and gather your belongings, your Grace. The salute is fired for the royal Spanish galleon.

(*Slowly Elizabeth rises.*)

ELIZABETH: I must be shut away. Even the Tower is not enough for her. I must be shut away. (*Suddenly she turns and blazes at Bedingfield.*) A true knight! Then you shall gather my belongings Master Bedingfield, with all chivalry for I swear I will not.

BEDINGFIELD: Madam I . . . er I. (*He stutters on for a moment.*)

ELIZABETH: Do it.

(*Bedingfield turns and brings two men into the room to collect the belongings as the cannon continues.*)

BEDINGFIELD: Your Grace, I do only what her Majesty commands. We must go with all speed and the people must not see you.

ELIZABETH: God bless the people.

(*Outside cell door. Elizabeth walks straight out of the cell and then turns so that all will hear.*)

ELIZABETH: And God bless her Majesty, my loving sister.

30

Interior, royal bedroom. Night.

The royal bedroom at night. The ladies-in-waiting are excited and hurry in all directions with the clothes that they have taken from the Queen. Mary sits in bed tre-

mulous. A lady is sprinkling handfuls of rose petals over the pillows. Another lady is snuffing candles so that only one or two, stategically placed, remain. There is, outside the room, the sound of fanfares and laughter. Suddenly all the bustle is over. The ladies, grouped, are in deep curtseys before Mary. She waves them to leave. The fanfares end. She is alone. She touches her face and the hair that streams over her shoulders. She is torn between terror and hope now that the moment has come. Push on her frightened, hopeful, ageing face, and on a fresh candle burning near the bed. Mix to: the candle half-burned, pull to show her still sitting, still staring towards the door. There are tears on her cheeks. Mix to: the candle almost gutted, and pull to show that she is asleep with her mouth open, gasping at her bad dreams. A sound, and she wakes. It is difficult to wake from the heavy, sad sleep. She begins to focus, and then she sees him. Spontaneously the unloved, incipiently mad woman smiles. She opens her arms in welcome.

MARY: Philip, husband.

(Cut to her point of view. Philip, magnificent and sombre, standing pensively looking towards her. He is framed full length by the posts at the foot of the four poster. His expression does not change from the formal mask befitting the future King of Spain, the Netherlands etc. etc. He inclines his head slightly to acknowledge her. He is about to do his duty. He is not required to appear to enjoy it.)

31

Interior, door to ante-room.

A door is unlocked by a key on a large ring which carries many keys, all large. Door opens. Closes. Is carefully re-locked.

Interior, ante-room. Day.

Bedingfield and Elizabeth enter.

He chooses the next key. He has to concentrate hard. He passes Elizabeth with a slight bow, but not aware of her as he concentrates on the door out of the ante-chamber. She is looking at him with detestation. She is pale and heavy-eyed and her nerves are bad. Outside the door there is a guard. The guard stands aside as Bedingfield comes to unlock it. The guard is very much at attention. As Bedingfield is choosing the key. Elizabeth suddenly bursts out:

ELIZABETH: Gaoler!

(Bedingfield is shocked. He is aware of the guard hearing what is said and he is no match for Elizabeth.)

BEDINGFIELD: Your Grace.

ELIZABETH: Tyrant. I go mad with the sound of everlasting keys in locks—

BEDINGFIELD: I must obey my—

ELIZABETH: The sound of arms and of guards changing. The voices in the night crying the hour and that all is well. All is not well with me, gaoler.

(Bedingfield drops to one knee.)

BEDINGFIELD: Your Grace, I beg you not to name me such.

ELIZABETH: You are such. I am allowed no quill, no ink, no paper.

BEDINGFIELD: The council has most strictly ordered—

ELIZABETH: The Queen will not hear me. You will convey no appeals from me to your masters.

(*Bedingfield produces his much thumbed and creased memorial of instructions from Mary*.)

BEDINGFIELD: Your Grace, read, see. Here, as I have shown you before, these are my instructions. They are written in the Queen's Majesty's own hand and I darest not—

ELIZABETH: I know them. I have them by heart. Item: I am not cleared of suspicion. Item: I must be kept without conference with any person. Item: I must talk to no man, woman or child without your choosing and always in your presence, gaoler. Item: you must record for the council and render faithfully in writing every word I speak and every action I make—

BEDINGFIELD: Your Grace, forgive me, I dare not do otherwise. (*He rises and goes to unlock the door*.)

ELIZABETH: I am worse treated than any common prisoner in Newgate. What other citizen is forbidden any appeal? What other citizen is kept shut up for many months without evidence or witness against him?

(*Bedingfield opens the door and indicates that she should enter the chamber. She rises and goes to door*.)

I see I must continue this life without all worldly hope.

32

Interior, small room. Day.

She enters a small chamber. Cecil is there looking severe in dress and manner. Elizabeth is surprised and hopeful all in one second, and then cautious in the next. Cecil looks towards Bedingfield, expecting him to close the door on them and leave them alone. Instead Bedingfeld enters and begins laboriously to lock the door on the inside. Cecil realizing suddenly kneels to kiss Elizabeth's hand and as he rises makes a slight gesture of warning, his fingers to his lips. When he speaks his tone of voice appears to be sharp and hostile.

CECIL: Your Grace, the Queen's Majesty is angered by your silence.

ELIZABETH (*complete innocence*): I am a poor prisoner at Woodstock, Master Cecil. My only comfort is to walk daily in the pleasant fields of the Holy Scriptures. I am sorry that her Majesty is angry.

(*From here the information which is vital for him to convey is underlined, not for stress, but to make clear the spine of the scene.*)

CECIL: Her Majesty is merciful. Confess that Wyatt and his rebels had certain knowledge of your favour and you will be forgiven and set free.

(*Elizabeth continuing to be pure and innocent begins sadly to shake her head, mainly for Bedingfield's benefit, and Cecil goes on:*)

You may trust that promise, *for the Queen is big with child and desires happiness through all the land when an heir is born to her.*

(*The news is a terrible blow. Elizabeth begins to weep at the destruction of all her hope. She cannot contain the tears. She despairs. She just has the wit to use the tears as if in contrition. When she replies she can hardly get the words out.*)

ELIZABETH: I would not cause my loving sister one hour of trouble at this moment of joy for all true subjects, but I cannot sin against God and my honour by confessing what is false.

(*Bedingfield is affected by her distress.*)

76

CECIL (*producing a document*): I am sorry to find you so stubborn, madam, I have one further charge. Here are listed those of your household who resist the true church.

(*She takes it from him uncaring. He presses her trying to get her full attention.*)

You must tell these ignorant fools and knaves that this realm has bowed itself in humble penitence and supplication before Cardinal Pole, the Pope's legate, and has received a solemn absolution.

(*Still weeping and hardly hearing him.*)

ELIZABETH: I will do as you say.

(*Cecil realizes that she has not understood the danger.*)

CECIL: Tell them further that the Lord Chancellor, Bishop Gardiner—

(*Elizabeth becomes alert at the name of her most implacable enemy.*)

—has passed through Parliament a bill of heresy—*and those who do not conform, madam, no matter how innocent they seem in other matters, will be burned to death.* Tell them also that no one, *high or low,* will be spared. That great heretic Archbishop Cranmer recanted only from fear and in the false hope that he would be spared the flames.

ELIZABETH (*involuntary*): Oh God. Is he burned? Is the old man burned.

CECIL: At the last he denied his recantation; he defied the true church and thrust first into the flames the hand that had signed the papers.

77

(*Silence as she fights for control.*)

So warn your servants, madam, that false repentance which is a mockery of the living body of Christ upon the cross will be . . . smelled out and the offenders will die for it.

(*She has it all now. She controls herself.*)

ELIZABETH: They shall be told. They shall conform as I do, and am most happy to see, Master Cecil, that you have been guided back to the true faith.

(*He permits himself the slightest touch of irony.*)

CECIL: Madam, I am proud to tell you that I so plainly saw my former errors and made amends, that I, of all men, was chosen by our gracious sovereign to escort the Pope's good Cardinal from exile back to this penitent land.

(*Elizabeth is desperate to speak even for a single minute in private with Cecil. She turns to Bedingfield.*)

ELIZABETH: Sir, I beg you to order my chaplain to prepare to say mass so that Master Cecil and I may receive the most comfortable sacrament together before his journey back to Court.

(*Bedingfield hesitates. Cecil solemnly weighs in.*)

CECIL: I would take it most kindly, Master Bedingfield.

(*Bedingfield unlocks the door and goes. Elizabeth runs to see the door is shut. The despair overwhelms her and she is hysterical and out of control.*)

ELIZABETH: What shall I do? What shall I do?

CECIL: Stand firm.

ELIZABETH: I cannot. She is with child. All my hopes

are dead. I cannot bear to be shut up without hope, year after year, until I am old and withered. I must escape.

CECIL: Impossible. You must give them no excuse to bring you to trial.

ELIZABETH: Then I will go into exile. Help me. You must help me. Go to de Noailles. He will arrange matters. I will go to France. I will be welcome there.

(*Her voice has been rising. Suddenly Cecil cuts in with complete authority and stops her head.*)

CECIL: Be silent. Be still.

(*A pause as she stands shivering and weeping. Cecil speaks coldly and without sympathy to sting her.*)

I swear to you that if you hope to ascend the throne of England you must never leave the realm.

ELIZABETH: I will never be queen.

CECIL: The Queen is old. The Queen is often sick. The child may be stillborn or die as your brother, Edward, died.

ELIZABETH: That is possible.

CECIL: De Noailles is not your friend. De Noailles and his master, the King of France, have only one friend, and she is the Queen of Scots. If you flee to France you will never return. You will be a prisoner and the Scottish Queen will reign here after Mary, your sister.

ELIZABETH: That is true.

CECIL: And above all, you are the hope of the people. If you run like a coward, you will lose their love and you will kill their hope.

ELIZABETH: Is it true? I have spoken to no man save

my gaolers these many months. I believed myself
abandoned by all but God.

(*Outside there is the sound of feet.*)

CECIL: It is true.

(*Bedingfield enters the chamber to see Elizabeth in an
abased attitude.*)

ELIZABETH: I beg you, Master Cecil, tell my sister that
I prostrate myself before her, and I rejoice at the news
and pray she may be delivered of a healthy male child
to rule this kingdom.

BEDINGFIELD (*very seriously*): Amen.

33

Interior, gallery. Night.

*There is a red glow upon the windows of the gallery
of the palace at Whitehall. The gallery is empty. Sound
begins. High pitched and thin and cutting the nerves.
A sound of nightmare. Of falling in nightmare into
the void. The door of the ante-room bursts open and
suddenly, shockingly, a half-demented figure runs sobbing and gasping half the length of the gallery, rushing
madly at the camera and then collapsing, huddled up,
knees pulled up. At the fall the sound effects stop and
the natural sound of the woman gasping and sobbing
is heard and the voices, and the door being banged wide
open and the Queen's four attendants shaken out of
sleep come running to kneel by her. They try to lift
her and she lies spread across their arms with her now
lank, now greying hair spread out, and her face greasy
with sweat, her eyes glazed with the pain in her swollen
belly. She is half crazy. It is the beginning of her death.
The flames redden the windows from far away.*

MARY: *Mea culpa, mea culpa, mea maxima culpa.* I am

past my time and the child is dead in my womb. I have sinned and God punishes me. I have tolerated heretics and I carry death in my womb. Mary, Mother of God, intercede for me. I will burn the heresy out of the land and be forgiven. I must bear a son.

(*They lift her and she screams. Cut to the far end of the gallery and there stands Renard, sombre. Cut to Mary who cradles her belly in her arms and prays in Latin as they carry her towards the ante-room. Cut to Renard again as Philip joins him. They are near a window and the light from outside and from a torch on the wall plays on their faces.*)

RENARD: She is not with child. She has a growth in her womb. The family is cursed. The doctors despair.

PHILIP: I must leave this land.

RENARD: Your Highness must remember the purpose for which you came to England.

PHILIP: I have done my duty. I do not find her agreeable.

RENARD: She is virtuous and she is the Queen.

PHILIP: She is old, ugly and barren, and I can neither get the Crown Matrimonial nor any right to the succession.

RENARD: Consider. If Elizabeth succeeds she will make an alliance with France. If Elizabeth is destroyed or set aside the crown will go to the Queen of Scots.

PHILIP: So I waste my time here. My father is dying. I am going home.

RENARD: There are two pressing reasons that you should stay. First, you may prevent more of these stupid burnings.

(*They are looking through the windows.*)

81

PHILIP: She is too devout to hear reason!

RENARD: They are so prejudicial to the Catholic party that I fear for our lives—

PHILIP: And the second?

RENARD: To befriend Elizabeth, your Grace.

(*Philip is surprised.*)

PHILIP: It has been your earnest endeavour to have the lady dead.

RENARD: She is young. She is pleasing in appearance, full of wit and learning and the people love her. She is now our best hope.

PHILIP: She is also a prisoner and I have no power to order her to court. The Queen and the Council are implacable.

(*Renard knows what is not generally known. Philip, who had a heart of ice and was known to smile only once, upon hearing the news of the massacre of the Huguenots, was also a lecher.*)

RENARD: She has, by all reports, a passionate nature, your Grace.

(*Philip licks his lips!*)

I believe that the Queen who loves you more than her life, could be persuaded to bring the lady to court.

(*Philip nods. Renard looking towards the door through which Mary was carried.*)

If the princess becomes queen, Parliament, the Church and the people will combine to have her married to a proper prince.

PHILIP: I must see her.

34

Interior, gallery. Day.

Elizabeth with Bedingfield arriving in the gallery of the palace at Whitehall. As they are coming in there is a cry behind of 'make way, make way, make way for the Lord Chancellor'. The cry is urgent, and a litter is carried into view with Gardiner lying in it. He has had a stroke and is dying. Cut to Gardiner's point of view. Elizabeth looking down and turning her head to see him pass. Cut to Elizabeth's point of view from above of Gardiner looking up. Turning his head slightly as the litter passes. Cut to a close up of Gardiner as he tries to lift his head. He is too ill, his head falls sideways and the soul is half out of him. Cut to Elizabeth triumphant. She has seen him out. Bedingfield kneels to her.

BEDINGFIELD: Madam, I take my leave of you.

(Elizabeth is very happy.)

ELIZABETH: Master Bedingfield, if ever I have need to keep someone close captive I will send for you.

BEDINGFIELD: The discharge of this my service were the joyfullest tidings that ever came to me, as our Lord almighty knows.

(Elizabeth bursts out laughing at his earnest and lugubrious cry.)

35

Interior, ante-room. Day.

Philip in profile, his face lit by light from the slit through which he is looking. Over this the laughter echoes. Ease to show that Philip is at a spy hole. From the spy hole show Elizabeth being dressed by two maids. Cut between Philip's face and reactions and the light-hearted dressing sequence. Elizabeth is almost naked at the beginning of the scene. The shots of her should not be of full length, but show a certain rowdiness, almost tomboy quality, with clothes fluttering in the air, things being tugged and stretched.

Interior, Elizabeth's bedroom (Whitehall.) Day.

ELIZABETH (*caught in mid-sentence*): And I am to wear (*Tug.*) my finest gown (*Tug.*) for the benefit of the great prince (*Tug.*) of Spain by order of the (*Tug.*) Queen herself?

(*She runs to a dressing table and picks up some jewels to wear when the maids suddenly hush and the door to the adjoining room opens. Mary is there. She is now past forty, looks dreadfully ill and far older, and is unhappily set in her bigotry. Elizabeth, past twenty, is at her peak of attraction and at this moment flushed with freedom and the light-heartedness of freedom after years of strain and fear. Elizabeth prostrates herself. Mary sharply claps her hands at the maids who go. Cut to Philip watching keenly. Specifically watching as the women face each other when Elizabeth rises, show from his point of view, first a close up of the tormented face of his wife and then the flushed and delightful face of Elizabeth. Mary makes no attempt to dissemble. She was always more direct and honest than Elizabeth in her dealings.*)

God preserve, your Majesty.

MARY: You still do not confess your offence.

ELIZABETH: Were I guilty of the slightest offence against the honour, authority and administration of your Majesty I should be consoled by the thought that my troubles were a just punishment.

MARY: Then you maintain that you have been wrongfully punished.

1. The young Princess Elizabeth (Glenda Jackson) (*The Lion's Cub*).

2. Queen Mary Tudor (Daphne Slater) (*The Lion's Cub*).

3. The celebration of Thomas Seymour's marriage to the Queen Dowager, Catherine Parr, with (left to right) Lady Tyrwhit (Nicolette Bernard), Thomas (John Ronane) and Catherine (Rosalie Crutchley) (*The Lion's Cub*).

ELIZABETH: I must not say so, but innocent and loyal as I am I feel cut to the quick at the disgrace of even being thought capable of such a fault.

MARY: No doubt you will tell others you are wrong-fully punished and so add to the charges of tyranny against me.

ELIZABETH: No, if it please you. I have borne the burden, and I must bear it.

MARY: So you say. God knows where the truth lies.

ELIZABETH: If I am lying then I request neither favour nor pardon at your hands.

Interior, ante-room. Day.

Cut to Philip. He is deeply distressed. Cut back.

Interior, Elizabeth's bedroom. Day.

MARY: I tell you plainly, madam, that though I can prove no fault in you I will not have you near me. My husband wishes to see you. After that I will send you not only from this Court, but from this land.

(*Mary leaves. Elizabeth sinks to sit on a stool, holding her head. There is a sound. She looks up. Philip is standing before her. The panel through which he has entered is partly open. For once she is at a loss. She does not rise. Philip kneels, takes her hand, kisses it with more than is formally required, and then looks up at her. Elizabeth is very cautious and silent.*)

PHILIP: The Queen's Majesty, my dear wife, is unwell.

(*Elizabeth is still silent.*)

She cannot bear a child.

(*Elizabeth is sure it is a trap.*)

ELIZABETH: I pray God that it is not true.

(*Philip rising and bringing her to her feet.*)

PHILIP: The lady is barren.

ELIZABETH: Why am I sent for?

PHILIP: I am returning to Spain. My father is dying. I shall be king in my own right before you see me again. I believe you to be much wronged. I am your friend and I will speak for you to the Queen.

(*Elizabeth is about to launch one more of her loyal set pieces:*)

ELIZABETH: In all my life I have done nothing to imperil the person of the Queen or the commonwealth—

(*She would go on to say—'Of this realm'. Philip calmly places a finger on her lips and she stops.*)

PHILIP: Princess, what is passed is dead. We must now make other shifts.

(*She is silent and disconcerted.*)

It is my joy to find you both beautiful and full of wit. Wise in statecraft and true in religion. You have all the virtues lady and you have a loving prince for your friend.

(*He kisses her on the cheek. Philip goes. Elizabeth sits and bursts out laughing.*)

86

Interior, royal bedroom. Day.

In the Queen's bedchamber, the Queen sits at her dressing table with Philip near. She is very angry.

MARY: I will banish her from the kingdom.

PHILIP: I do not wish it.

MARY: I will have her married to some petty prince far from this realm.

PHILIP: I do not wish that.

MARY: You found her pleasing?

PHILIP: I found her innocent.

MARY: Ah. As innocent as her mother.

PHILIP: Treat her gently as her rank demands.

MARY: She is the illegitimate child of a criminal who was punished as a public strumpet. She is no sister of mine. She shall not inherit this realm. She has bewitched you.

PHILIP: Tomorrow I sail for Spain.

MARY: Oh God.

PHILIP: If you wish to see me again treat her gently.

(Mary turns from the stool and kneels before Philip holding him tight with both arms:)

MARY: Don't desert me. I live only for your company and for your safe return.

(He disengages.)

PHILIP: Bring her with you to Greenwich tomorrow. It will calm the violent feelings against you and every Catholic if she is seen to ride by your side.

(*She remains on her knees.*)

Good night, madam.

(*Look down at her. As the door closes. Cut to:*)

Exterior, Elizabeth and Mary riding. Day.

A low shot looking up at Mary and Elizabeth both finely dressed mounted on horseback, each horse held by a groom in livery. See them against a blue sky. A mast or masts, banners blowing or rigging in the background. Trumpets are sounding a fanfare and the bosuns' pipes begin to shrill. The cries of sailors and the sound of a crowd, but all we see are the sisters, Mary weeping and trying to hide it. Mary turning her horse away from the river.

MARY: I pray to God he returns before I am too old to bear him a son.

ELIZABETH: Your Majesty, I will take my leave and keep myself as you order me, from your sight.

MARY: Do so.

(*Then she suddenly bursts out.*)

My husband would have you treated gently.

(*She controls herself. Impulsively she takes a ring from her finger. It is next to the finger on which she wears her betrothal ring of gold and black.*)

Take this. Wear it. Think of me.

(*Elizabeth takes the ring and puts it on. Mary looks at her betrothal ring.*)

88

MARY: You will know that I am dead if this betrothal ring is brought to you, for I never take it from my finger.

ELIZABETH (*impulsively*): Sister, it is hard to bear the long months away from court. The time is full of rumours and terrors and any villain may start a plot and use my name and I am helpless to defend myself.

MARY: You will never more be accused unheard. My husband speaks well of you.

ELIZABETH: Good sister, acknowledge the act of succession. Keep me with you.

(*Pause.*)

MARY: I will die first.

(*Elizabeth turns her horse out of frame. Push in on Mary then down until the hand with the betrothal ring fills the frame.*)

37

Interior, royal bedroom. Day.

A cross filling the frame. Pan up the cross to the hand which lies on the counterpane holding the rosary to which the cross is affixed. See hand and ring. Hold a beat. The rosary slips from the fingers.

Exterior, horses galloping at Hatfield. Day.

Horses galloping through the frame. Show the galloping legs and the spurred boots driving the horses on. There is dust and the shouting voices of riders. Cut to hands with whips, using them, and then to the straining of faces of one or two of the riders, courtiers. Elizabeth, cloaked, is walking among trees. There is the sound of a horse and Cecil rides up. He dismounts and goes to her and kneels. He offers her the betrothal ring. She takes it. She takes off her hat and skims it high in the air. Over the trees ...

ELIZABETH: This is the Lord's doing. It is marvellous in our eyes.

CECIL: You are the only right heir by blood and lawful succession to the crown. I pledge myself to serve you as my only sovereign lady and queen.

ELIZABETH: You shall be my chief secretary of the Privy Council. This judgment I have of you. You will not be corrupted by any manner of gift. That you will be faithful to the state, and that without respect to my private will you shall give me that counsel which you think best. If you shall know anything necessary to be declared to me in secret then you shall show it to my-self only and assure yourself I shall not fail to be silent in my turn.

(Pause. Cecil rises.)

CECIL: There is much to do. I pray your Majesty is in good health.

ELIZABETH: Although I may not be a lion, I am a lion's cub and I have a lion's heart.

(She walks away towards house.)

THE MARRIAGE GAME

by
ROSEMARY ANNE SISSON

The Marriage Game was first shown on BBC Television on February 24 1971, as the second play in a series entitled *Elizabeth R*, with the following cast:

ELIZABETH	*Glenda Jackson*
ROBERT DUDLEY, EARL OF LEICESTER	*Robert Hardy*
BISHOP DE QUADRA	*Esmond Knight*
COUNT DE FERIA	*Leonard Sachs*
WILLIAM CECIL	*Ronald Hines*
EARL OF SUSSEX	*John Shrapnel*
DUKE OF NORFOLK	*David Strong*
MARY SIDNEY	*Caroline Harris*
HENRY SIDNEY	*Anthony Ainley*
AMYE DUDLEY	*Stacey Tendeter*
MRS PINTO	*Clare Austin*
KATHERINE ASHLEY	*Rachel Kempson*
DOCTOR BURCOT	*Denis Carey*
SIR JAMES MELVILLE	*John Cairney*
LETTICE KNOLLYS	*Angela Thorne*

TWELVE LORDS *Terry Rendall, Bernard McConville, Rodney Cardiff, Christopher Holmes, Roger Minnis, Donald Groves, Peter Richardson, John Higgins, Ross Huntley, Giles Melville, Ian Calvin, Roger Charles*

SIX LADIES *Brenda Gogan, Linzi Scott, Jaqui Rawley, Julia Stratton, Susan Patrice, Diana Chapman*

THREE SERVANTS *Jo Hall (female), Lawrence Faerer, Ricki Reeves*

TWO RED GUARDS *Trevor Lawrence, Andrew Dempsey*

THREE BLACK GUARDS *Laurie Goode, Steven King, David Pelton*

MR BLOUNT *Roy Brent*

Producer Roderick Graham
Director Herbert Wise
Designer Richard Henry

CHARACTERS

ELIZABETH I

ROBERT DUDLEY, EARL OF LEICESTER

BISHOP DE QUADRA

COUNT DE FERIA

SIR WILLIAM CECIL

EARL OF SUSSEX

DUKE OF NORFOLK

MARY SIDNEY

HENRY SIDNEY

AMYE DUDLEY

MRS PINTO

KATHERINE ASHLEY

DOCTOR BURCOT

SIR JAMES MELVILLE

LETTICE KNOLLYS

INTERIORS

Room at Penshurst
Privy chamber
Corridor
Bedchamber
Presence chamber
Spanish Ambassador's room
Room in house at Kew
Hall/landing/stairs at Cumnor Place
Living-room, Cumnor Place
Bedroom, Cumnor Place
Mary Sidney's room

EXTERIORS

Queen's barge
Country
Street

1

Exterior, countryside. Day.

Robert Dudley, on a superb white horse. He is twenty-five years old, a dark, handsome man, with a touch of the gypsy about him. He and the horse dance joyously along the wintry road to Hatfield.

2

Interior, Spanish Ambassador's room. Day.

Bishop de Quadra, a Spanish Grandee of the Church, stands by the window. He turns as Count de Feria hurries in, a small, stupid, self-satisfied man.

DE QUADRA: Well? Did she see you?

DE FERIA: Oh yes! She saw me. For a few moments. A few moments, me! The Spanish Ambassador! She begged me to forgive her. 'So many kind friends have come to see her.'

DE QUADRA: And have they really?

DE FERIA: You would think the road to Hatfield was a Pilgrims Way, and she a saint. They cannot ride there fast enough, nor bow low enough when they arrive.

DE QUADRA: This is a black day for us, Count de Feria, and for our Master.

DE FERIA: It may be so, Bishop.

DE QUADRA: *May* be? The day when we exchange a faithful daughter of the Church, King Philip's wife, for a Protestant heretic?

DE FERIA: Heretic, maybe. But she is young, and must have a husband.

DE QUADRA: Will she allow King Philip to choose for her?

DE FERIA: I think she will. I think she must.

3

Exterior, countryside. Day.

Robert rides towards Hatfield. Robert canters down hill. Pan him through sun's flare.

4

Interior, room at Hatfield. Day.

Elizabeth comes forward to meet William Cecil, a cautious, slightly plump, man of thirty-eight. She is twenty-five and plainly dressed, but there is a glow of excitement in her face.

ELIZABETH: Well, my Secretary?

(Cecil kneels.)

CECIL: Your Majesty, you do me too much honour.

(She raises him with both hands, eyeing him thoughtfully.)

ELIZABETH: I think you will find more pains than honour in serving me. I mean to be a monarch for use and not merely for show. I shall wear you for my work-a-day garb, and I mean to wear you hard.

CECIL: Your Highness may wear me out, if it pleases you to do so.

ELIZABETH: One thing I will promise you. When there is something you want to say for my private ear alone, then I alone will hear it, and no one else ever will—

(*She glances round, and we see that there are others in the room, including Sussex, Norfolk and Robert.*)

—no, not even the other members of my Council.

(*Robert's face shows that he doesn't like this much. Elizabeth turns towards him, smiling.*)

How is my Master of Horse?

(*He falls on both knees, but smiles boldly up at her.*)

ROBERT: How is my mistress of hearts?

(*She laughs delightedly. The flattery is broad enough for her to take it as elaborate courtly flattery and yet there is just a gratifying touch of serious meaning in his voice. Elizabeth raises Robert with one hand.*)

ELIZABETH: Will you find me a beautiful horse to ride to London?

ROBERT: The best in the land!

ELIZABETH: A white one, I think.

(*Robert is slightly thrown by this. Has she seen his horse?*)

ROBERT: I have the very— Ah, but he is not a horse for a woman to ride.

ELIZABETH (*swiftly*): You rode him!

(*So she did see him.*)

Don't I ride as well as you?

97

(*Robert hesitates. He is the best horseman in the land.*)

ROBERT: When we were both eight, you rode as well as I did—

ELIZABETH (*annoyed*): But now—

ROBERT: But now you are a queen, and must take care.

ELIZABETH: I won't be imprisoned by being a queen. (*Glaring at him.*) No one will ever imprison me again!

ROBERT (*grinning at her cheerfully*): I believe you!

ELIZABETH: I will buy your horse. (*Looking at him sideways.*) Shall I buy it with the money you lent me when I needed it?

ROBERT: Did I lend you money?

ELIZABETH: And sold some of your land to do it.

ROBERT: I have forgotten.

ELIZABETH: I haven't. I never will.

(*She turns aside with him into the window embrasure. Throughout the play, she is never alone with him— only apart. Sussex, a sturdy, sensible man of thirty-two, watches them morosely, glancing at Cecil.*)

SUSSEX: Robert Dudley! I don't like it. We should never forget that he's Northumberland's son. There's no nobility to inherit there—only treachery and ambition.

CECIL: He has enough to satisfy him for the moment.

SUSSEX: You think so? Master of the Queen's Horse?

CECIL: It keeps him close to her, my Lord Sussex, and always showing to advantage. He's a good horseman.

SUSSEX (*grimly*): Yes. They say that managing a horse is like managing a woman.

(*Deliberately looking at Cecil.*)

And the Queen is a woman.

CECIL: You don't think—

SUSSEX: She is a woman.

(*Elizabeth is serious now, looking out of the window. Robert has stopped flattering her, and watches her sympathetically.*)

ELIZABETH: I used to walk on the leads of the Tower sometimes, and look towards the door of your room, and wonder whether you ever walked there, too. Once or twice a little boy brought me flowers. But then he came to me one day and said, 'Lady, I can bring you no more flowers'. I suppose they were afraid the flowers came from you, and might have a message in them.

ROBERT: The flowers did come from me, and there was always a message in them.

(*Elizabeth looks at Robert, frowning a little.*)

ELIZABETH: I never know when you are speaking the truth.

ROBERT: Does it matter?

ELIZABETH: Yes. I like to know what the truth is, and then I can decide whether or not to believe it.

ROBERT (*laughing*): The truth is that you will go to London in two days' time, riding on my horse and over my heart, and into the hearts of all your people.

5

Exterior, street. Day.

Elizabeth rides at the head of a procession, waving and smiling at the cheering crowds.

6

Interior, Spanish Ambassador's room. Day.

De Feria disgustedly listening to peals of bells out of the window. De Quadra placidly sitting watching him.

DE FERIA: She smiles and laughs and calls out to the common people like a dairy maid at a fair! A Queen should have more dignity.

DE QUADRA: Has she chosen her Council yet?

DE FERIA: Her Council! She has chosen William Cecil as her Principal Secretary and that traitor, Robert Dudley, as her Master of Horse. Thomas Parry, an old domestic, is Treasurer of her household, and that woman, Katherine Ashley, known for her treachery in Queen Mary's lifetime, is First Lady of the Bed-chamber.

DE QUADRA: But, her Council! The men who will govern for her. Will she have any of Queen Mary's Councillors?

DE FERIA: No one knows.

DE QUADRA: No one knows?

DE FERIA: They all waited upon her at Hatfield, and she was very gracious to them all. She said she meant to have a smaller Council than her sister's. She begged those who were left out to forgive her, since it derived from no unkindness towards them on her part.

DE QUADRA: But *which*? Which did she leave out?

DE FERIA: She didn't say. They departed, still not knowing. It's absurd. But what else is to be expected when the government of a country is in the hands of a woman, and she a mere girl, who is sharp, but altogether lacking in prudence!

(*Close up of de Quadra's face, almost expressionless, he turns his head towards de Feria.*)

DE QUADRA: But, Count de Feria—

(*De Feria turns to look at him.*)

—while none are chosen, all may hope. And meanwhile she smiles and laughs and calls out to the common people, and every day she sits more firmly on the throne, and every day she has less need of our Master's help to keep her there.

7

Interior, privy chamber. Day.

A few noblemen sitting round a table, including Sussex, Cecil and Norfolk, a proud, stupid and rash young man of twenty-two. The big chair at the end of the table is empty.

CECIL: My Lords, since we have much weighty business today, I would suggest that we should put aside the appointment of officers and turn our attention to the three main questions—

(*He is interrupted as the door is opened from outside.*)

OFFICER: The Queen's Grace!

(*Elizabeth stands, smiling in the doorway. They all get to their feet.*)

101

ELIZABETH: My Lords, we are minded to join our Council today.

(*Norfolk gets behind the big chair with great rapidity, holding it for Elizabeth, who sits, with a charming smile for him.*)

My Lord of Norfolk.

NORFOLK: Your Highness!

(*Elizabeth folds her jewelled hands on the table, as the men all sit.*)

ELIZABETH: Well, Master Secretary, what business today?

(*Cecil looks at a sheet of paper.*)

CECIL: Three main matters, your Highness, among some lesser ones. First the reform of the currency.

ELIZABETH: The currency. Yes, that must be seen to without delay.

(*The men glance at each other, smiling slightly. Not a woman's matter, this.*)

SUSSEX: It won't be easy. The coinage is greatly debased.

ELIZABETH: No matter what it costs we must ensure that the people know that the coins of the realm are legal tender, as I will always be to them. If my people cannot trust the coins they cannot trust me.

SUSSEX: Very well, your Highness, we will . . .

ELIZABETH: Set out on paper the measures you propose, and I will study them.

(*The lords exchange startled glances.*)

What next?

CECIL: A matter I mentioned to your Majesty yesterday. The appointment of your Majesty's judges.

ELIZABETH: You are quite right. Justice has often been debased, as well as the coinage, and the people have suffered from it. Judges must learn to give justice freely, as they receive it from their Prince. They must have a care over my people. They are *my* people. Everyone oppresses and plunders them without mercy, and they cannot revenge their wrongs or help themselves. The judges must take care of them, take care of them, for they are my charge.

(*There are tears in her eyes and the Council are all moved. She turns to Cecil and smiles.*)

What next?

CECIL (*carefully reading from the paper*): Thirdly, the matter of the Queen's marriage.

(*Elizabeth unfolds her hands and strikes the table a neat blow with the side of her hand.*)

ELIZABETH: Leave that aside.

SUSSEX: Your Highness, the question of your marriage must be discussed . . .

ELIZABETH: But not in this place or at this time. Leave that aside.

8

Interior, Spanish Ambassador's room. Day.

De Feria and de Quadra where we left them.

DE FERIA: I shall write to King Philip. If he means to marry her, it must be done at once.

9

Interior, presence chamber. Day.

The pattern of Elizabeth's court is now visible. Attractive young men and pretty girls, all beautifully dressed, stand around talking and laughing, to form a background to Elizabeth and Cecil, who talk apart. Among those who stand in the background are Sussex, Norfolk, Sir Henry Sidney, twenty-nine years old and a trifle solid, and Mary Sidney, his wife, Robert's sister, a very pretty, gentle girl of twenty-two.

CECIL: King Philip has qualms, because you are a heretic, and because he fears the marriage might involve him in a war with France over Mary Stuart's claim to the throne. He would insist that you should become a Catholic and return England to the Catholic faith.

(Elizabeth raises her eye-brows very slightly.)

He wishes you to obtain a secret dispensation from the Pope to allow you to marry your late sister's husband ...

ELIZABETH: He wishes *me* to do it?

CECIL: He would rather not be involved.

ELIZABETH *(demurely)*: Of course.

CECIL: And you must understand that because of his commitments in Spain and in the Low Countries, he could visit you in England only occasionally, and then only for a brief time, even though you might be pregnant.

ELIZABETH: In short, the perfect husband.

(She goes off into a peal of laughter. Cecil looks anxious.)

CECIL: But at the same time, your Highness, we mustn't . . .

(*She suddenly turns her eyes on him, and lifts up one commanding forefinger. She doesn't mind being taken for a fool by Philip, but she won't have it from Cecil. Cecil falls silent.*)

ELIZABETH: I will see the Spanish Ambassador now.

CECIL: Yes, your Highness. (*He bows and prepares to retire.*)

ELIZABETH: Cecil!

(*He pauses.*)

Are those the conditions he means to propose to me?

CECIL: No, your Highness. That letter from King Philip was meant for his Ambassador's eyes alone.

ELIZABETH: I see.

(*They eye each other with grave enjoyment. Cecil goes off. Elizabeth moves towards the Sidneys.*)

Mary!

MARY: Your Highness?

ELIZABETH: Where is that brother of yours? We gave him leave to go down into the country for a few days, and he has been gone more than a week.

MARY: I believe the roads to Oxford are very bad, your Highness.

ELIZABETH: If he doesn't come back soon, I shall send your husband after him—

(*Mary smiles at Henry.*)

—and then, after Harry, I shall send your brother Ambrose, like rolling cheeses down a hill, and in the end we shall probably lose them all, so you had better write to Robert and tell him to come back at once.

MARY (*smiling*): Yes, your Highness.

ELIZABETH: I can't think why he should want to go into the country at this time of year, anyway!

HENRY: His wife is moving into another house, and no doubt he felt it his duty to go and see that she was comfortable.

(*She turns away, but the Spanish Ambassador, de Feria, is just approaching with Cecil, so that may be why she doesn't seem to hear the remark. The others fall back a little, as Elizabeth holds out her hand to de Feria with a gracious smile. He kneels to kiss it.*)

ELIZABETH: Count de Feria! How pleased I am to see you! It is much too long since I saw you last!

(*Elizabeth raises him with feminine graciousness.*)

DE FERIA: It would not have been so long, your Highness, if I had lodgings at Court, as I always used to.

ELIZABETH (*astonished*): You are not lodged at Court? (*Glancing at Cecil.*) Why is this?

DE FERIA: I am told that there is no room for me now, and the result is . . .

ELIZABETH (*cutting in gaily*): The result is that when I do see you, it is all the more welcome! How is my dear brother, King Philip? (*Unwelcome emphasis on the word 'brother'.*)

DE FERIA: He is well, your Majesty, and I have messages from him which . . .

(*He glances round at the cheerful, frivolous young people about them.*)

. . . which I would prefer to tell to your private ear alone.

ELIZABETH (*gaily*): Oh, we are all friends here, to you and to King Philip. We can have no secrets from our friends.

(*De Feria hesitates, and then gives in with rather bad grace.*)

DE FERIA: King Philip wishes to become more than a friend to you . . . more than a brother.

(*She looks innocently enquiring.*)

(*Impressively.*) I am charged to bring you his dear love, and an offer of his hand in marriage.

ELIZABETH: You must forgive me. I had not expected this. I thought the difference in our religion must bar all thought of marriage. (*She looks astonished, turning aside in maidenly modesty. She really does it awfully well.*)

DE FERIA: King Philip is sure you will allow him to lead you once more out of darkness into the light.

(*Furious glances at each other from the Sidneys and Sussex. Elizabeth only smiles sweetly.*)

ELIZABETH: Then there is the matter of our relationship. A dispensation would be needed.

(*De Feria, disconcerted, throws a quick glance between Elizabeth and Cecil. Could they have read the letter? Impossible!*)

DE FERIA: These matters can be arranged.

ELIZABETH (*sadly pensive*): But dispensations are not always efficacious, as Catherine of Aragon found.

DE FERIA: I am sure that King Philip's love for you, and your tenderness towards him will conquer all obstacles.

(*Elizabeth gazes trustfully back at him, then looks away, briefly communes with herself, and turns back to him.*)

ELIZABETH: You have so taken me by surprise that I cannot give you an answer immediately.

(*She smiles shyly at Cecil and the others.*)

I must take counsel with my advisors, to see what is best for the kingdom. I am a queen, and cannot follow my own desires as an ordinary woman may do. If it were not so ...

(*A brief, wistful sign completes the sentence. Elizabeth holds out her hand.*)

Dear Count de Feria, take this answer to your Master, that if ever I consider marrying outside this country, I will think of King Philip of Spain.

10

Interior, hall landing at Cumnor Place. Evening.

Shooting upstairs to the empty landing.

ROBERT (*out of view*): I've told you before, it's impossible. The Queen doesn't like wives at Court.

(*Robert and Amye are walking along the landing. Close up of Amye's face, round and obstinate, very pretty as a young girl.*)

AMYE: Your sister is at Court with her husband.

ROBERT: Amye, my sister has been a friend of the Queen's since we were all children together.

(*They approach the living-room door, passing Mrs Pinto, the confidential maid.*)

Interior, living-room. Evening.

Amye and Robert enter.

ROBERT: The Queen's brother, poor Edward, died in Sir Henry Sidney's arms.

(*He picks up a book.*)

I'll take this back to London.

AMYE: Oh yes! You can take the book back, but not me! The Queen knows me. She came to our wedding.

ROBERT: That was a long time ago. When she was Princess Elizabeth. Things are very different now.

AMYE: Why?

ROBERT: She looks on me as her friend, her advisor. She does nothing without consulting me. Can't you see what an advantage that is to us? But there's always someone waiting to step into my place.

AMYE (*under her breath*): I wish they would.

ROBERT (*furiously*): Amye!

Interior, hall/stairs. Evening.

Mrs Pinto looks up quickly.

Interior, living-room. Evening.

Robert comes to sit down again.

You've forgotten what it was like before, haven't you? You've forgotten what it's like to be penniless. When you came to see me in the Tower, you had to borrow the money for the journey from your father. You've forgotten that, I suppose!

AMYE: He never grudged it. And at least I *saw* you then.

ROBERT: Well, you're seeing me now! You said you wanted to see me—here I am!

(She looks at him sideways, shrinking away a little. Robert softens.)

Amye, you know I love the country. When we were first married, we were very happy together in Norfolk, weren't we?

(She only looks at him.)

Do you think I want to live in the noise and stink of London? But this is my chance! I know her. I know her better than any man alive. She never has to pretend with me. That means more to her than anything.

AMYE: And what happens when she marries?

ROBERT: That depends on what happens now. The Queen must marry, whether she wants to or not, and I must have a say in her choice of a husband. I must see which way the wind blows, and add my puff to the others, or the husband will blow me out of Court. Whoever sits beside her on the throne must know that I helped to put him there.

(He had already stopped speaking to her, and is speaking to himself.)

110

AMYE: People are saying that you don't want her to take a husband, that you want to marry her yourself.

ROBERT (*exasperated out of all discretion*): How can I marry her? I am already married!

Interior, hall/stairs, Cumnor Place. Evening.

Mrs Pinto, attentive.

11

Interior, presence chamber. Day.

De Feria confronting Elizabeth with Cecil, Sussex, Henry Sidney, Mary Sidney and others in attendance.

ELIZABETH: News, my dear Count de Feria?

DE FERIA: Yes, your Highness. King Philip, despairing of the prize he first sought, has taken in marriage . . .

ELIZABETH (*wistfully*): He despaired very soon. That great love you spoke of, could it not last four months?

(*She heaves a pathetic little sigh, and turns away. De Feria looks at her, alarmed, and glances for support to Cecil and then to Sussex. Henry and Mary see her face, as we now do, convulsed with laughter. She turns back to de Feria, still not quite serious.*)

But I send my best wishes for happiness to him . . . (*Smiling outright.*) And even more to his wife!

DE FERIA: King Philip wishes me to say that his dearest hope is that the prize which he himself may not enjoy might yet be won by his nephew, the Emperor's eldest son, the Archduke Ferdinand.

ELIZABETH: Any relative of my dear brother Philip

must be dear to me. But, Count de Feria, I must tell you that if I could choose for myself—

(*De Feria's face shows sudden, acute attention.*)

—the single state is dearer to me than any husband. I do not mean ever to marry.

(*She sees Katherine Ashley approaching carrying some materials.*)

Ah, Kat, is that the stuff for my gown? Let me see it. Mary, come and see. Spanish velvet. (*Smiling back at de Feria.*) See how many good things come out of Spain.

(*She and Mary and other young women gather round Katherine Ashley, laughing and talking, and looking at pieces of velvet. De Feria casts his eyes up to heaven.*)

DE FERIA: Velvets and gowns! What has this to do with ruling a Kingdom?

(*Sussex turns to look at Cecil.*)

SUSSEX: Cecil, does she mean it?

CECIL (*smiles*): If you were a suitor, my Lord Sussex, and the lady said, 'I won't marry you because I love another', you would be offended. But if she said, 'I am minded never to marry—'

SUSSEX: Meaning, 'Until the time comes—'

(*They both turn, smiling, to look at Elizabeth, and both stop smiling, as they see that Robert has joined the group and that he and Elizabeth are laughing at each other.*)

The lions of Europe come courting her and what do they find? That mongrel cur always yapping at her heels.

ELIZABETH (*calling out*): Count de Feria, come and help us choose.

(*De Feria approaches, with a reluctant smile. The whole thing is terribly beneath his dignity.*)

DE FERIA: Your Majesty, I really—

ELIZABETH: It isn't easy, you see, to find a colour to go with this awkward hair of mine.

ROBERT: Yes, it is awkward hair.

(*Elizabeth turns her head to look at him.*)

It catches the eye. Wherever you go, we all turn to look after you, like daisies to the sun. Isn't that so, Count de Feria?

(*De Feria stumped again.*)

ELIZABETH: His tongue is not so nimble as yours. He prefers truth to compliment.

(*It is a reproof, and there is a sudden silence. Anyone but Robert would be abashed, but he looks boldly back at her.*)

ROBERT: How fortunate he is, then, to be here, where both are one!

(*She looks at him sternly and then suddenly bursts out laughing and he laughs, too.*)

Will you dance with me this evening, your Majesty?

ELIZABETH: Yes. But only because you dance better than any other man.

ROBERT: As you dance better than any other woman.

113

ELIZABETH: We are well matched then.

(*She says it with an air of daring and then bursts out laughing again and he laughs, too, and kisses her hand and she keeps hold of it, as they bend together over the velvets, which Katherine Ashley is holding. She glances uneasily at them.*)

SUSSEX: One of these days I'll beat him like the dog he is!

CECIL (*glancing at him*): The Queen would not like that. It would spoil the game. (*He goes forward and catches Elizabeth's attention.*) Your Highness, a letter has just come which I should like you to read at once.

ELIZABETH: A letter? Oh? (*In high good humour.*) Is it written in Latin, or French, or— (*Glancing round triumphantly.*)—Swedish?

(*She goes off, followed by Cecil. De Feria gazes after her.*)

DE FERIA: Swedish? Why did Her Highness . . . ?

ROBERT (*amused*): It is rumoured that Crown Prince Eric of Sweden is another suitor for the Queen's hand in marriage.

(*De Feria looks at him in dismay.*)

12

Interior, Spanish Ambassador's room. Whitehall. Day.

De Feria looks at de Quadra.

DE FERIA: She is worse than ten thousand devils. Even Cecil says he doesn't know what she means to do. And as for me—I think they know in Spain what happens at the English Court before I do! Well, you are the new Spanish Ambassador. I wish you joy of the task.

DE QUADRA: No matter what she says, she must marry. No woman can rule a Kingdom. And, moreover, she must—if she can—bear children.

(*De Quadra looks at de Feria, and says:*)

If she can?

DE FERIA (*shrugging*): Some say she cannot, but most believe that she can.

DE QUADRA: At all events, she must marry. It is only a matter of bringing pressure to bear on her advisors to make the right choice.

13

Interior, corridor. Day.

Elizabeth and Cecil enter.

ELIZABETH: Prince Eric of Sweden writes quite a lover's letter! (*Laughs delightedly.*) He writes better than the Archduke Ferdinand.

CECIL (*gravely*): Your Majesty, the Archduke Ferdinand would never become your husband unless you would consent to make England Catholic.

ELIZABETH: Then I might as well have married King Philip!

(*She laughs again, looking up at Cecil.*)

CECIL: But his brother, the Archduke Charles . . .

ELIZABETH: Would make fewer demands?

CECIL: He's in a less vulnerable position.

ELIZABETH (*swiftly*): Yes, he'll never be Emperor!

Interior, privy chamber. Day.

They walk through into the Privy Chamber. Cecil glances at her and decides to ignore her last remark.

CECIL: The only condition Archduke Charles would make . . .

ELIZABETH (*mildly*): Condition?

CECIL:—is that he should celebrate his own religion in public.

ELIZABETH: That seems reasonable. But I would never marry any man I had not seen.

(*Cecil looks at her, alarmed.*)

CECIL: Your Highness, he—

ELIZABETH (*innocently*): H'm?

CECIL: We could never expect the Archduke Charles to—to come courting—

(*Elizabeth laughs. The idea delights her.*)

He would have to be assured of success.

ELIZABETH: How could that be, when I haven't seen him?

(*She is still smiling, but slowly stops smiling. She stands up and moves a few steps away. Cecil hesitates and then moves after her. She looks back at him.*)

My sister married a man she had never seen. When he

4. Princess Elizabeth with the Earl of Sussex (John Shrapnel) in front of Traitor's Gate at the Tower (*The Lion's Cub*).

5. Queen Elizabeth I and Robert Dudley, Earl of Leicester (Robert Hardy) on the Greenwich road (*The Marriage Game*).

came to England, and saw her for the first time, his face showed—everything. She loved him, but he never loved her. (*Smiling bitterly*.) I think he loved *me* more than he loved her. Do you think I will chance a marriage like that?

CECIL: No, your Highness, we would never have you marry any man you could not love.

ELIZABETH: It is more important that he should love me. (*Pause*.) If I marry at all. (*She turns back to the table*.) I will answer the Prince of Sweden's letter. What does he look like? I have heard that he is very ugly—almost deformed.

CECIL: On the contrary, Highness, a very pleasant-looking man, with gold hair.

ELIZABETH: I shall tell him what I told him when my sister was alive, that I do not mean to marry.

CECIL: And what is the Imperial Ambassador to tell the Archduke Charles?

ELIZABETH: That I will never marry a man I have not seen.

Exterior, countryside. Day.

Elizabeth and Robert out hunting. They jump a log, pause, exchange looks and canter away.

14

Interior, bedchamber. Day.

Elizabeth and Cecil sit at a table. She is checking a list of accounts, while Cecil goes through a document written in his own hand, divided and sub-divided.

E

117

CECIL: I have set out the advantages and disadvantages of each marriage, under different headings.

(*She glances up at him and nods, changes a figure in the accounts and glances up at him again as he begins to read.*)

Prince Eric of Sweden—a Protestant marriage. His father is dying, and he will shortly be King. He would gladly come to England so that you can see him.

ELIZABETH: I have told him not to come.

CECIL: Meanwhile, he sends his brother, Duke John of Finland, with many rich gifts.

(*She smiles, gratified. He glances at her and continues.*)

This marriage would displease nobody, and would confirm your Protestant support but would bring no alliance with France or Spain. So, unless your Highness feels—

ELIZABETH: Is he really as handsome as you say?

(*Cecil opens and shuts his mouth. Elizabeth smiles and alters a figure in her accounts.*)

Tom Parry never could add two and two.

CECIL: Does your Highness mean always to audit your household accounts yourself.

ELIZABETH (*with a cheerful grin*): As long as Tom Parry is my Treasurer, yes!

(*She finds another mistake and alters it.*)

Well?

CECIL: The Archduke Ferdinand: the Imperial Ambassador assures me that he could never risk a Protestant marriage, so . . .

ELIZABETH: But he will be Emperor one day.

CECIL (*looking at her closely*): It would mean changing your religion.

ELIZABETH: We could settle these details later.

CECIL: He is not to be entirely discouraged, then?

(*She adds up a column of figures and changes the total and smiles at him.*)

ELIZABETH: Nobody should be entirely discouraged.

(*Cecil looks at her in despair.*)

15

Interior, corridor. Day.

Elizabeth is walking along, Cecil is just behind her and she listens to him without turning her head.

CECIL: Your Highness, sooner or later a decision must be made. You must marry.

ELIZABETH: Must?

CECIL: For the sake of your people.

ELIZABETH (*thoughtfully*): Yes. That is the only 'must'.

CECIL: Think of their terrors and uncertainties, think of the foreign invasions ...

16

Interior, privy chamber. Day.

... and civil war to which they will be subjected if the succession is not assured.

ELIZABETH: Succession? I have no intention of dying yet.

CECIL: Not yet, your Highness. Not for many years to come, please God. But you must consider the future.

ELIZABETH: Not I. You. (*She turns to him, smiling.*) You are the spirit who wanders abroad, gathering knowledge of the future from the stars. I am the earthbound mortal, the mere piece of clay, doing for the moment what must be done.

17

Robert, Mary and Henry Sidney, Norfolk and Sussex are waiting.

(*He looks at her as they move on into the presence chamber.*)

CECIL: Your Highness, even a spirit must have a habitation. Unless you listen to what I say, and act upon it . . .

ELIZABETH (*flashing dangerously out*): If I listen, it is enough!

CECIL: Yes, your Highness.

(*She softens and touches his cheek with the tips of her fingers.*)

ELIZABETH: Poor spirit! Do I vex you very much?

CECIL (*smiling*): Very much, your Highness. But a quiet spirit is a dead spirit, so I must not complain.

ELIZABETH (*with a tiny snap*): No. You must not complain.

(*A clerk comes towards Cecil with a letter. He takes it and glances at Elizabeth.*)

CECIL: From France.

(*He glances at her enquiringly. She nods, and he begins to open the letter. She becomes aware of Robert's eyes on her and turns to look at him.*)

ELIZABETH: Robin!

(*He comes towards her.*)

ROBERT: My Queen?

(*She takes a few steps away and he goes with her. She stops and looks at him.*)

ELIZABETH: You stare at me too much. Your eyes are always on my face.

ROBERT: Where else should they be?

ELIZABETH: Looking about to see how you may serve me.

ROBERT: If there is any way that I can serve you, I shall see it first in your face.

ELIZABETH (*smiling*): Very well. I will bestow upon you the most important title in the Kingdom.

(*Although he knows she is joking, that flash of ambition still shows in his eyes.*)

I shall call you my eyes.

(*In spite of himself, the disappointment shows, but he*

conceals it and laughs. Then he sees that she is not laughing.)

Robin.

(He looks at her enquiringly.)

When you stop looking at me—

ROBERT: I never will.

(He takes her hand and kisses it. Cecil comes with the letter and she turns to him, the movement bringing her closer to Sussex as well.)

CECIL *(out of view)*: Your Highness. The King of France is dead.

ELIZABETH: Then—

CECIL: Mary Stuart is Queen of France. It is said that she and her husband mean to lay claim to the throne of England as well.

ROBERT: God's teeth! Young King Francis is certainly ambitious. At fifteen years of age to claim the crowns of France, Scotland and England!

ELIZABETH: He should take care how he tries to take my crown, or I'll take a husband that'll make his head ache!

(She walks away and Mary Sidney and the other ladies go with her.)

ROBERT: Husband?

(Sussex is grimly pleased by his discomfiture. He glances at Cecil.)

SUSSEX: The Earl of Arran?

(*Cecil nods.*)

ROBERT: But he's in France! As the Protestant claimant to the Scottish throne, they'd never let him leave the country.

CECIL (*quietly gratified*): He is in London. In my house.

SUSSEX (*smiling*): Well done!

(*They both glance at Robert, whose face is expressionless.*)

So the Protestant Lords in Scotland, with our help, rise against the French Regent, declare for Arran instead of Mary Stuart—

ROBERT: 'With our help'? You know the Queen has a horror of war. She thinks it is an 'expensive business'.

CECIL: We shall never have another chance like this to throw the French out of Scotland, and our help could be given secretly.

SUSSEX: Then if the Queen marries Arran, England and Scotland will be united under one crown.

CECIL (*with a note of challenge*): I hope, Lord Robert, that we shall have your support in this matter with the Queen.

ROBERT: I agree. We shall never have a better chance to throw the French out of Scotland.

SUSSEX: And the other? The marriage?

ROBERT: The Queen will never marry any man she does not love.

(*He walks away. Sussex and Cecil look after him.*)

123

SUSSEX: Thank God he is married!

CECIL: He is childless. The marriage might be annulled.

SUSSEX: Is it true that the Queen has given him a present of £12,000?

CECIL: 'To help meet his expenses.' Admittedly, he has many.

SUSSEX: He is like a gypsy, going about to see what he can pick up. He will take from his mistress. He will take from his friends. If he were not as suspicious as he is rapacious he would take from himself!

CECIL: When the Queen marries, all this will be over.

SUSSEX: If she marries within the kingdom. That's why Dudley dislikes the idea of Arran—a husband always at her side, to protect her against predators like himself. He'd prefer a foreign husband with lands to look after abroad, while he himself plays the part of Prince Consort in England!

18

Interior, Mary Sidney's room. Day.

Robert stands in the doorway, looking every inch a King. He stands and walks as he rides, with athletic style and elegance. He sees his sister, Mary Sidney, who sits doing some embroidery, and goes towards her. She turns, delighted.

MARY SIDNEY: Robert!

ROBERT: How is my best of sisters?

MARY SIDNEY (*smiling*): That sounds as though you want something from me.

ROBERT (*laughing*): So I do!

(*He sits down, with a little sigh of relief, and watches her as she sews. He finds her company restful.*)

MARY SIDNEY: Do you know where the Queen has gone today?

ROBERT (*a hint of reluctance*): She's gone to Cecil's house.

MARY SIDNEY (*puzzled*): Secretly?

ROBERT: There is someone he wants her to meet.

MARY SIDNEY: It's unusual for her to go anywhere these days without you.

ROBERT: Yes.

(*Pause.*)

MARY SIDNEY: Robert.

ROBERT: Mmm?

MARY SIDNEY: People are talking.

ROBERT: It is a human custom.

MARY SIDNEY: They are talking—gossip.

ROBERT: That is a human vice.

MARY SIDNEY: Robert, what they are saying is scandalous.

ROBERT: Then that is treason.

(*He smiles, but she is very serious.*)

MARY SIDNEY: Yes, when it is about the Queen. Harry's

friends have been writing to him from France and Scotland even from Ireland. Robert, the Queen must marry!

ROBERT: I know. That's why I want your help.

(*She looks uneasy, and concentrates on her sewing.*)

You know how devious the Queen is. Since she was three years old, she has had to hide her true feelings and now, when she has set her whole heart on marrying . . .

MARY SIDNEY: Not you Robert . . .

(*He puts his hand on hers.*)

ROBERT: The man she really wants to marry is the Archduke Charles.

(*She looks up at him in relief.*)

19

Interior, Spanish ambassador's room in Whitehall. Day.

De Quadra talking to Norfolk.

NORFOLK: Are you sure of this, Bishop?

DE QUADRA: I had it from Lord Robert's own sister.

NORFOLK: Lady Mary Sidney?

DE QUADRA: Her husband, Sir Henry Sidney, is very close to the Queen also.

NORFOLK (*doubtfully*): Yes.

DE QUADRA: The Queen, like any other woman, does not wish to seem to yield too easily. The Imperial Ambassador has allowed himself to be put off by an appearance of unwillingness. He has given up, just when he should have urged his suit more strongly.

NORFOLK: Did Lady Mary say that the Queen would be willing to change her religion?

DE QUADRA: She didn't speak of it. But you and I know, my Lord Norfolk, that she is a Catholic at heart. She lights candles in her private chapel.

NORFOLK: A Catholic marriage would solve all our problems! But the influence of Cecil and the Protestant Lords is very strong.

DE QUADRA: All the more reason for forcing her to do what in fact she truly wants to do!

NORFOLK: Forcing her? (*Alarmed.*) Bishop, I—I'm not sure that . . .

(*He pauses, thinks it over, and looks uneasy. De Quadra nods.*)

20

Interior, presence chamber at Greenwich. Day.

De Quadra confronting Elizabeth. Cecil, Robert, Sussex, Norfolk, Henry Sidney, and Mary Sidney in attendance.

DE QUADRA: The Archduke Charles will be very happy to come to England, your Highness.

ELIZABETH (*gracious smiling*): And I shall be very happy to see him.

DE QUADRA: But if he comes, he will come as your future husband.

ELIZABETH (*smiling*): Ah, as to that—

DE QUADRA: Anything else is unthinkable!

(*Elizabeth is brought up short. She glances at Cecil, and then begins to smile again.*)

ELIZABETH: I have often told the Imperial Ambassador—

DE QUADRA: The Imperial Ambassador does not know your Highness as well as I do.

ELIZABETH: But he knows how to listen.

(*It is a mild rebuke and doesn't check De Quadra.*)

DE QUADRA: The true ambassador, your Highness, listens to what is meant, and not only to what is said.

ELIZABETH (*beginning to smile again*): Then I will say again, and mean it, that if the Archduke Charles cares to come to England as our guest—

DE QUADRA: As your guest, and as the husband of your choice.

(*Cecil looks at him, puzzled.*)

ELIZABETH: I have not said that!

DE QUADRA: But you have invited the Archduke Charles to your court.

ELIZABETH (*smiling*): I have said he is welcome.

DE QUADRA: *Very* welcome, your Highness, I hope.

(*Elizabeth's smile fades, as she feels increasingly pushed into a corner.*)

ELIZABETH: He is welcome as any other guest would be.

DE QUADRA: I am glad to hear it. I shall write to King

Philip and tell him that you have invited the Archduke Charles to England, and that he comes here as your future husband.

(*A look of absolute panic comes into Elizabeth's face.*)

ELIZABETH: If he comes on those terms, he had better not come at all!

DE QUADRA: Your Majesty . . .

ELIZABETH: He said he would like to come. I have never invited him. I have never said I would marry him. I have never said I would marry anyone! Never!

(*She moves towards the doors.*)

DE QUADRA: Your Majesty . . .

ELIZABETH: Enough!

(*She storms to the door. Mary Sidney is about to follow her out but Elizabeth turns and makes it clear she does not wish to be followed. De Quadra, immensely discomposed, takes a few steps after her, and Norfolk joins him. The others gaze after Elizabeth.*)

SUSSEX: What got into the man? What gave him the idea that she had said she would marry the Archduke Charles?

(*Mary Sidney looks at Henry Sidney and they both look at Robert.*)

CECIL: If you knew the trouble I have had to bring her to the thought of marriage! Now every suitor will be anathema to her for the next three months.

SUSSEX: But how could the Spanish Ambassador be such a fool? He had been here long enough to know the Queen. If you have a high-spirited, delicate young mare who is afraid of jumping, you don't cram her at the highest fence in the field! Any horseman knows that!

(*He stops short. He and Cecil look at Robert, who looks innocent and surprised.*)

HENRY SIDNEY: Yes. Any horseman knows that.

ROBERT: Perhaps the Ambassador is no horseman.

(*Norfolk returns furious.*)

NORFOLK: Lord Robert, one day someone will plunge a dagger in your heart!

MARY SIDNEY (*still looking at Robert*): If he can find it.

(*She walks away. Robert looks after her, and does, after all, look a little uneasy.*)

21

Interior, bedroom, Cumnor Place. Evening.

Amye lies on the bed. The room is in darkness. Robert stands in the doorway leading to the living room. He is silhouetted against the light and peers into the darkness.

ROBERT: Amye? Amye?

(*A note of irritation creeping in:*)

Are you lying down again?

(*He pushes the door wider open, the light falls on Amye, lying flat on her back.*)

Always lying in a darkened room, it's no wonder you have these sick fancies!

(*She suddenly sits up clutching her breast.*)

AMYE: Sick fancies? Is this a sick fancy? This lump here?

(*Robert gives a slight involuntary grimace, and then makes a heroic attempt to be sympathetic.*)

ROBERT: How is the pain now?

AMYE: Better.

ROBERT: I want to talk to you.

(*She gets up slowly, she looks crumpled and untidy, and he frowns as she goes past him.*)

I have to go back to London.

AMYE (*turning to him*): But you've only just arrived!

ROBERT: Cecil is going to Scotland to negotiate the peace. The Queen will need me with her while he's gone. I hoped to see Antony Forster while I was here, but I can't wait. Give him a message when he comes back.

(*She sits staring at the table.*)

Amye.

(*She slowly looks up at him.*)

I want this debt settled at once. They're only small men, and they can't afford to be out of their money.

(*He gives her a piece of paper. She stares at it blankly.*)

Tell Forster to arrange it with Flowerdew. He'll have to sell some wool, but even if it means selling at a loss, tell him I want it done at once.

(*She nods slowly and puts the paper down.*)

You won't forget?

(*Amye doesn't answer. She has forgotten already.*)

I wish you would get out more—see more company.

(*He puts a large package on the table, wrapped in a linen cloth.*)

I brought a present for you. Open it.

(*She looks at him, and slowly unwraps it to show a pair of velvet gloves.*)

Do you like them?

(*She nods slowly. He sighs, and goes towards the door.*)

I must go.

AMYE: Not now! Not this evening!

ROBERT: I must. She looks for me every minute of the day.

(*Amye comes to take hold of him.*)

AMYE: Let me come with you. She's given you a house in Kew. I could live there!

ROBERT: The Queen wouldn't like it.

AMYE (*suddenly screaming out*): She knows you're married! She came to the wedding!

(*They stare at each other in silence for a moment, and then he softens.*)

ROBERT: Get out a little more. Wear your new gloves. Enjoy some company. That was the whole idea of your sharing this house. Wasn't it? That you should have company. There's Mistress Owen, there's Anthony Forster and his family . . .

AMYE: Them! What do they care for me? They are all your people! If killing me would do any good, they'd do it!

ROBERT: Amye!

(*He touches her and she cries out in pain.*)

Do you want to destroy me?

(*She looks at him, his face seems to ask something of her. She averts her eyes. He opens the door and goes.*)

Interior, hall, landing, stairs, Cumnor Place. Evening.

Robert comes downstairs. Mrs Pinto is there, listening.

22

Interior, the Queen's bedchamber. Night.

Elizabeth is in a rich bed-gown, and her hair is down. She turns, delighted at the sight of Robert in the doorway.

ELIZABETH: Robin! Robin! You're back!

(*He kneels.*)

ROBERT: My own Queen!

ELIZABETH: You are welcome!

(*And she gives him both her hands and he kisses them.*

Then she puts one hand on his shoulder and from there round the back of his neck, so that as he rises, she is almost in his arms.)

ROBERT: I am covered in mud.

ELIZABETH: I've missed my eyes.

ROBERT: They have seen you all the time.

(*They still use the language of courtly love, but she is in love with him now, and taking pleasure in being in love with him. Move away to find that they are not alone in the room as we might have thought. Kat Ashley is there, and Mary Sidney and three or four pretty young girls all busy with dresses and jewels and ruffs.*)

ELIZABETH: Kat, show Lord Robert the pearl brooch. Come and see the latest present Duke John of Finland has given me.

(*Kat opens a small oak box by the bed and takes out the brooch.*)

ROBERT: You put it in your treasure-box!

ELIZABETH: Of course. Where else would I put it? It came with King Eric's love.

KAT: It's beautiful, isn't it?

(*She gives it to Robert, who looks at it, and gives it back to Elizabeth.*)

ROBERT: Not to me. I'm jealous of every other man who gives you presents.

(*Elizabeth laughs and gives the brooch back to Kat.*)

ELIZABETH: Put it over there, Kat.

134

(*Kat closes the box and takes the brooch across the room.*)

I have a present for you.

(*A quick hopeful look from him.*)

I have had your room changed, as you wanted.

(*He looks delighted. Mary Sidney and Kat are busy avoiding each other's eyes.*)

ROBERT: You are the kindest mistress in the world.

ELIZABETH: You look exhausted. You must go to bed.

ROBERT (*glances at her bed*): I wish—

(*He stops. Kat and Mary Sidney exchange horrified looks, and the young girls catch their breath. But Elizabeth laughs, delighted, flirting with danger as well as with him.*)

ELIZABETH: Wishes are not horses.

ROBERT: Come riding with me tomorrow morning!

ELIZABETH: No, I must see the Bishops.

ROBERT: Let someone else meet them. I have an Irish horse for you to try.

ELIZABETH: Is he faster than my gelding?

ROBERT: Much too fast. But you like danger.

ELIZABETH: So I do. (*Challenging him.*) But I never fall!

ROBERT (*smiling*): Alas! You never do!

(*She laughs and hugs him.*)

135

ELIZABETH R

ELIZABETH: Good night, my eyes.

(*He kisses her. They break. Then they kiss again.*)

ROBERT: Good night, my Queen.

(*She slowly frees herself, then turns away, smiling. Robert bows low, and she sees him in the mirror. He goes out. The women have been held motionless. They now bustle about as Elizabeth sits at the dressing table in front of the mirror.*)

ELIZABETH: 'Covered in mud'. How absurd! As if it mattered! He is still handsomer than any other man. Don't you think so, Kat?

KAT: Yes, your Highness.

(*Mary Sidney silently hustles the other young girls out of the door. Elizabeth looks at Kat.*)

Your Highness, I beseech you . . . Forgive me! Forgive me! I must say it! Lord Robert Dudley is married, your Highness! To give him the freedom that you do . . .

ELIZABETH (*indignantly*): What freedom have I given him?

KAT: He comes into your bedchamber, and you go to his. And now to move his room near to yours . . .

ELIZABETH: His room was unhealthy! You said so yourself. He is a good servant to me . . .

KAT: The whole of England . . . the whole of Europe is saying that he is more than that!

(*Elizabeth sits staring straight ahead, and then speaks very quietly.*)

ELIZABETH: Then the whole of Europe is wrong, as you know, and . . .

136

(*She looks at Mary Sidney in the mirror.*)

. . . and many others besides. I love him dearly, as I
have often said. And he loves and cares for me as . . .
(*Her voice shows that this is not quite such sure ground.*)
. . . as a subject should love and care for his Prince. I
take pleasure in his company, and I have been to his
bedchamber and he has come to mine. But there are
always others with us. I have never gone there alone.

(*Old King Henry VIII suddenly rises up in her, and
she stands up, towering over the kneeling Kat.*)

Though if I had chosen to do so, there is no one in the
whole world who could have stopped me!

23

Interior, landing, Cumnor Place. Day.

*Amye with Mrs Pinto on the landing at the top of
the stairs. Other servants standing in the hall below.*

AMYE: And I say that you shall all go, and go today!

MRS PINTO: But, my Lady, we never go to the fair on a
Sunday! It's so noisy and crowded, and all the riff-
raff will be there.

(*She glances at the servants below, who move and
glance at each other uneasily.*)

Mrs Odingsell says *she* won't go today!

AMYE: Mrs Odingsell can do what she likes! I say, all
my household shall go!

MRS PINTO: My Lady, what about your dinner? There
will be no one here to . . .

AMYE: I shall have dinner with Mrs Owen.

MRS PINTO (*relieved*): And then you'll stay in her part of the house until . . .

AMYE: No! Why should I? My Lord said that I should share the house for the sake of company . . . not to be spied on.

MRS PINTO: No, my Lady, of course not! I . . . (*She glances at the servants again.*) You want us all to go, then?

AMYE (*screaming*): Yes, go! Go!

(*Amye goes to her room. Mrs Pinto hesitates, then goes quietly upstairs to look through half-open door.*)

24

Interior, sitting-room. Cumnor Place. Day.

(*Amye, in pain.*)

AMYE: God help me! God deliver me! God deliver me!

(*Mrs Pinto turns away, troubled.*)

25

Interior, corridor. Day.

De Quadra meets Cecil.

DE QUADRA: I understand that you have achieved a superb Treaty, Sir William, while you were in Edinburgh.

(*Cecil bows.*)

Will Mary Stuart ratify it?

26

Interior, room in Paris. Day.

Mary Stuart sitting reading through a paper. She is in mourning, and wears white.

MARY: The French to leave Scotland, and I to give up all claim to the English Crown? (*She looks up.*) Never! Never!

27

Interior, corridor. Day.

Cecil and de Quadra.

CECIL: Queen Mary is now committed to it. She must.

DE QUADRA: Your Queen must be very pleased.

CECIL (*angry and upset*): Pleased, Bishop? I think she hardly knows or cares. Not a penny have I received for all the expense of my journey. I have borne the whole cost of it myself. It will cripple me for years to come. I return, and what do I find? The Queen can think of nothing but Lord Robert Dudley!

DE QUADRA (*solemnly concealing his gratification*): It is very bad, certainly, for her reputation. No one in Europe can talk of anything else.

CECIL: Perhaps you could speak to her, Bishop. She won't listen to me, now.

(*He isn't looking at de Quadra so misses the look of pleasurable amusement on his face. A moment later de Quadra is very grave again.*)

DE QUADRA: Is it true Lord Robert's wife is ill?

CECIL: Yes. She has a cancer in her breast. What will come of it all, God knows.

DE QUADRA: Ah.

28

Interior, hall/landing/stairs, Cumnor Place. Night.

Voices and laughter in the darkness. The door opens and Mrs Pinto comes in with other servants.

MRS PINTO: Quiet now, or you'll wake my Lady! Joan, Peter . . .

(*As she steps forward Mrs Pinto falls over something on the floor. She sees in the moonlight that it is Amye, lying dead at the foot of the stairs.*)

My Lady! (*Gasps.*) My Lady!

29

Interior, a room in Paris. Day.

Mary throws back her head and gives a screech of laughter.

MARY: The Queen of England is going to marry her horse-keeper, and he has killed his wife to make room for her!

30

Interior, corridor. Day.

Robert approaches down the corridor. He goes into the privy chamber.

Interior, privy chamber/bedchamber. Day.

Robert crosses the privy chamber to the bedchamber door. It opens. Elizabeth, in the bedchamber, turns and sees Robert, who remains in the privy chamber.

ELIZABETH: Go away! What are you doing here? Go away from me!

ROBERT: You don't think—you don't believe that I...?

ELIZABETH: What does it matter what I believe? You shouldn't have come here, until...

ROBERT: Until what?

(*No reply.*)

Who told you?

ELIZABETH: Cecil.

ROBERT: He always knows everything first.

ELIZABETH: The Spanish Ambassador knew as well.

ROBERT: How could he?

ELIZABETH: Rumour. (*Bitterly angry.*) Rumour! It killed her before...

(*Stopping short, and then continuing with a change of tone.*)

... before she was dead.

ROBERT: Elizabeth...

(*She turns on him a terrifying glance. He takes a step backwards.*)

Your Majesty...

141

(*She turns away from him, clasping her hands.*)

ELIZABETH: You must go, go out of London, and . . .

ROBERT (*blazing out*): If you like, I will go to the Tower!

ELIZABETH (*turning back and stopping him*): What good would that do? They would only think that you were guilty, and that I knew about it!

(*Robert stares at her in horror as she turns away from him.*)

ROBERT: I have sent Blount to Cumnor Place. I have told him to find out exactly what happened. Exactly. And I have said that if anyone is guilty, they are to be brought to trial.

(*He looks at her, she doesn't move.*)

I've told him to send for her brother, so that he can see that everything is properly done.

(*Elizabeth still doesn't move.*)

What more can I do?

(*She turns to him.*)

ELIZABETH: Go to Kew and stay there.

(*He stares at her, completely shattered, then turns and walks away into the corridor.*)

31

Interior, Kew. Day.

Robert sits, alone and dejected, by the window.

32

Interior, bedchamber, Greenwich. Evening.

Elizabeth sits alone, worried and miserable. Kat and Mary Sidney watch her anxiously from across the room.

33

Interior, stairs/landing, Cumnor Place. Day.

Mrs Pinto at the foot of the stairs with Thomas Blount.

MRS PINTO: She was a good, virtuous gentlewoman, and I have many times heard her pray to God upon her knees to deliver her from desperation.

(*Blount looks quickly up the stairs, and Mrs Pinto catches hold of his sleeve in agitation.*)

No, Master Blount, never think that . . . or I shall be sorry to have said so much! It was the pain that made her desperate. I am certain that my Lady's death was from pure mischance.

(*Blount starts to move away upstairs.*)

34

Interior, bedchamber. Day.

Elizabeth and one of her ladies. There is a knock at the door. The lady-in-waiting goes to open it to admit Cecil. He bows.

CECIL: Your Majesty. The Jury brought in a verdict of accidental death.

(She gives a sigh of relief, then stiffens.)

ELIZABETH: Of course. What other verdict could there have been?

(He looks at her sideways. She knows very well, and so does he.)

CECIL: But . . .

ELIZABETH *(turning on him)*: But?

CECIL *(hesitating)*: Your Highness, there is still a great deal of talk. It is said that if you marry Lord Robert Dudley, your good name will be gone forever.

ELIZABETH: I have never said that I will marry him.

(Suddenly turning on Cecil the anger she feels against Mary.)

You know very well that I have always said that I would marry no one!

35

Interior, Kew. Evening.

Robert is pacing up and down the room. He turns slowly and sees Cecil.

ROBERT: Cecil!

CECIL *(bowing)*: My Lord. *(Gently.)* I came to see . . . how you were.

ROBERT *(really touched)*: That was very good of you.

(He gestures to Cecil to sit down, and sits down himself.)

I haven't heard from the Queen. Not a word! Does she say I may come back to court?

(*He sees from Cecil's face that he may not.*)

I am her Master of Horse! I have duties which should be attended to.

CECIL: A little patience, Lord Robert.

ROBERT: Patience! When things are being said about me, which . . .

CECIL: I can assure you that the Council has done all it can to protect your good name.

ROBERT: But the Queen? She doesn't believe . . . ?

CECIL: No! Certainly not. She has always protested your innocence most vehemently.

(*Robert looks immensely relieved. For the first time he thinks of her and not himself.*)

ROBERT: How is she?

CECIL: She is not well. Nervous distress always affects her physical well-being.

ROBERT: I can't bear to be away from her at such a time.

CECIL: A little patience.

ROBERT: I will never forget your kindness in coming to see me.

CECIL (*gently, smiling*): Lord Robert we are both servants of the Queen. And in the end she will always do what she means to.

36

Interior, corridor, Greenwich. Day.

Norfolk and Sussex stand talking.

NORFOLK: Well, at least that's the end of the Gypsy!

SUSSEX (*slowly*): He didn't kill her. The Jury brought in a verdict of accident but all the circumstances point to suicide.

NORFOLK: What does it matter what actually happened? The talk and the scandal are enough to finish him forever. She can never marry him now.

(*Elizabeth comes out of her room, followed by Cecil, Kat, Mary Sidney and girls. Sussex and Norfolk bow low as she passes, but she doesn't look at them. She walks down the gallery with a face of desolation. Sussex gazes after her, then turns to look at Norfolk and speaks with deliberation.*)

SUSSEX: She must take a husband and have an heir. If Dudley is the only man whom she can love, and who can arouse her desire, then in God's name, let her marry him, and be happy!

37

Interior, presence chamber. Day.

Elizabeth sees Robert coming along the corridor towards her. He kneels.

ROBERT: Thank you! Thank you for letting my poor eyes look on your face again.

ELIZABETH: My face was the poorer, because they were not there.

(The words are spoken only for each other. He puts his face down on her hand and she moves her other hand almost to touch his head.)

38

Interior, corridor. Day.

De Quadra talking to Cecil who carries a roll of papers.

DE QUADRA: Does she mean to marry him, in spite of all?

CECIL: I don't know, Bishop. I don't know. *(Glancing at the papers he carries.)* I know she means to give him an earldom.

DE QUADRA: An earldom? That looks like the first step.

CECIL: We shall see.

(He bows a farewell and moves into the presence chamber, where Elizabeth sits at a table in the alcove.)

39

Interior, presence chamber with walls. Day.

A cheerful, laughing group is around her, consisting of Robert, Henry Sidney, Mary Sidney, Sussex, Norfolk and others.

ELIZABETH: King Eric of Sweden has sent me a beautiful New Year's gift of ermine. What shall I send him in exchange? My heart perhaps?

ROBERT: Impossible! That is already engaged elsewhere.

(She looks up at him laughing as Cecil comes up.)

ELIZABETH: Well, Master Secretary, why that grave look?

ROBERT: Cecil always looks grave. It gives him an air of importance.

(Elizabeth looks at him sharply, and turns back to Cecil.)

CECIL: Your Highness promised to give your answer to the Pope's invitation to the Council of Trento.

ELIZABETH: Did I? *(Pause.)* It is very kind of the Pope to invite me to a gathering of Catholic Princes.

ROBERT: If you accept, it will make your Protestant subjects very angry.

ELIZABETH: *Angry?* Princes are angry. Subjects obey. *(To Cecil.)* How if I refuse?

CECIL: Then I must tell your Highness that there is a serious risk of a rebellion among your Catholic subjects, especially in the North.

ELIZABETH: And—King Philip?

CECIL: Would not discourage such a rising.

ROBERT: Are we to jump at King Philip's bidding?

(Elizabeth is silent. She suddenly looks up at Cecil with a complete change of tone.)

ELIZABETH: And what other business have you for us today?

(Cecil wants to continue the subject, sees that she doesn't mean to, and puts the papers before her.)

148

CECIL: The letters patent, your Highness.

(*He puts the papers before her. Robert and the rest of the group exchange happy looks; Elizabeth is aware of them. She looks carefully at the top paper, picking up her pen.*)

ELIZABETH: 'Our well-beloved subject, Robert Dudley...' M'm. 'The Earldom of...'

(*She suddenly throws down the pen, picks up a knife and slits the paper straight up the middle.*)

No! I will not do it! No!

(*They stare at her, aghast.*)

CECIL: Madam—

ROBERT: Your Highness—

ELIZABETH: No!

ROBERT (*almost beside himself*): But *why*? Why?

ELIZABETH: Do you want a reason? Then I will give you one! The Dudleys have been traitors for three generations, and I do not choose to raise another one above his station to threaten me again!

(*He stares at her in a stupor of rage and confusion. Elizabeth looks at the next paper.*)

'Ambrose Dudley—Earl of Warwick'. Yes. That I will sign.

(*Robert turns and walks away. She picks up the pen, dips it in the ink, and signs with a bold 'Elizabeth R.' She puts the pen down, looks at Robert's back, smiles, gets up and goes towards him. He turns.*)

ROBERT: You have destroyed me!

ELIZABETH (*smiling*): Oh no. No. (*Gently touching his cheek.*) The bear and the ragged staff is not so easily overthrown. Is it?

ROBERT: How can you treat me as you do?

ELIZABETH: How? (*Very tenderly, but still smiling.*) Because I love you.

(*She walks past him towards the corridor. He looks after her with a new look of hope. Cecil is at the door and holds the curtain aside for her.*)

CECIL: Your Majesty, the Pope's invitation . . .

(*She looks at him in silence, looks thoughtfully at Robert and then at Henry Sidney.*)

ELIZABETH: Harry! I want a word with you.

(*Henry Sidney hurries to join Elizabeth and Cecil as they go out.*)

40

Interior, Spanish Ambassador's room. Whitehall. Day.

Henry Sidney being entertained to wine by de Quadra, who is just refilling his glass.

HENRY SIDNEY: The Queen has been invited by the Pope to take part in the Council of Trento.

(*De Quadra looks at him, bottle poised.*)

We all know King Philip would like her to accept.

DE QUADRA: So would her Catholic subjects. I am assured that if she refuses, there will be an uprising.

HENRY SIDNEY: Tell me, de Quadra, would King Philip

feel inclined to support a marriage between Lord Robert Dudley and the Queen?

(*De Quadra, still looking at him, puts the bottle down.*)

DE QUADRA (*cautiously*): King Philip has always valued the services which Lord Robert performed for him in past times.

HENRY SIDNEY: Suppose that, in exchange for King Philip's support over this marriage, which the Queen greatly desires . . .

(*De Quadra looks at him quickly.*)

. . . Lord Robert were to urge the Queen's attendance at the Council of Trento, instead of opposing it, as he has done hitherto?

DE QUADRA: But—how greatly does the Queen desire the marriage?

41

Interior, privy chamber. Evening.

Elizabeth sitting with de Quadra.

ELIZABETH: I see, Bishop, that I must make you my confessor. I have a great esteem and affection for Lord Robert Dudley.

(*She meets de Quadra's watchful eye.*)

What would King Philip think of such a marriage?

DE QUADRA: Unofficially, your Highness . . . I can say that King Philip would welcome such a match. If your Highness would care to write to Madrid, asking King Philip to express his sentiments . . .

(*Elizabeth looks at Cecil, seated across the table.*)

42

Interior, Spanish Ambassador's room. Day.

Cecil is standing confronting de Quadra.

CECIL: Her Highness, like any other woman, hardly cares to make the first move in affairs of matrimony. But if King Philip would write and urge her to marry Lord Robert Dudley, this would make it easier for her to have her heart's desire.

DE QUADRA: Would this match please you, Master Secretary?

CECIL: Would it please King Philip?

43

Interior, presence chamber (as a corridor). Day.

De Quadra and Norfolk.

DE QUADRA: My Lord of Norfolk, the Queen has refused to attend the Council of Trento.

NORFOLK: Yes.

DE QUADRA: And you promised King Philip that if she refused the Pope's invitation, the English Catholics would rise in protest.

NORFOLK: I think they would have done so, but . . .

DE QUADRA: But, what?

NORFOLK: They don't like Lord Robert Dudley.

DE QUADRA: Well?

NORFOLK: When they heard that King Philip was

supporting a marriage between Lord Robert and the Queen . . .

DE QUADRA: Not publicly! He never gave his approval publicly!

NORFOLK: Word got about that King Philip would give the marriage his support in exchange for the Queen attending the Council of Trento.

DE QUADRA: And so the English Catholics thought it better that she should not go.

NORFOLK: Yes.

DE QUADRA: Tell me, my Lord of Norfolk, is the Queen the kind of woman who would use her lover's unpopularity for her own ends?

NORFOLK: The Queen is . . .

(*Struggling to cope with matters far beyond him.*)

. . . the Queen.

44

Exterior, the Queen's barge. Night.

An impression of an ornamental gallery, with lanterns and water-lights, and an impression of other lights, music and laughter. Elizabeth sits in the boat, with Robert beside her, both laughing. De Quadra and Cecil enter to sit with them.

ELIZABETH: No, no, we cannot possibly drown. We have the power of Spain and the Church on our side. Haven't we, Bishop?

(*Sound of water, and the boat rocks.*)

Robin, your water festival will sink us yet!

153

(*He takes her hand to steady her, and then holds on to it.*)

Here we are, in the company of the Bishop. Why shouldn't we two be married, here and now? Would you do it, Bishop?

DE QUADRA: Gladly, your Highness, if that is what you wish.

(*Robert catches his breath. Behind the laughter is the realization that it could be done.*)

ROBERT: Then why do we delay? Here's the ring!

(*He prepares to draw a ring off his finger.*)

ELIZABETH: Ah, but I'm afraid the Bishop doesn't know the English marriage service well enough.

(*De Quadra looks from one to the other, hardly able to believe they could joke about such a thing.*)

ROBERT: I will teach it to him.

ELIZABETH: And what will you teach me?

ROBERT: What can I teach you? You learnt the way to my heart long ago, and nothing else matters.

ELIZABETH: But I have so many hearts. What shall I do with yours?

(*Robert and Elizabeth move away leaving de Quadra gazing at Cecil in a state of total bafflement.*)

DE QUADRA: Does she mean to have him or not? She still declares that she will marry no one, but—in God's name, Master Secretary, what is she about?

(*Cecil looks at him and smiles.*)

CECIL: Her Highness, Bishop, is like a beautiful fish in

the river. We see the silver glint, the exquisite curve, the dart and flash, and receive the impression of gaiety and liberty. But the freedom is an illusion. Turn and twist as she may, all the time she is being drawn to the bank by that implacable thread—the absolute necessity of marriage, the absolute need to provide for the succession.

(*De Quadra slowly nods. There is perspiration on his forehead. He wipes his hand across it.*)

Bishop, are you ill?

45

Interior, bedchamber. Evening.

Elizabeth is in bed, feverish, but sitting up. Mary Sidney and Kat in attendance, and Doctor Burcot by the bed, a short irascible German doctor.

BURCOT: My Liege, you have the smallpox.

(*She stares at him in a fury.*)

ELIZABETH: You lying knave! Get out of my sight! Get him out of here! Tell me that I have the smallpox when it is nothing but a chill. You are a scurvy knave fit only to doctor cattle! God's blood, if you stay here I will pour your own medicine down your throat. Get out! Get out!

46

Interior, corridor. Night.

In the darkness a sense of bustle, agitation and distress. Servants hurry backwards and forwards. Sussex, his doublet unlaced, meets Cecil.

SUSSEX: How is she?

(*Cecil cannot speak.*)

She is not . . . ?

CECIL: No. No. But . . .

SUSSEX: You know de Quadra is dead?

CECIL: The doctors say she will not live.

47

Interior, bedchamber. Night.

Elizabeth lies in bed, held in Mary Sidney's arms. Kat kneels beside her.

KAT: Your Highness? (*Pause.*) Your Highness?

(*Elizabeth's eyes are not quite closed, but show no consciousness. Kat looks despairingly at Mary Sidney.*)

Shall I let the Council come in?

(*Mary Sidney nods. Kat goes to the door and Cecil comes in, with Henry, Sussex, Norfolk and others. They gather round the bed. Elizabeth opens her eyes.*)

ELIZABETH: Is that my Council?

MARY SIDNEY: Yes, your Highness.

ELIZABETH: I am going to die, aren't I?

MARY SIDNEY: Oh, your Highness!

ELIZABETH: My Lords.

CECIL: My Liege.

(*They gather round, agonized.*)

ELIZABETH: Lord Robert Dudley is to be Lord Protector of England. (*Hasty glances of dismay.*) He is to receive twenty thousand pounds a year.

(*All carefully not looking at each other.*)

And I want five hundred pounds a year to be given to his servant, Tamworth, who sleeps in his room.

(*They can't resist a glance or two at this, and Elizabeth even dying, is aware of it.*)

Although I loved Lord Robert dearly, I call you all to witness that nothing improper has ever passed between us.

(*She moans and closes her eyes. Kat comes to bathe her forehead, but Elizabeth pushes her aside.*)

No! Promise me, my Lords—promise me—that you will do all I ask.

CECIL: We promise, your Highness. We promise.

ALL: I promise.

(*They withdraw in great uneasiness as Kat indicates with a nod that they should go.*)

48

Interior, corridor. Night.

SUSSEX: What can we do?

CECIL: Pray that her Highness may not die.

49

Interior, corridor. Night.

Doctor Burcot, cross and dishevelled, just got out of bed, being hurried towards the privy chamber by Sussex. He stops outside the door.

BURCOT (*huffily*): She called me a knave. I am a master of the art of medicine.

SUSSEX: Then practise your art. Now!

(*Burcot looks down and sees Sussex holding a dagger at his back. He looks at Sussex, makes an irascible German noise, and goes into the privy chamber.*)

Interior, privy chamber. Night.

They go through to the bedchamber door.

50

Interior, bedchamber. Night.

Mary Sidney and Kat Ashley on each side of Elizabeth. Burcot comes in, and looks at her.

BURCOT: Hah! Almost too late, I see. (*He looks round the room.*) Make up the fire. Wrap her in red flannel and lay her in front of the fire.

(*Mary Sidney and Kat stare at each other.*)

Quickly!

(*Kat goes to get the red flannel. Mary Sidney begins to lift Elizabeth in her arms.*)

51

Interior, privy chamber. Night.

SUSSEX: Should we send for Lord Huntingdon?

NORFOLK: Or Lady Catherine Grey?

CECIL: My Lords, we must make a firm decision, and stand by it, before the King of Spain forces a ruler upon us.

SUSSEX: Or before Mary Stuart invades from Scotland.

(*They look at each other.*)

CECIL: The truth is that the Queen is about to die, leaving no bearable successor.

52

Interior, bedchamber. Night.

Elizabeth wrapped in red flannel, being laid back in bed by Kat and Mary Sidney, supervised by Burcot. Burcot gives Mary Sidney a black bottle, and she gives Elizabeth a drink from it.

ELIZABETH: That is comfortable.

(*She sighs, and leans back, and then sees her hand. It has a few red spots on it. She starts up again, horrified.*)

Kat! What's that?

KAT: Hush, your Highness! It is a good sign. The doctor says it is a good sign.

BURCOT: Hah! What is a few spots? Would you rather be dead, my Liege, or have a few spots?

(*Kat and Mary Sidney lay Elizabeth down. Mary Sidney relinquishing her, stands up. She wipes her own face with her hand, and then sees that her hand, too, is covered with red spots. She puts her hands over her face. Move behind her to find Kat smiling joyfully down at the sleeping Elizabeth.*)

53

Interior, privy chamber, Greenwich. Night.

Burcot comes bustling out, and Sussex and Cecil fall upon him.

BURCOT: Yes, she will live.

(*He nods at them, and bustles off with Norfolk.*)

SUSSEX: We're safe!

CECIL: For the moment.

Interior, bedchamber. Day.

Elizabeth looks at herself in the mirror. She peers at what she thinks is a scar, and then sighs in relief.

54

Interior, presence chamber. Day.

Sussex, Norfolk and Robert in the Alcove.

NORFOLK: The Commons says they won't grant her any money until she agrees to marry.

SUSSEX: Well—perhaps they're right. The Queen must marry, and she must have an heir.

ROBERT: She has imprisoned a member of the House of Commons for saying just that.

NORFOLK: She—she can't do that.

ROBERT: She has done it.

SUSSEX: We must give the Commons our support. (*Looking at the others.*) After all, if the Queen dies without succession, we shall be the first to go.

55

Interior, bedchamber. Day.

Kat is kneeling at Elizabeth's feet, arranging her dress. There is a knock and one of the ladies admits Cecil. He bows.

CECIL: Your Highness, the deputation is here from the Houses of Parliament.

56

Interior, presence chamber. Day.

An extremely uneasy little group waiting for Elizabeth. It includes Sussex, Norfolk, Robert and the Speaker of the House of Commons.

NORFOLK: Who is going to speak first?

(*They look at each other.*)

ROBERT: No matter who speaks first, I can tell you who will have the last word!

NORFOLK: You. (*Pointing to Sussex.*)

(*The others look annoyed. Elizabeth comes out, with Cecil behind her. She pauses, eyeing them defiantly.*)

ELIZABETH: Well, my Lords? Master Speaker?

(*Sussex glances at the others, and unwillingly steps forward.*)

SUSSEX: Your Highness, out of the love they bear you, your Houses of Parliament, both Lords and Commons, humbly beg you to marry.

(*He is about to say more. But Elizabeth pounces like a lion.*)

ELIZABETH: How dare they send such a message, and how dare you bring it! Do you say I am not married?

(*A moment of shock, and instinctive glances at Robert. Elizabeth draws a ring off the fourth finger of her left hand.*)

Here is my ring! It was put on my finger at my Coronation. (*She puts it back again.*) I am married to England! I am married to my people!

(*They look at her, speechless. How can they reply to that?*)

It has pleased God to lay his hand on me, so that my life hung by a thread. I am not afraid of death. I have as much courage as my father. And if it had not been for the love I bear for my people, I would gladly have died. As for the succession, just as I have taken loving thought and care for my people in every other way, so when the time comes, I will take care of that.

(*Uneasy glances at this. Nobody likes to say that she might leave it too late.*)

If God puts it in my mind to marry, then I will marry, but I will marry no one who does not love my people as dearly as I love them myself, and for my own part, as I have often said, it will please me best if at the last a marble stone shall record that this Queen, having reigned such and such a time, lived and died a virgin.

(*She seems to have finished. They glance at each other again, and Norfolk unwillingly prepares to put his oar in, but Elizabeth seeing his intention, rips the whole thing apart on a note of rising fury.*)

I am an absolute Princess, and I will marry at no man's bidding, so you may put that thought clean out of your heads! And I take it very unkind in you all, knowing as you do my heart, and my love for my people, to come and harry me in this way! I had not expected it of you.

(*She turns on Robert unexpectedly.*)

I had not expected it of *you*, my Lord! I thought that if all the world turned against me, you would not!

ROBERT (*horrified*): I? I would die for you!

ELIZABETH (*exasperated*): What has that to do with it?

(*She sweeps away down the gallery, pauses, and turns.*)

Master Speaker!

(*The Speaker, apprehensive, steps after her, and bows.*)

I have freed that Member of Parliament from the Tower. I am sorry that his rudeness made me forget myself. And for the money that my Commons grant me, to show my love for them, I will remit a third part of it.

(*The Speaker, completely taken in, smiles, delighted, and bows again. Elizabeth goes on and out. Cecil and the lords stand looking after her.*)

163

CECIL: I think Mary Stuart will have her second husband before the Queen has her first.

57

Interior, privy chamber. Day.

Elizabeth subtly preening herself as she talks to Sir James Melville, an attractive Scotsman. Sussex, Norfolk and Robert in attendance, and ladies-in-waiting. With them is Lettice Knollys, a good-looking, high spirited girl of twenty-one, with the air of good humour which sensuality often gives. Elizabeth is dressed in the Italian style with her hair down.

ELIZABETH: Of what complexion is your Queen, Sir James?

MELVILLE: Not so white as yours, your Highness.

(Elizabeth smiles.)

But she is held to be a very lovely lady.

(Elizabeth nods graciously.)

ELIZABETH: Queen Mary is of my height, I believe?

MELVILLE: A little taller.

ELIZABETH: Then she is too tall.

(Melville bows politely. Elizabeth moves a few steps away, showing off her walk and her dress, and glances back as Melville follows her.)

You have seen me dressed in the French style, and the English, and now the Italian. Which do you prefer?

(Melville affects to consider carefully.)

MELVILLE: The Italian, Madam, shows you to best advantage.

164

*(She is pleased, and smiles again. See Lettice conceal-
ing a smile. Melville decides he can talk business again.)*

Queen Mary is to understand, then, your Highness, that
if she were to marry the young French King, her late
husband's brother . . .

ELIZABETH: I should consider it an unfriendly act.

MELVILLE: You would not have the same objection to
her marrying the Archduke Charles?

(Elizabeth's face suddenly rigid.)

Or to Don Carlos of Spain?

ELIZABETH *(turns)*: I know nothing of Don Carlos.

MELVILLE *(smiling)*: Indeed, your Highness? I thought
there was not a Prince in Europe who had not been
your suitor.

*(A quick glance from Lettice to Robert inviting him
to share her amusement. He avoids it. Elizabeth turns
to Melville, smiling.)*

ELIZABETH: Is your Queen fond of dancing?

MELVILLE: Very fond, your Highness.

(Pause, feeling that more is expected of him.)

She dances well, but not with the stateliness of your
Majesty. *(He is about to return to business.)*

ELIZABETH: She is a fine musician, I suppose?

MELVILLE: Er—she is generally thought to play very
well, for a queen.

(Elizabeth is struck by this observation.)

58

Interior, corridor. Night.

*Melville is being brought along the gallery by Norfolk.
Melville is glancing at him, puzzled. Norfolk puts his
finger to his lips, as they reach a curtain, from behind
which comes the sound of music.*

59

Interior, bedchamber. Night.

*She plays brilliantly, and Melville's face expresses an
appreciation of this, mingled with amusement. He steps
quietly through the curtain, and stands listening. Elizabeth, as though just seeing him, breaks off, stands up,
and comes towards him.*

ELIZABETH: Sir James Melville! (*Aiming a playful
bow at him.*) What are you doing here?

MELVILLE: Deriving great pleasure, your Highness,
from your music.

ELIZABETH: You have no business to be here! I never
play before men. I only play to enliven myself when
I am alone. (*Glancing sideways.*) . . . As I daresay
Queen Mary does.

MELVILLE: She plays well—but your Highness must
take the prize.

ELIZABETH (*gratified*): And yet there is a greater prize
which Queen Mary may win if she will.

(*Melville is suddenly attentive.*)

60

Interior, a room in Edinburgh. Day.

Close up of Mary throwing her head back and laughing. She is reading a letter, highly amused at its contents, turns it over, reads some more, laughs again, and then suddenly sits up, staring at the letter.

MARY: She suggests that I should marry—*whom*?

(*She looks up with a face of astonished indignation.*)

61

Interior, presence chamber. Evening.

Robert standing between two Lords in their parliamentary robes. He advances and kneels down. During the following speech from Cecil, Elizabeth rises from her canopied chair and places a mantle round Robert's neck. As she fastens it, she tickles his neck. With a slight roll of the eye, he maintains his gravity, Melville watches.

CECIL: 'We Elizabeth, by the Grace of God Queen of England and Ireland, Defender of the Faith, of our special grace and certain knowledge and mere motive, have erected, preferred and created the said Robert Dudley as Earl of Leicester, and by these present erect, prefer and create him the name, status, style, title, honour and dignity of Earl of Leicester, with all and singular the pre-eminences, honours and other things whatsoever of such status of Earl of Leicester appurtaining, we give and concede by these present to him the said Robert Dudley, of the same style, title, honour and dignity . . .'

62

Interior, a room in Edinburgh. Day.

Mary dictating a letter.

MARY: 'My very dear cousin, Elizabeth,—' (*With all her charm and warmth.*) '—with regard to the Earl of Leicester, the praise you give him must commend him to me, and whom you love, I must love also. I must tell you frankly that I had not thought to marry a subject—no, not even the Earl of Leicester—but yet I mean in this, as in all things, to be guided by your best judgment and advice'.

(*Slow close up to see the smile slowly giving way to an expression which shows just how little she means to take any advice given by Elizabeth.*)

63

Interior, bedchamber. Night.

Robert, looking sleek and satisfied, standing by the fire, talking pleasantly to Cecil. Elizabeth stands a little way away talking to Melville.

ELIZABETH (*her eyes on Robert*): And what do you think of my—new creation?

MELVILLE (*smiling*): I think the Earl of Leicester adorns his place even more than Lord Robert Dudley did.

ELIZABETH (*suddenly turning on him*): And yet I think you like Lord Darnley better!

(*Melville, catches his breath, taken completely by surprise. He makes good recovery.*)

MELVILLE: No one could like a pale-faced boy more than such a handsome man as Lord Robert.

(*Elizabeth looks at him.*)

ELIZABETH: I hope Queen Mary doesn't.

MELVILLE: Queen Mary wishes to please you, but she fears Lord Robert himself has no enthusiasm for the match.

ELIZABETH: Why do you say that?

MELVILLE: He has always made it clear that he hopes to marry elsewhere.

(*Elizabeth's eyes rest on Robert's face. He is smiling.*)

ELIZABETH: I have often said I do not mean to marry.

MELVILLE: No, your Highness, for now you are both King and Queen, but if you married, someone else would be King.

(*She looks at him and smiles.*)

However, if you would name Queen Mary as your successor—

ELIZABETH: You forget, Sir James, I was myself 'successor' when my sister was alive. I know well what plots were formed about my name and in what danger she stood from me—and she knew it, too. I have no wish to put myself in a winding sheet while I am still alive. (*She moves to the bed.*) But I will send my cousin a special present as a token of my goodwill.

(*Elizabeth goes towards the treasure box and Melville follows her. She sits on the bed, opens the box and takes out a miniature portrait. Melville leans forward to look at it.*)

MELVILLE: My Lord's picture? Is this what you mean to send to Queen Mary?

169

(*He nods and smiles, glancing at Robert.*)

Of course, you have the original.

(*Elizabeth sits with her eyes on Robert. Her hand closes on the miniature.*)

ELIZABETH: When Queen Mary has the original, I shall need the picture. (*She puts it back in the treasure box and bangs the lid shut, and stands up, putting the box down.*)

MELVILLE: Then your Highness doesn't mean to send my Queen a special present?

ELIZABETH: If Queen Mary will be guided by me, then in time, everything I have will be hers.

(*She walks to join Robert and Cecil by the fire, leaving Melville gazing after her, dumbfounded.*)

64

Interior, bedchamber. Day.

Elizabeth and Cecil with Kat.

CECIL: Your Highness, she has married Lord Darnley.

ELIZABETH: How could she do such a thing, when I have offered her the Earl of Leicester?

CECIL: I believe the Earl sent to her secretly denying his suit.

(*She slowly becomes furious.*)

ELIZABETH: He did *what*? Where is he?

(*Cecil indicates the privy chamber and she storms to the door.*)

Interior, privy chamber. Day.

Robert gossiping with Lettice, and one or two other lords and ladies. Elizabeth goes straight up to him. Cecil stays by the door.

ELIZABETH: Is it true about you and Queen Mary?

ROBERT: Er . . . I . . . er . . .

ELIZABETH: I told you that you were to marry her.

ROBERT: The choice was not entirely mine.

ELIZABETH: No, it was mine, as your prince, to tell you what you, my subject, should do. Did I give you leave to write to her?

ROBERT: Who said I did?

ELIZABETH: Do you say you didn't?

ROBERT: If I wrote it was only to . . .

ELIZABETH: Did you say you wouldn't marry her?

ROBERT: No, I . . . (*Gives a quick involuntary look to Cecil.*) Could I say I loved her?

ELIZABETH: At my command—yes! How dare you! How dare you interfere with my plans? That is what has left her free to marry against my will, and to marry Lord Darnley, who has a claim to the thrones of both Scotland and England! You are a traitor! (*She storms out into the corridor.*)

Interior, corridor. Day.

Sussex and Norfolk in a group, talking to Henry Sidney just outside the door. Elizabeth comes out, speaking to Robert as he follows her out.

ELIZABETH: You are a traitor! (*Glaring at Henry Sidney*.) And so are all who wish you well!

(*Sussex and Norfolk move hastily away from Henry as Elizabeth goes off up the corridor. Robert and Henry glance at each other and stand looking after her. Halfway up the corridor she pauses by a young man, Thomas Heneage, who is bowing to her. She takes his arm and they walk away together up the corridor.*)

65

Interior, Penshurst. Day.

Mary Sidney sits embroidering a shirt her face in a shadow. Robert sits opposite.

ROBERT: Was ever a man in such a dilemma? The Queen abuses me because I didn't press my suit on Queen Mary, but if I had done so—

(*He stands and he shudders at the thought.*)

My dear sister, I sometimes think the whole thing was a plot by Cecil to put me out of favour with the Queen.

MARY SIDNEY: You are not really out of favour?

ROBERT: She won't speak to me, or to anyone who wishes me well. She blames me for Queen Mary's marriage to Darnley. But if she wanted to stop it, why did she let him go to Scotland? (*Sits on edge of table.*)

MARY SIDNEY: Perhaps because only half of her wanted to stop it.

(*He looks at her and smiles. Brief pause.*)

ROBERT: One thing she wants with her whole heart is for you to come back to Court.

MARY SIDNEY: No! Never!

ROBERT: She misses you. I miss you, too. The countess of Essex is good-natured enough, but—

MARY SIDNEY: Lettice Knollys was never good-natured.

ROBERT: She likes me.

MARY SIDNEY: She likes any man!

(*Robert smiles. Mary Sidney frowns. Pause.*)

ROBERT: The Queen has been giving her favours very freely to Thomas Heneage.

MARY SIDNEY: Yes, so I heard.

ROBERT: Two can play at that game. I think I shall try what a little jealousy can do—enjoy a flirtation of my own.

MARY SIDNEY (*quickly*): Not with Lettice Knollys!

(*As she turns, we see her face, terribly pock-marked. Door slams.*)

66

Interior, the gallery. Greenwich. Day.

Lettice and Robert talking and laughing in the alcove. Elizabeth with a group of young men further down the gallery.

LETTICE: Why not, my Lord, if it pleases you? But I'm sure you have more—important things to do.

ROBERT: Could anything be more important than being with you?

LETTICE: That depends what you think is important.

ROBERT: You are important to me, Lettice.

LETTICE: Am I? More important than the Queen?

ROBERT: There are many queens at Court, and you are one of them.

LETTICE: I may have to leave Court soon.

ROBERT: You could not be so cruel. You know your going would turn a garden into a desert.

LETTICE: And what about my poor husband, all alone in Ireland?

ROBERT: It is enough for him to be your husband. He shouldn't expect more.

LETTICE: What would you expect if you were my husband?

ROBERT: The warmest bed in Christendom!

(*She laughs heartily. Elizabeth has been moving up the gallery. Robert affects not to notice, and leans closer to Lettice.*)

And if I were your husband, I would share it with nobody.

LETTICE: If *you* were my husband, you wouldn't have to!

(*Elizabeth strikes him a furious blow on the shoulder with her clenched fist.*)

ELIZABETH: Do you turn your back on me?

ROBERT (*turning to confront her*): *You* turned your back on *me*!

ELIZABETH: Yes, so I did, and so I will, whenever it pleases me to do so!

(*They glare at each other, both in a blazing temper.*)

ROBERT: Your Majesty, I ask permission to leave the Court.

ELIZABETH: Yes, go, go.

(*She half turns away, and then pauses and turns back.*)

No I cannot part with you. I need you with me.

(*Robert looks relieved. His temper begins to subside.*)

You see, you are like my little dog. When people see you, they know I am near by.

(*Elizabeth walks out, followed by Kat, into the privy chamber. The others disperse. For a moment Robert stands motionless, then he walks violently into the privy chamber.*)

67

Interior, privy chamber. Day.

Kat is in the doorway of the bedchamber and tries to stop Robert as he strides to the bedchamber.

KAT: Lord Robert, the Queen doesn't wish to be . . .

(*He pushes past her and goes in.*)

ELIZABETH: How dare you come in here!

175

68

Interior, bedchamber. Day.

ROBERT: How dare you try to keep me out!

ELIZABETH: By God, my Lord, you presume too far! I tell you that I will have no master here, and only one mistress. I made you what you are. I gave you what you have. If you try to take more, I will destroy you utterly.

(*He turns aside, and is suddenly in tears. She sees it, and turns to him.*)

Robin!

(*She is crying too. They cling to each other.*)

How could you talk of leaving me?

ROBERT: Do you think I want to? (*Suddenly in despair.*) What do you want of me?

ELIZABETH: Only to be here.

ROBERT (*angrily*): While you give your favours to Thomas Heneage?

ELIZABETH: I'll send him away.

ROBERT: And after him, who will it be? And how many more? You ask too much of me! For eight years I have loved you, been faithful to you, thought of no one but you. For six years I have begged you to marry me. If you were not Queen—

ELIZABETH: If I were not Queen—?

ROBERT: I should know what to do. I should know what to say to you.

ELIZABETH: What would you say?

(*He releases her and steps back.*)

ROBERT: I would say, come to St. Swithin's Church-yard, opposite the Earl of Oxford's house. Come on Wednesday, at eleven o'clock exactly. If you come, then we will be married and I will love you for ever. But I won't wait for you. If you don't come at eleven, I shall leave, and never care for you again.

(*He goes out.*)

Exterior, porch of St. Swithin's Church. Day.

Robert stands waiting. An impression of a number of men at arms around, waiting with him. He glances up-wards. Shot of the church clock at ten to eleven. Robert walks a few steps away and then back again. Church clock strikes eleven. He listens to it intently, and then stands quite still, waiting. Shot of church clock at twenty past eleven. Robert glances up at it, straightens up, pauses, and then walks through the gate. Mix to: Church clock at eleven forty-five. Elizabeth, heavily cloaked and followed by two girls walks through the gate. She pauses, looking about her, her face expres-sionless.

Exterior, a country road leading to Greenwich. Day.

Robert rides slowly along the road with a number of servants. A servant rides at a gallop after them, and overtakes them. They stop, and he speaks to Robert. Robert looks back along the way he has come. Mix to: A coach travels along the same stretch of road beside a tallish hedge. It reaches the place where Robert stands waiting. His men, on horse back, are a little distance away. One servant, dismounted, holds Robert's horse.

177

Exterior, outside the coach. Day.

The coach stops, and Elizabeth looks out of the window as Robert comes to her.

ROBERT: You came—but too late.

ELIZABETH: You waited—but not long enough.

(*He opens the door, and takes her hand. She descends, puts her arms round him and kisses him very simply and lovingly. They take a step or two away.*)

ROBERT: My servant told me that you had gone by river and landed at the Three Cranes.

(*She nods.*)

Did you mean to come late?

ELIZABETH: God knows what I meant.

(*They are silent for a moment, looking at each other.*)

ROBERT: When you were eight years old, you told me that you would never marry.

ELIZABETH: Did I?

ROBERT: I didn't believe you. To decide such a thing at eight years old!

ELIZABETH: Have you forgotten what happened when I was eight years old?

(*His face shows comprehension.*)

ELIZABETH: She was dragged screaming down the corri-dor.

ROBERT: Catherine Howard.

ELIZABETH: She was always kind to me. More like a sister than a step-mother. She tried to reach my father to beg for her life, but they wouldn't let her speak to him. He was her husband, but they wouldn't let her speak to him. They dragged her away, and then they cut off her head. I learnt then how dangerous life was.

ROBERT: You and I have both known what it is to have an axe fall very close to our own head, and yet to live.

ELIZABETH: But never to live safely again.

ROBERT: Yielding can bring a kind of safety. You would learn that on our wedding-night.

(*There is a long pause before she looks up at him.*)

ELIZABETH: As my mother did?

(*She never mentions her mother so this is a shattering little sentence, and Robert knows what it means to her to say it. He gazes at her, and can find no answer. See in his face the gradual realization that this is her final answer.*)

ROBERT: Elizabeth.

ELIZABETH: As I am now, I depend on no one's good-will for my life. Except the goodwill of the people, but I have always known how to keep that. I have known it since I was eight years old.

(*Pause.*)

ROBERT (*very gently*): Shall we go back to Greenwich?

(*She gazes at him.*)

ELIZABETH: My eyes! My dear loving eyes! (*Smiling.*) Yes. Let us go back to Greenwich.

(*They turn back to the coach. He takes her hand, to*

179

help her in. She pauses, and turns to him in sudden panic.)

ELIZABETH: Robin?

(He smiles at her.)

ROBERT: I am here.

(The panic leaves her face. He hands her tenderly into the coach, and springs after her.)

Exterior, a country road. Day.

The coach bowls along the road, gets smaller and smaller and it leaves us.

Exterior, the coach. Day.

Close up of Elizabeth's face, calm and assured, gazing out of the window, with Robert beyond, his eyes on her face.

SHADOW IN
THE SUN

by
JULIAN MITCHELL

G

Shadow in the Sun was first shown on BBC Television on March 3 1971, as the third play in the series *Elizabeth R*, with the following cast:

ELIZABETH I	*Glenda Jackson*
THE EARL OF LEICESTER	*Robert Hardy*
LORD BURGHLEY	*Ronald Hines*
SIR FRANCIS WALSINGHAM	*Stephen Murray*
THE EARL OF SUSSEX	*John Shrapnel*
SIR CHRISTOPHER HATTON	*Bernard Horsfall*
CATHERINE DE MEDICI	*Margaretta Scott*
DUKE OF ALENÇON	*Michael Williams*
JEAN SIMIER	*James Laurenson*
FENELON, THE FRENCH AMBASSADOR	*John Hughes*
LETTICE KNOLLYS	*Angela Thorne*
LADY COBHAM	*Jill Balcon*
DWARF 'ELIZABETH'	*Mary Patricia Finn*
DWARF 'LEICESTER'	*Albert Horton*
PREACHER	*Kenton Moore*
JACQUES	*Leslie Lawton*
COURT OFFICIAL	*James Urquhart*

DANCERS   *Eva Ronen, Jill Bathurst, Unity Grimwood, Clare Welch, Joy Hope, Alan Starkey, Bob Harvey, Danie Retief, Arthur Sweet, Royston Maldoom.*

Producer Roderick Graham
Director Richard Martin
Designer Peter Seddon

CHARACTERS

ELIZABETH I

LORD BURGHLEY

THE EARL OF SUSSEX

THE EARL OF LEICESTER

SIR CHRISTOPHER HATTON

SIR FRANCIS WALSINGHAM

CATHERINE DE MEDICI

THE DUKE OF ALENÇON

JEAN SIMIER

FENELON, THE FRENCH AMBASSADOR

LADY COBHAM

LETTICE KNOLLYS

MALE DWARF

FEMALE DWARF

PREACHER

COURT OFFICIAL

SIMIER'S SERVANT

ALENÇON'S SERVANT

TWO DOCTORS

LADIES

COURTIERS

MARIE

INTERIORS

Brief outline of plot:

Elizabeth has broken off all relations with France because of the St. Bartholomew's Eve Massacre when thousands of Huguenots (Protestants) were massacred in Paris. Meanwhile Don John, the Spanish leader in the Netherlands, has died and the Spanish troops are in disarray. Now is the time for France to lead the rebels to victory against the Spaniards. But to retain the balance of power in Europe an alliance with England is necessary. Hence the idea of a marriage between Elizabeth and the Duc d'Alençon (the younger brother of the King of France). Simier (Alençon's agent) comes to England to negotiate the marriage. Apart from the French alliance, England still needs an heir to the throne and the marriage negotiations proceed satisfactorily. Leicester, who is very close to the Queen, is against it, but we discover that he himself has married secretly.

Alençon comes to England and he and Elizabeth go through a ludicrous but delirious courtship. However, public opinion in the country is strongly opposed to a marriage with a Catholic prince and even the Council is divided so there is some delay. Alençon is now offered the Dutch crown and the alliance again becomes urgent to prevent France becoming too powerful. Finally France and England agree to an alliance but France insists it must be ratified by the marriage. Leicester objects, so Simier tells the Queen that Leicester is married. Elizabeth, shocked, immediately announces that Alençon will be her husband. She orders Leicester to be taken to the Tower. Sussex persuades her not to send him, and at the same time Elizabeth asks Sussex for his help. She does not want to marry, and wants the Council to extricate her from the commitment. Alençon is very angry but he is bought off for £60,000 and returns to the Netherlands.

1

Interior, long gallery. Day.

*The whole court is assembled in the long gallery, every-
one dressed in the deepest mourning. There is a little
nervous whispering, a sense of tension, expectation.
The outer door is flung open. At once there is silence.
All heads turn to look.*

COURT OFFICIAL: His excellency, the Ambassador of
France!

(*At once all eyes turn away and down, everyone stares
at the ground. Fenelon, the French Ambassador,
appears at the door. He has been waiting four days
for an audience, and knows it's going to be difficult.
But he wasn't prepared for this. He stops abruptly,
shocked by what he sees. The long gallery is silent as
death. He has to pass all these people to get to the
Queen. As his eye travels down the rows of courtiers,
it seems a very long way to the presence chamber,
where, framed through the distant door, Elizabeth is
waiting. Fenelon licks his lips nervously, then starts
down the gallery.*)

2

Interior, presence chamber. Day.

*Fenelon seems very small and distant through the door
into the long gallery. Elizabeth is standing in the middle
of a half-circle of her ladies and councillors. She looks
grim. Among those surrounding her are Burghley,
Leicester, Sussex, Hatton, Walsingham, Lady Cobham
and Lettice Knollys. The only sound is the distant noise
of Fenelon's footsteps.*

187

3

Interior, long gallery. Day.

Fenelon is trying to keep his dignity as he walks at proper ambassadorial pace past the courtiers. The sweat is beginning to show on his brow.

4

Interior, presence chamber. Day.

Elizabeth is looking rigidly ahead. Leicester glances enquiringly at her, but she has eyes for no one but the approaching Fenelon. Everyone lowers their eyes to the ground. Leicester looks under his brows across at Lettice Knollys. She catches his glance. They exchange a very fleeting smile, then both look anxiously towards Elizabeth. But she has seen nothing of this little flirtation. She is at her grandest, enjoying this opportunity to show her real feelings about something for once. Lettice and Leicester lower their eyes again. They have, however, been observed by Sussex, who does not approve.

5

Interior, long gallery. Day.

Fenelon's steps sound thunderous as he approaches the presence chamber.

6

Interior, presence chamber. Day.

Elizabeth is ready. As Fenelon enters the presence chamber, she takes a few steps towards him. But she does not offer him her hand. Fenelon bows. We see his face, thoroughly scared. When he rises from his deep bow, we see what he sees—the stern, sad, majestic face of Elizabeth.

7

Main titles

Superimpose camera main titles:

> Shadow in the Sun
> by Julian Mitchell

8

Interior, presence chamber. Day.

Elizabeth has led Fenelon towards the window, away from the others.

ELIZABETH: So it is true. Six thousand dead.

FENELON: Once the Huguenot conspiracy was discovered, your Majesty . . .

ELIZABETH: I have been conspired against myself. By Catholics. I haven't found it necessary to slaughter them in thousands.

FENELON: Immediate action was called for, ma'am. The King was persuaded his life was in imminent danger. Justice required the severest measures.

ELIZABETH: Did it require the murder of women and children?

FENELON: The people were so outraged when they heard of the plot, your Majesty, they took matters into their own hands.

189

ELIZABETH: Are you telling me the King of France cannot govern his own subjects in his own capital city?

(*Fenelon cannot answer.*)

And were the Huguenots not his subjects, too?

FENELON: They were rebels and traitors, ma'am.

ELIZABETH: Even the children?

(*It comes out with fierce feeling. Elizabeth is genuinely upset, and takes a moment to recover herself. She hates any waste of life.*)

The King of France must show the world that they were traitors, Fenelon. That it was not malice and hatred which took so many innocent lives.

FENELON: Your Majesty . . .

ELIZABETH: And if he cannot, I tell you this . . . there is a God in heaven will avenge them.

FENELON: No one is more concerned than his Majesty to put right any wrong, ma'am. He is most anxious that there should be no misunderstanding abroad. This was purely an internal matter, a French matter. No enmity whatever was intended towards England or any of the Protestant powers.

ELIZABETH: The King of France is an honourable man, and if he assures me that that is so, then I accept it.

(*Fenelon looks relieved.*)

But if he can be persuaded to abandon six thousand of his natural subjects, I fear he may also be persuaded to abandon his alliance with a foreign queen.

FENELON: On the contrary, ma'am. He hopes very

much that you will not think the alliance between our countries is in any way affected.

ELIZABETH: Then tell him . . . tell him we are deeply grieved for his loss of so many loyal subjects.

(*The audience is over. She gives him her hand. He takes it gratefully and kisses it. Elizabeth withdraws towards the privy chamber. Fenelon's look of relief changes to one of apprehension as the councillors approach him, led by Burghley.*)

BURGHLEY: The massacre of St Bartholomew's Eve will go down in history as the greatest crime since the crucifixion. You will tell your master I said so.

FENELON: My Lord Burghley . . .

LEICESTER: There can be no further question of a marriage between the Queen and the Duke of Alençon. I hope that is fully understood in Paris.

FENELON: Naturally, my Lord. But, my Lord . . .

BURGHLEY: There is nothing more to be said.

(*The councillors turn away to follow Elizabeth. Fenelon hesitates, then turns to go.*)

9

Interior, long gallery. Day.

The courtiers are now all looking towards the door into the presence chamber. Fenelon appears in it. He had forgotten he would have to run this gauntlet again. He hesitates again, wipes his brow, then hurries down the gallery past the silent, hostile courtiers. The doors slam.

191

10

Interior, privy chamber. Day.

Elizabeth is in conference with her councillors—
Burghley, Leicester, Hatton, Sussex and Walsingham.

LEICESTER: The axe, ma'am. It must be the axe.

ELIZABETH: No.

HATTON: The massacre was only the first step. The next is to put Mary on your throne.

SUSSEX: For your own safety, ma'am—

ELIZABETH: Oh, my safety!

BURGHLEY: It would be an opportunity to deal with the problem once and for all, ma'am.

WALSINGHAM: And it would please a great many of your subjects.

LEICESTER: The Puritans are clamouring for revenge in kind. And they're right. We should teach our Papists how they do things in France.

HATTON: Even the bishops are for it.

ELIZABETH: We will have no massacre, or talk of massacre, here. Catholics and Protestants, they are all my loyal subjects, and I shall protect them equally.

SUSSEX: The Queen of Scots is neither loyal nor a subject, ma'am.

ELIZABETH: She is my guest.

LEICESTER: The sort that will cut your throat in the night!

ELIZABETH: She is my guest. If she abuses my

hospitality . . . again . . . (*Pause*.) . . . then we will have to think again.

(*The councillors look at each other in despair.*)

WALSINGHAM: Is it wise to wait and see?

ELIZABETH (*smiling*): Always, Walsingham.

BURGHLEY: Very well. But I believe we should alert the coast, and put the navy to sea.

ELIZABETH: Then attend to it. But the navy is to be instructed not to attack French shipping.

(*Pause*.)

LEICESTER: You're not still thinking of the Duke of Alençon?

ELIZABETH (*smiling again*): No, Robin.

BURGHLEY: If your Majesty only had an heir, the Queen of Scots would no longer be such a threat to us.

ELIZABETH: I want no husband. I am married to my country. I don't want my subjects to feel jealous. As they are loyal to me, so am I to them.

(*It is the end of the subject and of the meeting.*)

11

Interior, presence chamber. Day.

Lettice Knollys is waiting with Lady Cobham for the meeting to end. She sees the councillors beginning to come out from the privy chamber.

LETTICE: Now we shall know, at last.

(*She leaves Lady Cobham and goes over to Leicester and Sussex.*)

LEICESTER: We should send an army to the Netherlands. We should support Protestants everywhere.

SUSSEX: You know it's out of the question.

LEICESTER: Why?

SUSSEX: You should look in at the Treasury sometimes, Leicester.

(*Leicester turns away in disgust and finds Lettice. He brightens at once.*)

LETTICE: Well, my Lord? Is it decided? Does she keep her head or lose it?

LEICESTER: Neither. We wait and see.

LETTICE: Oh, then she keeps it.

LEICESTER: And as the Queen always waits, and as there is always something else to see, I suppose she will keep it for ever!

LETTICE: Her Majesty is decidedly indecisive. About so many things.

LEICESTER: Well, in her, nature and policy so combine, you cannot tell one from the other.

LETTICE: Are you as disappointed as you seem, my Lord?

(*Leicester recognizes the double entendre for what it is.*)

LEICESTER: Can't you tell? Can't you see it in my eyes?

LETTICE: Oh, I have never dared to look in your eyes. I have always understood they were my cousin's.

LEICESTER: Oh, her Majesty lets me use them for myself at times. You may look.

LETTICE: Oh, no. Suppose she were to make up her mind after all? She might not like what her eyes saw then.

(*Elizabeth has come out of the privy chamber and is going into the long gallery. They follow her.*)

LEICESTER: Well, I am the Queen's to command in all things, of course, but—

12

Interior, long gallery. Day.

They come through into the long gallery.

LETTICE: I have heard it said that she will let you command her.

LEICESTER: Then you have heard wrong. No one has ever commanded her, or ever will.

LETTICE: Not even in the bedchamber?

LEICESTER: Not even there. If she marries now—and she won't—it will only be for policy.

LETTICE: And are you good policy or bad?

LEICESTER: Well—she will never marry me.

LETTICE: You must have a policy of your own, my Lord. Is it to marry? Or to burn?

LEICESTER: Oh, I burn.

LETTICE: I believe I feel your heat.

LEICESTER: I am a furnace. Lettice—

LETTICE: What will the Queen say, if she finds her eyes on another?

LEICESTER: Nothing. Because she will not know. Will she?

(*Elizabeth is looking at a paper which Burghley has handed her. She looks round for Leicester.*)

ELIZABETH: Robin!

(*Leicester bows to Lettice and goes to the Queen.*)

13

Interior, French royal apartments. Night.

Two dwarfs, one dressed as Elizabeth, the other as Leicester, are acting a parody of their courtship.

DWARF ELIZABETH: Robin! My eyes! My ears! My nose! My mouth! My arse!

(*Catherine de Medici, the Queen Mother of France is watching the performance with the greatest delight. With her is Fenelon, who is less amused.*)

CATHERINE: Answer her, Leicester!

DWARF LEICESTER: Use me as you will, my beauteous virgin queen. All my parts are at your service.

DWARF ELIZABETH: Oh, would that you would use me as I would you would!

(*Dwarf Leicester advances lecherously.*)

No, no, forbear! I am a queen! And yet I am a woman, too. Come, then, my love. But no!

DWARF LEICESTER: By all the saints in heaven, I'll make your mind up for you!

DWARF ELIZABETH (*coyly*): I am too narrow for a man.

DWARF LEICESTER: It's not a man I'm looking for.

(*He advances on her again. Jean Simier enters and comes quietly to whisper to Fenelon. Simier is young, handsome, charming, the intimate adviser of Alençon.*)

DWARF ELIZABETH (*cowering*): Treason! Treason!

DWARF LEICESTER: Yield! Or I draw my weapon!

(*Dwarf Elizabeth shrieks with mingled delight and terror as he pursues her.*)

CATHERINE: Bravo! Bravo!

FENELON: Your Majesty, the Duke of Alençon is here.

CATHERINE: Good. I will see him. (*To Dwarfs.*) Go on, Leicester! Have at her, man!

FENELON: I believe, ma'am, it might be as well not to act the play before the Duke.

CATHERINE: No? He might find it instructive. (*But she claps her hands.*) Thank you—thank you. We will see the rest tomorrow.

(*The dwarfs look disappointed.*)

DWARF LEICESTER: Won't you see where I carry her off to bed, ma'am?

CATHERINE: Tomorrow. Give them something, Fenelon.

(*None too pleased, Fenelon gives the dwarfs money and they withdraw.*)

SIMIER: It will take a larger man than that to carry off the Queen of England, ma'am.

CATHERINE: I think my son is big enough, though, Simier. I hope he's in a better mood.

SIMIER: He is obedient to your Majesty's wishes, as always, ma'am.

(*Alençon enters. He is short and pockmarked, but full of energy and spirit, a frustrated younger son.*)

ALENÇON: Well, what is it this time? Am I to be shut up again for being a naughty boy? Or is it my head you want?

CATHERINE: Francis, I am your mother. Remember the commandment.

ALENÇON: Which one? Thou shalt not kill?

FENELON: That is no way to speak to the Queen, my Lord.

CATHERINE: I thought you said he was obedient, Simier.

SIMIER: I said, as always, ma'am.

ALENÇON: When I was told you'd sent for me, I wondered if it was the start of a new massacre. I thought perhaps I ought to flee. But then, I've fled so often—it wouldn't be dignified to run away again. So here I am—*Mother*. At your service. (*Ironic bow.*)

CATHERINE: Oh, you're very clever, Francis—very sharp. You could do yourself an injury.

ALENÇON: I don't need to. There are so many other people ready to do it for me.

CATHERINE: Your quarrels with your brother do serious injury to France.

ALENÇON: I never quarrel with the King. It would be disloyal. He quarrels with me.

FENELON: My Lord, there are quarrels, let us say, and they do great harm.

ALENÇON: Then speak to him, not me. I don't start them.

CATHERINE: There wouldn't be any quarrels if you left Paris.

ALENÇON: Oh, so it's exile! I told you I was never summoned to hear good news, Jean.

FENELON: The Queen has excellent news, if you will only listen.

ALENÇON: Is my brother dead?

FENELON: My Lord!

CATHERINE: Don John is dead. The Spaniards no longer have a general in the Netherlands.

ALENÇON: Is this true?

FENELON: Yes. It will take months for a new commander to be appointed and arrive.

ALENÇON (*crossing himself*): Then God be praised!

CATHERINE: I'm glad you cross yourself. You've always been so active for the heretics I thought perhaps you'd become one.

ALENÇON: The Huguenots aren't heretics, they're Frenchmen.

CATHERINE: Call them what you like. Now is your chance to prove their loyalty.

FENELON: If you lead them into Flanders, my Lord, you could drive the Spanish into the sea.

ALENÇON (*pause*): But the English would never allow that. A French Netherlands? They'd send an army at once.

CATHERINE: Not if you act intelligently for once.

(*Another pause. Alençon looks first at Fenelon, then at Simier.*)

SIMIER: I believe, my Lord, the Queen is reminding you that you're still a bachelor.

ALENÇON: But it's impossible! The negotiations were broken off after the massacre.

FENELON: The massacre was some time ago. Queen Elizabeth's memory can be very short when it suits her.

CATHERINE: You must realize, though, that we cannot finance you. The Treasury is empty, as you know—you've helped to empty it.

FENELON: But you are the known champion of the Huguenots, and if you guarantee freedom of worship for all Dutchmen of whatever faith—

CATHERINE: If you offer Elizabeth your hand—

FENELON: Think what it would mean for France, my Lord.

(*Alençon is finding it hard to take it all in.*)

SIMIER: It certainly opens up a prospect, my Lord.

ALENÇON: But what's behind it? There must be something else, Mother.

CATHERINE: You know it has always been my dream

that all my sons should be kings. Whatever you may think, that's what I've always worked for.

FENELON: You would have two crowns, my Lord—England and the Netherlands.

CATHERINE: But you must act at once, before the Spanish have time to reorganize.

ALENÇON: Yes—

(*He is extremely struck by the idea. Catherine smiles and gives him her hand.*)

CATHERINE: I shall help you all I can—my son.

(*Alençon kisses her hand without really knowing what he's doing. Catherine has to take the hand away to offer it to Simier.*)

Who knows? Perhaps Simier will be a Duke! The Duke of London and Antwerp!

(*Laughing, she goes out with Fenelon. The two young men are momentarily speechless.*)

ALENÇON: Well!

SIMIER (*bowing*): His Majesty the King of England, Wales, Ireland and the Netherlands! But I don't think I want to be Duke of London. Real English dukes are all counties, aren't they? May I be Lancaster and York, my Lord?

ALENÇON: You can be anyone you like! (*Pause, then abruptly.*) There's another kingdom you've left out.

SIMIER: Which one's that?

ALENÇON: France.

SIMIER: My Lord, I think you should be content with four.

ALENÇON: My brother will never have children. You don't get heirs by dressing up as a woman and prancing about with minions.

SIMIER: True. But he may dress up as a man one day. I think four is enough.

ALENÇON: Can Elizabeth have an heir? How old is she?

SIMIER: Well, old enough.

ALENÇON: But is she young enough?

SIMIER: That will be up to you.

ALENÇON: But can she? What's she like?

SIMIER: They say she's very—very majestic.

ALENÇON: She's not—she's not like my mother, is she?

SIMIER: My Lord, I think you'd better see for yourself.

ALENÇON: No. Not yet. What I need now is a spy, Jean. A loyal, devoted, love-struck, beady-eyed spy.

(*Simier looks at him, then points enquiringly to himself. Alençon nods. Simier bows with a deep flourish.*)

SIMIER: At your service—your Majesty!

14

Interior, presence chamber. Day.

Simier is kneeling before Elizabeth, presenting her with a casket of jewels. Also present are Leicester, Hatton and Lady Cobham.

SIMIER: The Duke of Alençon begs your Majesty with

all the fervour of a devoted heart to accept these trifling tokens of his most earnest admiration.

ELIZABETH: Trifling and earnest?

HATTON: He can hardly be both, ma'am.

ELIZABETH: If he is trifling, you must take this back again.

SIMIER: He is so earnest, ma'am, that if you send it back, you will break his heart.

ELIZABETH: Oh, then I accept. I would never willingly break a man's heart.

LEICESTER: You command so many hearts, you must break some.

ELIZABETH: But not willingly, Robin.

SIMIER: I wish I could tell you how happy this will make him, ma'am.

ELIZABETH (*looking at the jewels*): Tell him he makes *me* very happy. Tell him, he is a jewel among princes, and I will wear him on my sleeve.

(*She holds a jewel against her sleeve.*)

SIMIER: He would rather be closer to your heart, ma'am.

ELIZABETH: Here, then?

(*She moves the jewel to her heart.*)

SIMIER: A little higher, ma'am. He would hang there with all his soul.

HATTON: What?

SIMIER: I do not speak for myself, Sir Christopher, though I wish I dared.

203

ELIZABETH: You speak quite well enough for me.

SIMIER: If my master were here—

ELIZABETH: Well? What would he say?

SIMIER: That he was jealous, ma'am.

LEICESTER: Of whom?

SIMIER: Of these jewels, my Lord. Because they will lie where he would lie himself.

LEICESTER: The Duke is very forward for one who has never so much as set eyes on her Majesty.

SIMIER: I am only his echo, my Lord, his feeble imitation, but I swear report alone was enough for him to know—

HATTON: To know what?

SIMIER: Where he would lie.

ELIZABETH: You are very bold for an echo. What is your name?

SIMIER: Simier, ma'am.

ELIZABETH: Oh, then you're not an echo, you're an ape.

LEICESTER: He's a monkey, certainly.

ELIZABETH: No, no, he is an ape, his master's ape. And now he shall be mine, too.

(*She gives him her hand*.)

SIMIER: I am your creature in everything, ma'am.

HATTON: Is an ape a suitable messenger of love? Shouldn't his master speak his lines for himself?

LEICESTER: Yes, marriage by proxy is one thing, but wooing . . .

SIMIER: My master only wishes he were here.

ELIZABETH: Then why isn't he?

15

Interior, French royal apartments. Night.

Fenelon is with Queen Catherine.

FENELON: She calls him her ape.

CATHERINE: What does that make my son?

FENELON: The King of England . . . perhaps. But he must go there himself. She insists she will do nothing without seeing him first.

CATHERINE: Will she like what she sees?

FENELON: Well, she likes what she's heard. (*Pause.*) She's very capricious. And he is young.

CATHERINE: Young! Oh, yes, he's certainly that! But . . .

FENELON: A queen without an heir cannot be too choosy about looks, ma'am.

CATHERINE: Well, I wouldn't have him.

FENELON: Not even for your country?

CATHERINE: Well . . . (*She laughs.*)

FENELON: Of course, she's very fond of saying she's married to England.

205

CATHERINE: Well, if she wants a baby, she'll have to be divorced. I only hope Francis can manage *his* part. She *is* forty-five.

(*The two dwarfs come in.*)

DWARF LEICESTER: Will you see our new play now? I'm the Duke this time.

CATHERINE: No. I think we'd better not have any plays about the Queen of England for the time being.

DWARF LEICESTER: But, your Majesty . . .

CATHERINE: I said, no more plays.

(*She goes out with Fenelon. The dwarfs look at each other in dismay. Dwarf Elizabeth bursts into tears. Her husband takes her in his arms to comfort her.*)

16

Interior, long gallery. Day.

Sussex comes over to Walsingham, looking thoroughly pleased with himself. Leicester is at a window, frowning.

SUSSEX: He's coming! He's set out at last!

WALSINGHAM: But will he get here? They're offering two to one against in the city.

SUSSEX: Generous odds.

WALSINGHAM: Will you take them?

SUSSEX: I never gamble, if I can help it, Walsingham. But if I did—well, two to one would tempt me.

WALSINGHAM: What about three to one against the marriage ever taking place?

SUSSEX: Even more tempting.

WALSINGHAM: Do you think so? I think it would be money thrown away.

(*Leicester has been listening.*)

LEICESTER: You're not usually so cautious.

WALSINGHAM: He want's too much. Sixty-thousand a year and a coronation—it's impossible.

SUSSEX: Well, sixty-thousand is too much, of course, though he will have to have something. But as for the coronation—some formal recognition of his position will have to be made.

LEICESTER: And what do we get in return? Nothing!

SUSSEX: We get a very great deal. We get the Netherlands, at very little expense to ourselves. We get peace with France, and Spain removed from our doorstep. We get prosperity.

WALSINGHAM: It's a good thing you're *not* a betting man. You let your hopes get the better of your judgment.

SUSSEX: We get an heir, Walsingham.

LEICESTER: Or lose the Queen in the attempt.

SUSSEX: Many women of her age have had fine, healthy children.

LEICESTER: Many others have died.

WALSINGHAM: I'd rather we had a childless queen than a queenless country.

LEICESTER: With a French Catholic regent!

SUSSEX: You exaggerate, as usual. The Duke is notorious for his tolerance. All he asks for himself is for mass to be said in his private apartments. No one can object to that.

WALSINGHAM: The whole country objects.

SUSSEX: A few puritans. They don't rule here yet, and I hope they never will.

LEICESTER: I'd rather they ruled than the French.

SUSSEX: There is no question of that. He will be her husband, nothing more.

WALSINGHAM: Well, I'm willing to bet my whole estate he won't be.

LEICESTER: Of course he won't.

SUSSEX: You're wrong, Leicester.

LEICESTER: No. I know the Queen. She'll never marry anyone.

SUSSEX: No? You've been away from court—important business, no doubt. You'll find things have advanced in your absence. We're beyond diplomacy this time. We're down to human nature.

(*Leicester looks suddenly shaken.*)

17

Interior, bedchamber. Day.

Elizabeth is looking pale and rather frightened. Present are Lady Cobham, two ladies, Burghley and Simier. In the background, two doctors are waiting, in black robes.

ELIZABETH: Is the Earl of Leicester here?

LADY COBHAM: Shall I go and see, ma'am?

ELIZABETH: Yes. No. No, it doesn't matter.

(*Burghley looks crossly at Simier.*)

BURGHLEY: Surely we can dispense with this, Simier. You see how much it upsets her Majesty.

SIMIER: I wish it could be avoided, my Lord. But it is only right that the Duke should know his prospects before he commits himself further.

BURGHLEY: Everyone agrees the prospects are excellent.

SIMIER: Then what can be the objection of confirming them with her Majesty's own physicians?

ELIZABETH: You sound like a horse-coper, haggling over a brood-mare.

SIMIER: We are commanded to be fruitful and multiply, ma'am.

ELIZABETH: It makes me no better than a beast.

SIMIER: No, no. We are halfway to the angels, all of us, and you . . .

ELIZABETH: It's an uncomfortable, straddling sort of place, with our heads in the clouds and our . . . our feet in the mire.

SIMIER: We must endure the condition in which God has placed us, ma'am. If we were pure spirit we could not multiply. There is no marrying in heaven.

ELIZABETH: Which is why, no doubt, we look forward to it.

209

BURGHLEY: These metaphysics are all very well, Simier, but ...

SIMIER: All the Duke wants is children, my Lord.

(*To Elizabeth. After pause:*)

I believe you want them, too.

(*Elizabeth does and she does not. She looks at the doctors with revulsion.*)

BURGHLEY: The whole nation would rejoice in your Majesty's joy.

(*Elizabeth makes up her mind.*)

ELIZABETH: Very well. The Duke shall have his assurance. And as many children as my womb can bear.

(*She gives Simier her hand. He kisses it and withdraws with Burghley. He goes through the door first. As Burghley is about to follow him, Elizabeth takes a small step towards him.*)

Burghley ...

BURGHLEY: Ma'am?

(*She gives him a small smile, really a plea for help.*)

If you wish to say no, ma'am, I will do my best to find some way round it.

(*This was all the help she needed.*)

ELIZABETH: No. No. Thank you.

(*Burghley bows and goes. Elizabeth turns and looks at the doctors. She winces, and puts out a hand to Lady Cobham.*)

I am ready, gentlemen.

18

Interior, privy chamber. Day.

(Burghley is presiding at the council table. Present are Leicester, Hatton, Sussex and Walsingham.)

HATTON: Oh, the Queen's serious enough about it. The question is, is he?

SUSSEX: I see no reason to doubt it.

WALSINGHAM (*glumly*): Nor do I.

BURGHLEY: He certainly gives every appearance of seriousness.

LEICESTER: I dare say! He has a great deal to gain from making a show of wooing the Queen. But have you considered how much more he might gain from marrying elsewhere? I'm sure he has.

SUSSEX: What? Who?

LEICESTER: There are princesses in Spain. They may not be queens, but they're young, and Catholic.

SUSSEX: Leicester, your suspiciousness amounts sometimes almost to madness.

LEICESTER: He's making demands already that he knows we can't meet. Every concession we make, he'll raise his price. And when we protest, he'll say it's we who aren't serious, break it all off, and hurry to Spain with a very convincing appearance of anger and disgust. Then France and Spain will be united against us, the Netherlands will be lost for ever, and those who urged this marriage on the Queen will have so much to answer for, they'll still be explaining in their graves.

(Pause Leicester looks extremely pleased with himself.)

211

HATTON: It's true he has dawdled over coming here.

SUSSEX: He has not dawdled! He couldn't come till the negotiations were properly advanced. The delay shows how seriously he's been taking them.

BURGHLEY: And he is coming now.

LEICESTER: Only to delay everything longer.

(*Elizabeth enters. She looks better now her medical ordeal is over. Everyone rises.*)

ELIZABETH: You will be glad to know, my Lords, that the doctors see no reason to suppose that I am different from other women.

LEICESTER: Then they are fools, ma'am. You are more precious to us than all the other women in the world.

ELIZABETH: I only mean that they foresee nothing to prevent me having children.

SUSSEX: Please God, your Majesty will have many.

ELIZABETH: Well, I cannot hope for very many, of course. But I can do my duty. And I mean to.

(*Elizabeth is about to go through, when she turns.*)

You are welcome back to court, Leicester. Will you come and tell me your news?

LEICESTER (*very faint hesitation*): I shall be delighted, ma'am.

(*He goes over to her and they go through. As soon as they have gone, the councillors relax.*)

HATTON: Does she know?

SUSSEX: I hardly think she would have smiled at him if she did.

BURGHLEY (*very sharp*): Know what?

HATTON: A secret.

BURGHLEY: I don't like not knowing secrets. What is it?

SUSSEX: He has done what he is so against the Queen doing.

WALSINGHAM: Oh, you mean Lettice Knollys.

BURGHLEY: His marriage is scarcely a secret, Hatton.

HATTON: Well, I did not imagine you didn't know.

WALSINGHAM: I'm sorry it seems so widely known, though.

SUSSEX: Her father insisted on witnesses. With reason, and very properly. But where there are witnesses . . .

BURGHLEY: It is not a crime to marry

HATTON: Do you think the Queen will agree with you?

BURGHLEY: Well, I do not consider it my business to tell her of it, and I shall not seek out opportunities to do so.

HATTON: Good Lord, nor will I!

WALSINGHAM: Nor will anyone in his senses.

SUSSEX: You need not look at me. Men were killed in the old days for carrying less awful messages.

BURGHLEY: Well, if none of us tell her.

HATTON: She's bound to find out eventually. And then . . . well. If I were Leicester, I think I'd spend a year or two quietly circumnavigating the globe.

WALSINGHAM: I doubt if his new wife would like that.

HATTON: If I were her, I'd go with him.

19

Interior, bedchamber. Day.

Elizabeth and Leicester, who is looking extremely uneasy.

ELIZABETH I'm sorry you won't look me in the eyes, Robin. But I understand.

LEICESTER (*alarmed*): Do you?

ELIZABETH: Do you imagine it's easy for me to look at you?

(*They do look. He is frightened. She laughs.*)

There's no need to be so frightened, I'm not going to banish you!

(*Leicester is immensely relieved. He falls on one knee and takes her hand.*)

But I must ask you to promise me something.

LEICESTER: Anything.

ELIZABETH: Not to be jealous. Or if you can't help feeling it . . . not to let it show.

(*Leicester is utterly confused. For a moment he hardly knows what she's talking about.*)

You know that the Duke of Alençon can never be more to me than . . . a husband.

LEICESTER (*just having the presence of mind to say it*): Must he be even that?

ELIZABETH: If I choose him to be.

LEICESTER (*rising*): But why should you? There's no need for you to marry.

ELIZABETH: Some people think there is. Ask your colleagues . . . Ask Sussex. He has a thousand reasons in favour of it. I half think it myself.

LEICESTER: But what do you feel in your heart?

ELIZABETH: I haven't consulted my heart. I haven't considered it. And I want you not to consider it, either.

(*Leicester knows what he must say, but it isn't easy.*)

LEICESTER: I must at least consider my own.

ELIZABETH: No! The Duke will be here, any day. I want you to act towards him as though . . . as though he *was* the considered choice of my heart.

LEICESTER: I don't think I'll be able to.

ELIZABETH: If I can, so can you. (*Pause.*) We know each other too well for me to command you, Robin.

LEICESTER: I have always obeyed you. I have wished sometimes I hadn't.

ELIZABETH: So have I.

(*She laughs.*)

LEICESTER: Will you let me, just once more, try to dissuade you?

ELIZABETH: No.

LEICESTER: I beg you . . .

ELIZABETH: No. I don't like you to beg. People beg for forgiveness. There's nothing you have ever done for which you need ask pardon. Do what I ask, Robin . . . that is all.

LEICESTER: It is a great deal.

ELIZABETH: If you love me . . .

LEICESTER: You know how much . . .

ELIZABETH: Yes. And you know how much I depend on your love, Robin. And will depend on it.

(*Hold on their look.*)

20

Interior, Simier's chambers. Day.

Simier comes in from his living quarters to his bedroom. There is a large bed, with curtains. There is a noise from the bed. Simier freezes. He draws his sword and tiptoes up to the bed. He flings back the curtain.

SIMIER: Spy!

(*Lying on the bed, fully dressed is Alençon. He opens one eye.*)

ALENÇON: Hello. (*Seeing the upraised sword he sits up, alarmed.*) Jean! What the devil do you think you're doing?

SIMIER (*lowering the sword*): I . . . I heard a noise. I thought you were one of Walsingham's spies.

ALENÇON: Well, I'm not. Put that thing down. It reminds me of Mother. (*He yawns and lies back again.*) God, I'm tired.

SIMIER: I wasn't expecting you till tomorrow.

ALENÇON: I rode all night. You can see how passionate I am by the state of my boots.

SIMIER: When did you arrive?

ALENÇON: An hour to two ago . . . I don't know. I've been asleep. Where have you been?

SIMIER: With the Queen. Look what I've brought you.

(*He produces a nightcap.*)

ALENÇON: What on earth is that?

SIMIER: The Royal nightcap.

ALENÇON: Good God!

SIMIER: I stole it, then confessed my crime, and begged forgiveness, saying until you could see her in it yourself, you would never sleep.

ALENÇON (*putting it on*): And I slept through the whole thing! (*He closes his eyes and crosses his hands across his chest.*)

SIMIER: My Lord, I think you should wake up.

ALENÇON: What for?

SIMIER: Don't you want to see the Queen?

ALENÇON: Mmm.

SIMIER: It would make a splendid impression if you were to stride through the royal apartments as you are, all dirty and dishevelled . . . if you threw yourself down

217

ELIZABETH R

at her feet. It would show how ardent you are, how . . .
(*Alençon has given no sign of having heard him.*) My
Lord?

ALENÇON: Mmm.

SIMIER: My Lord, don't you *want* to make a splendid
impression . . .?

(*All he gets is a snore. Simier is exasperated. He starts
trying to pull off Alençon's boots, but gets an angry
kick and a growling noise for his pains. He gives up
and goes to the writing desk. He picks up a pen and
paper, looks at the bed for inspiration, which he doesn't
get, then begins to write.*)

21

Interior, bedchamber. Day.

*Elizabeth is reading a letter. With her is Lady Cobham.
Elizabeth laughs at what she reads.*

LADY COBHAM: What mischief is your monkey up to
now, ma'am?

ELIZABETH: No mischief. The Duke is here, and wanted
to come and see me at once, all dirty and dishevelled
though he was . . . the monkey could hardly restrain
him, he says.

LADY COBHAM: Well, we shall have to get used to some
strange French manners I dare say.

ELIZABETH: But he got him to bed at last.

LADY COBHAM: Well, that is what he came for.

ELIZABETH: He says he wishes to God I were with him.

LADY COBHAM: So do I.

218

ELIZABETH: Listen to this . . . 'As he could then with greater facility convey his thoughts to you'.

LADY COBHAM: Facile, indeed, ma'am. We all know some thoughts lie too deep for words.

ELIZABETH (*doubtful*): And some words go far beyond the thoughts which inspire them.

LADY COBHAM: Oh, he cannot have come all this way only to talk, surely?

ELIZABETH: Well, to eat, too, anyway. I am invited to dinner.

LADY COBHAM: Nothing else?

ELIZABETH: I think that's enough for a first meeting. (*She goes to a mirror and looks at herself.*) I wonder if what they've told him goes anywhere near the truth.

LADY COBHAM: Oh, I shouldn't worry about that. They say he's not exactly the picture Simier's been drawing.

ELIZABETH: Oh, they say he's a hunch-back, they say he's deformed, they say anything that comes into their addled heads! So what have they said about me?

LADY COBHAM: You have nothing to fear, ma'am.

ELIZABETH (*looking at her pretty straight*): No? I am old enough to be his mother.

LADY COBHAM (*pause*): Many young men prefer a maturer woman.

ELIZABETH: Isn't that because 'maturer' women lust after younger men?

LADY COBHAM: If you're determined to see the dark side of everything, ma'am, I cannot argue with you.

ELIZABETH: Did I ask you to argue? (*She sees she is letting her nervousness get the better of her and recovers her poise.*) I want your advice, Anne. What shall I wear? I must look very . . . very . . . as I used to look. What do you think is appropriate?

LADY COBHAM: Oh, white, ma'am. You cannot possibly wear anything else.

22

Interior, Simier's chambers. Night.

Simier is setting things straight on the table in his dining-room. It is set for two, with gold plate. The crystal glasses glitter in the candlelight. A fire burns in the grate. Alençon comes in from the bedroom fidgeting with his collar.

ALENÇON: Do I look all right?

SIMIER: Irresistible.

ALENÇON: I wish I hadn't come on ahead of my trunks. These boots have such damned low heels.

SIMIER: Straightness matters more than inches, my Lord. Remember you are a soldier, a man of deeds, not a courtier.

ALENÇON: Doesn't she prefer courtiers? (*Seeing table he stops short.*) Why is the table only set for two?

SIMIER: Because you will be dining with her alone, my Lord.

ALENÇON: What?

SIMIER: I shall be here, waiting on you.

ALENÇON: Don't leave the room, whatever you do.

(*Simier hands him a goblet.*)

SIMIER: Here.

ALENÇON: What?

SIMIER: Dutch courage.

(*Alençon swallows it down and grimaces. The door opens and a servant appears.*)

SERVANT: Her Majesty the Queen!

(*Elizabeth enters, she is looking superb, dressed all in white, and glittering with diamonds. Simier bows deeply. Alençon doesn't bow. He advances boldly to meet her.*)

SIMIER: The Duke of Alençon, your Majesty.

ALENÇON: Oh, they lied to me! They lied!

ELIZABETH: Who, my Lord?

ALENÇON: They told me you were beautiful!

(*Elizabeth is extremely taken aback. Simier is so appalled he covers his eyes.*)

But you are above beauty, as an angel is above a man. The commonest woman may be beautiful, but you . . .

(*He falls to his knees and reverently kisses her hand. Elizabeth looks delighted. Simier uncovers his eyes.*)

SIMIER: My Lord, I told you her Majesty summed up the beauty of the world.

ALENÇON: Summed up? She exceeds it as the sun exceeds the moon.

ELIZABETH: Rise, my Lord, I beg you.

ALENÇON: I would rather stay here. I feel it is my natural place.

ELIZABETH: You carry courtesy too far. It is not fair.

ALENÇON: Fair? You are so fair . . .

ELIZABETH: You look at me. May I not look at you?

ALENÇON: I dare not let you.

ELIZABETH: Why? I hope they have lied to me, too, my Lord.

ALENÇON: About what?

ELIZABETH: About you.

ALENÇON: I don't know what they can have said, except that I am unworthy of you.

ELIZABETH: They've said . . . they've said you're ugly. Stunted.

(*Alençon springs to his feet.*)

ALENÇON: Who told you that? I'll kill him!

ELIZABETH: I see he was wrong. You stand as straight as an elm.

ALENÇON: You must tell me who it was.

ELIZABETH: Oh, no. I'm very grateful to him. He's succeeded in doing what I could not. He's got you off your knees, my Lord.

(*They look at each other, both thoroughly enjoying this game. They laugh.*)

SIMIER: Will your Majesty be seated?

ELIZABETH: Thank you, Simier. You have a very faithful servant here, my Lord. I find he has told me nothing but the truth.

23

Interior, presence chamber. Day.

The councillors are waiting for Elizabeth and Alençon to appear. Present are Burghley, Leicester, Sussex, Hatton and Walsingham.

WALSINGHAM: I wish someone would help me.

HATTON: Gladly, Walsingham—how?

WALSINGHAM: My problem is whether or not I'm supposed to know.

LEICESTER (*quick and suspicious*): Know what?

WALSINGHAM: That the Duke is here. My servants tell me it's a profound secret.

HATTON: I think you can admit to suspecting it.

LEICESTER: It would be better not to discuss matters of state with your servants at all.

WALSINGHAM: They talk of nothing else. And since the whole country does know he's here, it seems idle to deny it.

BURGHLEY: It is early days yet. The country will have to be won over to the idea of the marriage slowly.

SUSSEX: Once it realizes the benefits to be gained, it will be delighted, of course. But there are bound to be doubters at first.

WALSINGHAM: There seem a good many already. Have you not been to church this last week?

BURGHLEY: It is no business of preachers, either.

SUSSEX: Walsingham is a Puritan. The sermons he chooses to hear are as contentious as they are long.

(*Elizabeth enters with Alençon. With them are Simier and Lady Cobham.*)

HATTON: And here is his text.

(*Burghley and Sussex go at once to meet them. Leicester holds the other two back a moment.*)

LEICESTER: Burghley is right, Walsingham. Preaching should be confined to religious matters. (*He goes to join the Queen.*)

WALSINGHAM: Leicester surprises me. I should have thought—

HATTON: Ssh.

WALSINGHAM: But are we to let it simply happen?

HATTON: It's not simple. And whether or not it happens—

(*He shrugs. Walsingham looks peeved, but follows him over to the others.*)

ELIZABETH: My Lords, I cannot tell you with what pleasure it is I commend the Duke to you.

SUSSEX: We have awaited your coming with impatience, my Lord. We are truly glad to see you.

BURGHLEY: We all pray that the result will be as happy for our two countries as for her Majesty and you.

LEICESTER: Lord Sussex and Lord Burghley speak for us all. You are most welcome, my Lord.

ALENÇON: Thank you, thank you all. You make me feel what I hope very soon to be here—at home.

ELIZABETH: Oh, I hope we can do better than that for you. I understand your life at home has not always been—easy.

ALENÇON: Well—I am not unhappy to leave it. Because I could not imagine a greater happiness than to be here always.

LEICESTER: We cannot hope that you will give us so much happiness as that, my Lord.

ELIZABETH: What, Robin?

LEICESTER: The Duke will wish to be in the Netherlands, too, ma'am. I only hope he will allow me to go with him.

(*Elizabeth very pleased with Leicester.*)

ELIZABETH: That is handsomely said. But I could not let you both go.

LEICESTER: You would not be so cruel as to forbid me? Nothing else would hold me back.

ELIZABETH: I find it hard to forbid you anything, as everyone knows.

ALENÇON: Nothing would give me greater pleasure than to count the Earl among my commanders. Nothing would do so much to guarantee our certain victory. I hope you will not forbid him.

ELIZABETH: Oh, if you both plead against me, what can I say?

(*Everyone is looking extremely pleased with the way things are going, except Walsingham and Hatton.*)

LEICESTER: I wish you would tell me about your last campaign, my Lord.

ALENÇON: It was not glorious. But I think I can truth-

fully say that it was not inglorious, either. With a little
more money, a little more co-operation among the
Dutch themselves—

LEICESTER: Well, that would be worth an army in
itself. But tell me about your siege, my Lord. What
sappers did you have?

(*Leicester and Alençon move off together.*)

BURGHLEY: I can see that you are pleased with your
admirer, ma'am.

ELIZABETH: I think I like him more than any man I
have ever known.

HATTON: Oh, that is too unkind!

ELIZABETH: Oh, I love you, Hatton, I love all my
subjects. But the Duke is not my subject, and so—

HATTON: He is a better man? Surely you won't say
that.

BURGHLEY: I don't think you need quibble Hatton.
I think the Duke will be a subject soon.

SUSSEX: If indeed he is not one already. And I think
he is.

SIMIER: He is your Majesty's slave and vassal.

ELIZABETH: Oh, I don't want a slavish husband, Simier.
That would never do.

(*For once Simier can't find a way out of his compliment. He laughs and moves away.*)

SIMIER: I will remind you of that, ma'am, if you ever
find fault with his boldness!

(*Elizabeth smiles as he goes.*)

226

BURGHLEY: Your Majesty—

ELIZABETH: Yes, Burghley?

BURGHLEY: The Duke's personal charms are unquestionable—

ELIZABETH: Oh, they are. I mean to have him. You understand that?

BURGHLEY: I am delighted, ma'am, delighted.

ELIZABETH: Then what are you hesitating about?

BURGHLEY: I only wished to say, ma'am, that I hope you will not be so swayed by your heart as to make any promises as to the Duke's army—

ELIZABETH: Lord Burghley, do I really look so head over heels in love that you think I will promise anything without consulting you? (*She says it with amused but real affection.*)

BURGHLEY: Thank you, ma'am.

ELIZABETH: No one needs to teach me that marriage is a civil contract, as well as one before God and between two hearts. But you will allow, I hope, that it is happier if the hearts speak before the lawyers and preachers.

(*She looks over at Alençon, smiling. Burghley sees her look and says no more.*)

24

Interior, chapel. Day.

A puritanically dressed preacher is holding forth from the pulpit. In front of him is an hour glass. At the front of his congregation is Elizabeth. Among those with her are her ladies, Burghley, Sussex, Leicester, Hatton, Walsingham and several courtiers, among whom uneasy glances are passing.

PREACHER: You may know your enemy by his fair words and smiling countenance, for Satan cometh ever in beauteous raiment and bearing precious gifts.

(Elizabeth stirs angrily.)

God is not one, he saith, but many, and He hath not one altar, but many altars, and you may worship Him where you will. But I say unto you, the Lord God Almighty hath said, Thou shalt have no other God but me, and thou shalt cast down all other altars but my altars, and root out all other worship from the land.

(Elizabeth's fury is causing some anxiety among the councillors, though not to Walsingham or Leicester, who seem to approve the preacher's sentiments.)

Woe unto them who suffer the heretic to flourish in place of the godly! Who suffer their altars to be raised up where they should be cast down! Their idols and graven images to be established in the house of the Lord God of Israel! Woe unto them, I say, and I say again—

(Elizabeth has risen.)

ELIZABETH: And I say, Mr Preacher, that I will hear no more!

(She sweeps out. The preacher is terrified but defiant. He grips the front of the pulpit.)

PREACHER: I say—

(His courage fails him. Burghley hurries out after Elizabeth. Hatton is smiling behind his hand. Sussex is fuming. Leicester is expressionless.)

WALSINGHAM: Go on, sir. You have preached only thirty minutes. Surely you have more.

(*The preacher opens and shuts his mouth. Nothing will come.*)

25

Interior, passage outside chapel. Day.

Elizabeth is raging at Burghley and Sussex.

ELIZABETH: I will not have it!

BURGHLEY: No, ma'am.

ELIZABETH: I will not be abused in my own chapel, or told what to do by a canting, obstinate Puritan!

SUSSEX: Silence him, ma'am, for God's sake.

ELIZABETH: It is an insult to me—and an insult to the Duke.

BURGHLEY: Will you speak to the preacher yourself, ma'am, or—

ELIZABETH: I dare not trust myself.

SUSSEX: Send him to the Tower, ma'am.

ELIZABETH: I'd rather hang him!

BURGHLEY: If I may say so, ma'am, that would silence him, but not the multitude. I suggest banishment might be a better course.

ELIZABETH: No—wait—yes. There must be many vacant livings in the north. I suggest—Northumberland. Let him prate to the sheep. There are plenty of

Catholics up there. Let him try his skill at converting them.

BURGHLEY: An excellent suggestion, ma'am.

SUSSEX: Your Majesty is merciful.

(*Elizabeth feels much better.*)

ELIZABETH: He is never to come near the court again.

SUSSEX: It might be as well to issue a ban on such texts as lend themselves to this kind of preaching.

ELIZABETH: Then see to it.

(*Elizabeth, calm again, goes into garden. Congregation come out of church.*)

BURGHLEY: I wish you luck, my Lord.

SUSSEX: It should be easy enough.

BURGHLEY: I have heard hatred and vengeance preached on 'God is love'.

(*He goes to join Elizabeth as Sussex realizes the impossibility of his task.*)

26

Exterior, courtyard. Day.

ELIZABETH: Where have you been, my Lord? Where has this monkey been leading you?

SIMIER: Only to mass, ma'am. We have been worshipping God.

ALENÇON: I confess my heart was not in it.

ELIZABETH: Will you be converted to our way, then?

ALENÇON: My worship is only for you.

ELIZABETH: Oh, that is blasphemy in any religion.

ALENÇON: To say I love you?

ELIZABETH: Do you not love God?

ALENÇON: I love Him, yes, as a man must. But I love you out of choice.

ELIZABETH: I think that must be heretical.

ALENÇON: Oh, I worship you both. But the one is a duty, and the other a delight.

ELIZABETH: You should delight in your duty, my Lord.

SIMIER: She is too quick for you.

ALENÇON: Well, I am a lover, not a theologian. And God, who knows everything, knows me for what I am. (*Producing a diamond ring.*) Will you wear this, as a token of my true devotion?

ELIZABETH (*almost greedily*): Oh, Francis!

(*She is about to take the ring, then holds out her hand. Alençon slips the ring on, then kisses the hand. Elizabeth looks at it admiringly.*)

ALENÇON: It was my mother's.

ELIZABETH: Look how it glitters. It's like a star.

ALENÇON: You are the star, and its light is lost in yours.

LEICESTER: We all grow dim in her Majesty's presence.

231

SIMIER: Oh, don't say that. The Duke has his own way of shining. You will find him a sun, ma'am, when he rises.

ALENÇON: Forgive him, ma'am. He really is a monkey. He has no shame.

SIMIER: It would be a shame indeed not to tell the truth.

ALENÇON: He makes me jealous.

ELIZABETH: Why?

ALENÇON: Because he's your pet. I wish I were. Pets go with their mistresses everywhere.

ELIZABETH: Then you must be my pet, too. You shall be—my frog.

ALENÇON (*taken aback*): Oh, I'm too warm blooded for a frog, believe me.

ELIZABETH: No. You are a Frenchman, and so a frog.

ALENÇON: May I leap where I choose, then? I see no other advantage.

ELIZABETH: You are ignorant, very ignorant. Burghley—instruct the Duke.

BURGHLEY: The Romans, my Lord, used the frog for a love charm. It signifies mutual ardour and constancy.

ALENÇON: Oh, then I am a frog! I shall croak nothing but love! And as I am a beast now, not a man, I can worship you as a goddess without any fear of blaspheming!

(*Elizabeth laughs.*)

232

27

Interior, long gallery. Night.

Music. The long gallery has been converted to a ball-room for the evening. The whole court is present. Elizabeth is dancing with a group of courtiers and ladies, including Leicester and Hatton. In a window seat, half-hidden, are Alençon and Simier.

ALENÇON: How well are we doing, do you think?

SIMIER: Better than we could have hoped. Look!

(Elizabeth is making a loving gesture towards Alençon in the dance. She looks younger and happier than at any time in the play so far. Alençon bows and throws her a kiss.)

ALENÇON: I feel so damned silly, sitting here while everyone dances. It's absurd—everyone knows I'm in London.

SIMIER: Oh, it's just her way of doing things. She has to negotiate with the country as well as with you, and she never does anything directly.

ALENÇON: It's too devious for me.

SIMIER: It's very clever. The English don't like the French. She's breaking it to them as gently as possible.

ALENÇON: Not too gently, I hope. I can't wait for ever.

SIMIER: Well, she always said she had to see you before she'd go any further. And now she has.

(Alençon shivers and shuts the window.)

ALENÇON: It's very damp, England.

SIMIER: No damper than the Netherlands.

233

ALENÇON: I suppose that's why she calls me a frog. I'm to leap from one wet marsh to another. I hope I don't get rheumatism.

SIMIER: The Queen's bed will keep you warm and dry. Bow, my Lord!

(*Elizabeth is smiling across at them. Alençon bows back.*)

ALENÇON: She's a splendid woman, isn't she? She plays the game for all it's worth.

SIMIER: Well, it is worth a great deal.

ALENÇON: I'm glad I like her. It would have been hard going if I didn't.

SIMIER: It would have been even harder if she didn't like you.

(*The dance has ended and new groups are forming. Leicester is at the far end of the room in a group which, to his horror and fury includes Lettice. But he has to smile. She's smiling, too, but taunting him. The dance begins and they meet.*)

LEICESTER: I told you to keep away!

LETTICE: Oh, but I was invited.

(*They part for a moment, then meet again.*)

LEICESTER: You must leave! At once!

LETTICE: Oh, but I love dancing, you know I do. And I've had so little fun lately, stuck at home.

(*Again they part and dance to other partners before they meet again.*)

Isn't it a splendid ball!

LEICESTER: Lettice, as soon as this dance is over, you will make some excuse and—

LETTICE: But why? I'm enjoying myself.

LEICESTER: If the Queen sees you—

LETTICE: She has seen me. She was very friendly.

LEICESTER: Someone will tell her!

LETTICE: Oh, I shouldn't think so.

(*Again they part. When they meet again Leicester is determined.*)

LEICESTER: Get your cloak.

LETTICE: Oh, don't be so difficult Robin. I had to see the man she's going to marry. I think he will do, don't you?

(*Elizabeth meets Leicester. They volta.*)

LEICESTER (*mouthing*): Get your cloak.

(*Alençon is standing up.*)

SIMIER: Where are you going?

ALENÇON: To make a gesture.

(*He comes from behind his curtain and across the floor to Elizabeth. The music, which was about to start again, doesn't. Everyone watches.*)

Forgive me, ma'am, but I grew so jealous behind my curtain, I could sit still no longer.

ELIZABETH: My Lord!

ALENÇON: To see you dancing with other men was more

than my blood could stand. Either you must let me partner you, or you must join me in my hiding place.

(*Elizabeth is delighted. She gives him a formal curtsey.*)

ELIZABETH: I am honoured.

(*He leads her into the dance. The courtiers applaud. At the far end of the gallery Leicester is hurrying Lettice away. Elizabeth has seen none of it. Her eyes are all for Alençon as they lead the dance together. Sussex comes to join Simier.*)

SIMIER: Well, my Lord? How long will it be?

SUSSEX: Six months, Simier, not a day longer!

28

Interior, bedchamber. Night.

Lady Cobham is undressing Elizabeth after the ball.

LADY COBHAM: You named him perfectly, ma'am. When he was dancing, I thought he was going to leapfrog right over you!

(*Elizabeth smiles. She is tired.*)

ELIZABETH: Oh, yes, he will do very well, Anne. Very well indeed.

LADY COBHAM: When will it be?

ELIZABETH: When will what be?

LADY COBHAM: The wedding! Oh, I look forward to doing this for you on your marriage night! There'll be some leaping then, I'm sure!

(*Elizabeth smiles but doesn't answer.*)

Oh, he loves you, ma'am, there's no doubt about it. I've never seen such a diamond.

ELIZABETH: It was Queen Catherine's. I understood its meaning.

LADY COBHAM: It means he loves you. What else?

ELIZABETH: She wants me to have him. I was not sure.

LADY COBHAM: What does it matter what she wants? He's old enough to decide for himself.

ELIZABETH: Hardly.

LADY COBHAM: Ma'am.

ELIZABETH: Younger sons are never old enough to decide for themselves. You should know that.

LADY COBHAM: Well, then, I'm glad you've decided for him.

ELIZABETH: It was his mother who sent him. But for once Queen Catherine and I are agreed. I *shall* have him.

LADY COBHAM: Well, so long as he has you—and you love him—

ELIZABETH: Oh, I do, I do.

LADY COBHAM: Then when will it be, ma'am?

ELIZABETH: You ask too many questions. I'm tired. I want to go to bed.

LADY COBHAM: And so does he!

(*She hurries on with her duties, though.*)

You won't delay now, will you, ma'am? Surely—

ELIZABETH: If you delay much longer with my night-gown, Anne, I shall have to find a nimbler lady-in-waiting.

(*Lady Cobham is silenced. Elizabeth passes a hand across her eyes. It is all so difficult.*)

29

Interior, courtyard. Evening.

A game of blind man's buff is in progress. In the middle of the circle is Elizabeth, blindfolded. Among the players are Alençon and Simier, Lady Cobham, Leicester, Hatton, Sussex and other courtiers and ladies. Elizabeth turns slowly round, her arms stretched out in front of her, groping. The players laugh as they circle her, ducking out of the way as she approaches.

ELIZABETH: It isn't fair! I can't find anyone!

SIMIER: Here, ma'am!

(*He pushes Alençon towards her, but she misses him, turning towards Simier's voice.*)

ELIZABETH: Where? Where?

ALENÇON (*moving away*): Here!

SIMIER: Oh, love is even blinder than they say!

(*Hatton and Leicester are standing rather apart from the game.*)

HATTON: I'm glad there are no preachers or members of the Commons here. It is blindness like this which—

LEICESTER: Wait till he's gone. It's not much longer.

HATTON: But—

LEICESTER : Till then—keep quiet.

ELIZABETH : I know *that* voice! Robin? Robin? Where are you?

(*She comes towards him, groping the air. He moves away.*)

LEICESTER : Out of sight is out of mind.

(*Elizabeth stops dead.*)

ELIZABETH : What did you say?

LEICESTER : I said, I am out of your reach, ma'am.

(*Simier quickly pushes Alençon into Elizabeth. She stumbles at the impact, and falls, clinging to him, bringing him down with her. He gets quickly up, but she has him round the legs.*)

ELIZABETH : Ah! I have you now, Robin! (*She begins groping her way up him.*) Robin? No—

(*Her hands wander up and down Alençon as she gets to her feet.*)

No! It's Francis!

ALENÇON : Who else should you have? I am caught indeed. You may remove the bandage.

(*But Elizabeth doesn't remove it. She goes on feeling him.*)

ELIZABETH : I don't need eyes to tell me whom I love. (*She kisses him still blindfolded.*) Till you come back, Francis, my eyes will be blind with tears. (*She kisses him again, then tears off the bandage, laughing.*) Won't they, my Lords?

(*Her eyes are dry. Sussex and Simier are pleased, Leicester expressionless, Hatton shocked.*)

30

Interior, privy chamber. Day.

Leicester, Hatton, Sussex and Walsingham. They're tired and ratty and getting nowhere.

HATTON: She can't do it. I won't say it again. But she can't.

SUSSEX: Well, I shall go on saying that she must.

WALSINGHAM: We've had to put off Parliament once.

HATTON: Oh, it's not just Parliament. It's the people. They love her. It's their love which binds this country together. Destroy it, and you destroy the kingdom.

LEICESTER: Very well, but will you go and tell her the people forbid her to marry?

(Burghley enters. He looks exhausted as he slowly takes his place. Those standing go to their seats. The council is in session formally again. Burghley looks round enquiringly. One by one they shake their heads. Burghley sighs.)

BURGHLEY: My Lords, understanding that the country does not—as yet—love the Duke as she does herself, her Majesty asks for our advice. It is time we gave it.

LEICESTER: Must we?

BURGHLEY: I should have said, she commands it.

WALSINGHAM: In that case, may we take it that she herself doesn't know what to do?

BURGHLEY: It is never safe to assume her Majesty's feelings.

HATTON: If she wants to break it off, I'll be happy to take the blame. And I don't think it will be blame.

SUSSEX: Then suggest it and see.

LEICESTER: Oh, what does she expect us to say? That the country is crying out for her to marry? That the wedding won't most likely be celebrated with a massacre of catholics to make St Bartholomew's Eve look like Bartholomew Fair?

BURGHLEY: I see there is no point in further argument. But I must ask you this—if the Queen is determined to marry, will you support her or not?

HATTON: Of course. With the greatest mis-givings, but if she insists—

WALSINGHAM: Quite.

BURGHLEY: Leicester?

LEICESTER: Yes. But I hope to God she will listen to reason.

(*Burghley speaks quickly to prevent an outburst from Sussex.*)

BURGHLEY: I need not ask you, Sussex. I shall tell her Majesty, then, that we are divided and irreconcilable, except in loyalty to her. You do not make it easy for me.

HATTON: Do you imagine it's easy for us?

BURGHLEY: Well—I shall do my best.

31

Exterior, courtyard. Day.

Lady Cobham is reading a letter to Elizabeth.

LADY COBHAM: He says he is jealous of the letter, because it will touch your hand, and he cannot.

ELIZABETH: Here. (*She touches the letter.*) There, our hands have touched now. (*She frowns.*) It does not seem a very long letter.

LADY COBHAM: No. But he says he can hardly see to write because of the tears which fall ceaselessly from his eyes.

ELIZABETH: Oh, very gallant!

LADY COBHAM: I do believe there are little pans of salt scattered over the paper, ma'am. Of course, he was writing at sea. They may just be spray.

ELIZABETH: I will have the text without learned commentary, please.

LADY COBHAM: His affection for you will last for ever. He is, and will remain, the most faithful and affectionate slave who could ever exist on earth. And as such, on the brink of the troublesome sea, he kisses your feet.

(*Elizabeth looks at her feet, pleased.*)

ELIZABETH: Is that all?

LADY COBHAM: Perhaps the sea troubled him too much to write further. But there's one from your monkey, too.

ELIZABETH: Oh?

LADY COBHAM: He says the Duke made him get up early to discourse on your divine beauty, and about his great grief at leaving your Majesty, the gaoler of his heart and mistress of his liberty. Though without asking, he *takes* the liberty of humbly kissing your lovely hands.

ELIZABETH: Hands and feet! I wonder where they will venture next.

(*Enter Burghley.*)

Oh, Burghley, you must read my letter from the Duke. It is a rare garden of sweet-smelling compliments and love.

BURGHLEY: A pleasure, ma'am.

ELIZABETH: Well? You look more as if you had smelt something bad. What's the matter?

BURGHLEY: I have been with your council, ma'am.

ELIZABETH: Oh? And what do they say?

BURGHLEY: They say, they will follow your wishes in everything, ma'am.

ELIZABETH (*immediately and deeply angry*): What? I asked for their opinion, not their obedience.

BURGHLEY: They feel they cannot give it, ma'am. Not until they know exactly what you want.

(*Close up on Elizabeth boiling up with rage.*)

32

Interior, privy chamber. Day.

The councillors look like chastened schoolboys. Elizabeth is lecturing them severely.

ELIZABETH: I had expected better than this, my Lords, much better. Do you call yourselves my council, and will not give me advice when I ask for it? I tell you, I blame myself exceedingly that I was ever so simple as to let you consider the matter at all. All I get is wrangling and disputation.

LEICESTER: If your Majesty will only tell us what you did expect, we . . .

ELIZABETH: I expected a unanimous and universal request for me to proceed with the marriage, not haverings and doubts.

HATTON: Your Majesty, we are only concerned for the safety of the realm.

ELIZABETH: You dare, then, to doubt my wisdom in having a child of my own body? To inherit and continue the line of my father and grandfather? The line of Henry the Seventh who made this country one, and Henry the Eighth who gave us our religion . . . you would bring it to an end? I suppose you have had too much of peace and prosperity. You want civil and religious wars again, with son against father, and father against son . . . that is what we had before.

HATTON: Your Majesty . . .

ELIZABETH: My marriage would make this kingdom safer than a hundred thousand men.

WALSINGHAM: The people fear for their religion, ma'am.

ELIZABETH: So you hide behind the people, Walsingham, with your long, Puritan face. Well, I do not wish to see it. You would not dare to tell me to mine that you think so slenderly of me, that I am not to be trusted with the safety of the church, I suppose? If that is your opinion, you had better hide your face indeed.

(*Pause. No one dares to speak.*)

BURGHLEY: Your Majesty, you have only to say . . .

ELIZABETH: I have said! (*She bursts into tears.*) I am a woman . . . you must forgive me. You should understand . . . you have wives, you have children, you know what it is to love and be loved. It is your right . . .

every man's right. Yet you would deny me mine. In your wisdom, you would make *me* barren.

LEICESTER: Your Majesty . . . ma'am . . .

ELIZABETH: I have denied myself everything for my country. What have you denied that you will take this from me, too?

SUSSEX: Your Majesty, you know there is no doubt in my mind. Except one, I never thought to find there.

ELIZABETH: What? Will you betray me, too?

SUSSEX: Ma'am, we are unanimous in agreeing to support you whichever way you decide, if you will only say.

ELIZABETH: Say what?

SUSSEX: Whether you truly wish to marry the Duke, or not.

ELIZABETH (*weeping*): How can I say, if you will not advise me?

(*They look at each other in bewilderment. Elizabeth sees this, and it infuriates her because it is a reflection of her own indecisiveness.*)

ELIZABETH: Besides, I do not think it suitable to tell you my wishes. I looked to you to urge me, to beg me, to marry. But as you have kept your feelings from me, so shall I keep mine from you.

(*She leaves, the councillors getting hurriedly aside to let her through.*)

LEICESTER: Good God, I had not expected that.

WALSINGHAM: I feel whipped.

SUSSEX: So you should be.

HATTON: But where does it leave us? I really do not know.

BURGHLEY: It leaves us, my Lords, precisely where we were.

33

Interior, bedchamber. Night.

Elizabeth is receiving Simier. Lady Cobham is also present.

SIMIER: Your Majesty . . .

ELIZABETH: You've made good speed. I hope your master is well?

SIMIER: As well as he can be out of your presence, ma'am. He wishes he had wings to bring him back sooner. Every minute away from you is a torture to him.

ELIZABETH: Well, we must all undergo more rackings before this business is done. Anne, where are the articles?

(*Lady Cobham produces papers.*)

SIMIER: Are the councillors agreed, ma'am? This is excellent news.

ELIZABETH: The articles include the concession the Duke demanded. He and his household will be guaranteed the right to hold Catholic services in his private chapel.

SIMIER: He will be overjoyed.

ELIZABETH: There is, however, a new clause. I regret it, but it is essential.

SIMIER: What is it?

ELIZABETH: The articles must remain suspended for two months.

SIMIER: But, your Majesty ...

ELIZABETH: You are aware of the difficulties. I trust you will not make more.

SIMIER: But I don't understand why ...

ELIZABETH: I must have time to bring the people to consent to the marriage.

SIMIER: The people?

ELIZABETH: I have no choice. Believe me, if the Duke were here, I should marry him tomorrow. You may tell him that.

SIMIER: I cannot accept any alteration in the terms without his agreement, ma'am.

ELIZABETH: If you don't, they will never be accepted by Parliament. I tell you, two months will hardly be long enough.

SIMIER (*pause*): Very well, ma'am. But the Duke will be very disappointed.

ELIZABETH: I am myself.

SIMIER: Perhaps this will raise your spirits. (*Giving her a letter.*)

ELIZABETH: Thank you.

SIMIER: Will you not read it?

ELIZABETH: When I am alone.

SIMIER: Will you not look at the seal, at least?

247

(*Embedded in the seal is an emerald*.)

LADY COBHAM: Oh, ma'am. An emerald!

ELIZABETH: Like the jewel in the forehead of the toad! You are a good monkey, Simier, and a better messenger. Here. (*Takes off a ring and hands it to him*.) Give this to your lord and tell him . . . I love him.

(*Simier kisses her hand*.)

SIMIER: Two months will be an eternity.

ELIZABETH: Oh, they will pass. Like everything else. Thank you, Simier.

(*Simier bows and goes. Elizabeth looks tired and old*.)

LADY COBHAM: Shall I read the letter, ma'am?

ELIZABETH (*sitting*): No.

LADY COBHAM: What is the matter, ma'am?

ELIZABETH: Nothing.

LADY COBHAM: Let me help you.

ELIZABETH: No one can help me, Anne. I cannot even help myself. I am the Queen and I am alone. And that is what it is to be the Queen. (*She begins quietly to weep*.)

LADY COBHAM: Oh, ma'am, you must not let what the Parliament thinks or says upset you. You have only to speak to them firmly.

ELIZABETH: But I'm not firm, I'm weak. I have always been weak and done what other people wanted, so that now I hardly know what I want myself.

LADY COBHAM: Don't you? I think you do.

248

ELIZABETH: Yes. I want . . . I want to be young again, and . . . I want not to feel time like a dead child in my womb.

(*Lady Cobham is appalled. Elizabeth stares straight ahead, regarding her future, one hand slowly caressing the place where her baby would be.*)

34

Interior, room in Dieppe. Day.

Alençon is in bed asleep, with a girl. A servant knocks and enters. Alençon wakes and yawns.

ALENÇON: Well? What sort of a day is it? Can we put out again?

SERVANT: The gale still blows, my Lord. The captain says it may go on for a week.

ALENÇON: Then England might as well be China for all the hope we've got of getting there. (*He shakes the girl awake.*) Here . . . Minouche . . . time to get up.

GIRL: Mmm?

ALENÇON: Wake up. What's her name?

SERVANT: Marie, my Lord.

ALENÇON: Well, get her out. Tell her to come back tonight.

(*He gets up. As he does so the door opens and Simier comes in, soaked to the skin.*)

ALENÇON: Jean! How the devil did you get here?

SIMIER: I swam, I think.

ALENÇON: Bring him some brandy. And take . . . what's her name?

SERVANT: Marie.

ALENÇON: Take her with you.

(*The servant gets Marie up and out.*)

I've been trying to get across for three days. It's impossible.

(*He starts getting dressed.*)

SIMIER: Well, we had the wind behind us, of course. But . . . my Lord, I have done many things in your service, but that's the last time I cross the channel in a storm. I don't think I shall ever eat again. My stomach is in the stomach of a fish.

ALENÇON: Mine went the same way yesterday.

SIMIER: Well, it's a good thing you didn't come, my Lord.

ALENÇON: What's happened?

SIMIER: She's blowing hot and cold again. She loves you tenderly, but . . .

ALENÇON: But what?

SIMIER: She wants to marry you . . . I'm sure of that. Look . . . here's your proof. (*Producing garter.*) I nearly hung myself with it, but the ship was tossing so badly I couldn't make a knot.

ALENÇON: More underclothes! I shall have a wardrobe soon.

SIMIER: Well, she'll strip naked for you any time . . . that's what I mean. But she's frightened. They've been telling her you'll get them into a war with Spain.

250

ALENÇON: Who has?

SIMIER: Leicester and Walsingham mainly.

ALENÇON: So nothing's changed.

SIMIER: Yes it has. She doesn't seem to mind the prospect as much as they do. She's sending you thirty thousand pounds.

ALENÇON: Well! That's what I call a real love-token!

SIMIER: Yes and no. She wants a guarantee that if Spain attacks her, France will come to her aid.

ALENÇON: She's negotiating direct?

SIMIER: Walsingham's in Paris already.

ALENÇON: Is he? And what am I supposed to do meanwhile?

SIMIER: Capture every town you can.

ALENÇON: I knew my mother would thwart me somehow.

(*Enter servant with brandy.*)

SIMIER: You're not thwarted, my Lord. You're making excellent progress.

ALENÇON: Thirty thousand pounds won't last me long.

SIMIER: There'll be more. You should count your blessings.

ALENÇON: While I have them! Well, here's to Elizabeth. I'd rather have her money than her body any day!

SIMIER: Oh, I think you'll get both in the end. Elizabeth!

(*They drink.*)

251

35

Interior, French royal apartments. Day.

Fenelon is interviewing Walsingham. Catherine comes in.

CATHERINE: Is this the Lord Walsingham?

WALSINGHAM (*bowing*): Sir Francis, ma'am.

FENELON: I have been explaining the necessity of fixing a date for the marriage, your Majesty.

CATHERINE: Yes, Sir Walsingham, we must have a definite day.

WALSINGHAM: But, your Majesty . . .

CATHERINE: Alliances on paper are all very well. They serve their purpose, then they are torn up and thrown away. But a union between two houses is a bond of blood.

WALSINGHAM: I regret, ma'am, that under the circumstances the bond you speak of is not likely to have issue.

CATHERINE: Does Queen Elizabeth admit so much?

WALSINGHAM: It is . . . it is understood that such is the case.

CATHERINE: Well, I am sorry, very sorry. Not to have children, not to watch them grow and see them take their places in the world, as my sons have taken theirs . . . Well, you will tell the Queen how much I pity her, Sir Walsingham.

(*Walsingham bows . . . He would rather hang himself.*)

But it makes no difference to the need for the marriage.

I respect the feelings of your queen, but the alliance can only come into force at the altar.

WALSINGHAM: But that, ma'am, will be like an open declaration of war against Spain.

CATHERINE: On the contrary, it will prevent Spain from declaring war on us.

FENELON: Exactly. The Spanish may complain, but they will not dare do anything against us.

CATHERINE: Give the Queen my compliments and say, I am impatient for the day that I can call her . . . daughter.

36

Interior, bedchamber. Day.

Elizabeth is getting ready to see Alençon. Lady Cobham is helping her.

LADY COBHAM: Well, it won't be long now!

(*Elizabeth does not answer.*)

He's so impetuous! He just pulls on his hat and takes the first boat to come and see you . . . I wish my husband had wooed me like that!

ELIZABETH: A man who pulls on his hat on an impulse may pull it off again at a whim.

LADY COBHAM: Oh, ma'am, you know he loves you.

ELIZABETH: I know he says he does. Love! All my life men have been telling me they love me. But I am still a virgin. Almost an . . . (*She stops abruptly.*)

(*Enter Leicester.*)

LADY COBHAM: The Earl of Leicester, ma'am.

ELIZABETH (*pleased*): Robin! Is he here?

LEICESTER: Yes.

ELIZABETH: And will you conduct me to him?

LEICESTER: Not . . . Not immediately.

ELIZABETH: Oh? (*She waves her women away.*)

LEICESTER: It's not too late. You can send him away . . . you have every excuse.

ELIZABETH: But why should I? We're betrothed.

LEICESTER: I wish to God you weren't!

ELIZABETH: It's no use wishing. (*Pause.*) You have been very . . . kind, Robin. But we have gone too far to turn back now.

LEICESTER: Forgive me . . . but don't you mean to turn back eventually?

ELIZABETH: I don't see how I can. If I reject him, we have no alliance, and he marries a Spaniard. That has to be prevented, at whatever cost.

LEICESTER: He will stay single if you pay him. The other cost is too great.

ELIZABETH: Oh, it will not cost me so very much. Giving up things for my country has become my second nature. And my virginity is no use to me or anyone else.

LEICESTER: But what about your first nature?

ELIZABETH: Oh . . . I hardly know.

LEICESTER: I think you do.

ELIZABETH: You must not say such things.

LEICESTER: I would be ashamed not to.

(*Burghley comes in. He is not pleased to see Leicester.*)

BURGHLEY: Your Majesty ... the Duke is here, ma'am.

LEICESTER: Send him away! We don't need him!

BURGHLEY: I think we do.

ELIZABETH: Are you jealous, Robin?

LEICESTER: Of course.

ELIZABETH: I mean ... because of his victories?

LEICESTER (*pause*): That has nothing to do with it.

BURGHLEY: No, my Lord?

LEICESTER: We are talking about marriage, not war.

ELIZABETH: Oh, they're the same thing. But we are not committed irrevocably to either. Are we, Burghley?

BURGHLEY: Well, ma'am, we are getting precariously close to one or the other.

ELIZABETH (*laughing*): Then let us meet the danger face to face. Anne ... my rings. Thank you, Robin. You will conduct me to the Duke?

LEICESTER: I would rather be excused.

ELIZABETH: If I cannot be, neither can you. Won't you help me? I need you, Robin.

(*Leicester bows. Elizabeth adjusts her rings.*)

I am ready, my Lords.

37

Interior, presence chamber. Day.

Alençon, Simier and Sussex are waiting for the Queen.

ALENÇON: I'm glad to see so many smiling faces.

SUSSEX: Well, my Lord, in all confidence, they are not all to be trusted.

ALENÇON: That is hardly a secret, my Lord.

SUSSEX: No. But if you will take my advice you will not listen to promises. Don't leave England until you're married, or you never will be.

SIMIER: You mean, the Queen will never be.

SUSSEX: Well, take it as you will . . . this is the last chance.

ALENÇON: Oh, never fear. I won't budge till the Queen is well and truly bedded.

SUSSEX: As she will be, if you persist. She is very taken with your person, if I may so phrase it . . . It is only the politics which hold her back.

SIMIER: It seems unfortunate . . . If *I* may so phrase it . . . that the Duke's arrival has been celebrated in such an offensively Spanish manner.

SUSSEX: What do you mean?

(*Elizabeth's entry prevents an immediate answer, with her are Burghley and Leicester.*)

ELIZABETH: My Lord, you have been away too long. You are most welcome home.

ALENÇON: My Lady, I have burned to be here, and

now I see you, I am a blaze which shall never be put out.

SIMIER (*to Sussex*): The three Jesuits hanged yesterday will now be burning in hell.

SUSSEX: Oh, the Jesuits deserve what they get.

LEICESTER: There will be beacons on every hilltop to celebrate the wedding, my Lord.

ALENÇON: I shall walk in their light all my life.

SIMIER: There is a smiling face I don't like. I wish I could see that grinning above a blazing beacon.

(*Sussex looks shocked. Alençon and Elizabeth go on together into the long gallery, followed by everyone else.*)

But I think I know the match to light his pyre.

(*Sussex looks alarmed.*)

Oh, you needn't fear a general conflagration . . . just one very big, very satisfying, explosion.

(*He laughs at Sussex's puzzled face and follows the others.*)

38

Interior, Alençon's bedroom. Day.

Alençon is in bed again. Simier is trying to get him up.

ALENÇON: Nothing's changed. It's all ifs and buts, just as before.

SIMIER: My Lord, you will change nothing by lying in bed.

ALENÇON: What's there to get up for? More shilly-shallying. (*Picks up garter.*) Look at this damned thing. It may hold up a stocking and go round a leg, but it won't keep an army or go round a castle's walls.

SIMIER: She'll pay. Give her time.

ALENÇON: Meanwhile, I suppose she expects me to keep up my hopes with a garter! I hope it's stronger than my patience, that's all.

(*Jacques enters hurriedly, signalling frantically with his hands.*)

JACQUES: Her Majesty the Queen!

(*Alençon quickly pulls up the sheets as Elizabeth enters carrying a bowl of soup. Jacques goes out.*)

ELIZABETH: What? Still in bed?

ALENÇON: I was just . . . I . . . Simier, why the devil am I still in bed?

SIMIER: You are melancholy, my Lord.

ALENÇON: Yes, that's right. I'm melancholy.

ELIZABETH: Well, I've brought you some bouillon. That should make you more cheerful.

ALENÇON: How very . . . kind.

ELIZABETH: I'm told French women are always bringing their husbands little titbits. It keeps them sweet.

SIMIER: It was very well thought of, ma'am. He is rather sour today.

(*Elizabeth sees the garter.*)

ELIZABETH: Oh, you still have my garter.

ALENÇON: I keep it next to my heart, as a token that one day . . . one day . . . I shall see the leg it honoured. And the other one close beside it. Though not too close.

ELIZABETH: And so you shall.

ALENÇON: But when? I am melancholy because the day never seems to get nearer.

ELIZABETH: Well, we can hardly get on with the business, if you stay in bed.

ALENÇON: Where better for business?

ELIZABETH: That is for after the marriage, Francis. Before it, we use the council chamber.

ALENÇON: Day after day! I swear I shall never get out of this bed until *you* swear to marry me. I shall lie here, a gross and sprawling charge on your revenues, till I am guaranteed removal to the Royal bedchamber. I shall be wide awake there, I promise you.

ELIZABETH: If you stay in bed, it will affect your liver.

SIMIER: The liver is the seat of all emotions, ma'am. His is so affected already, only a long convalescence in the royal bed will ever put it right.

ELIZABETH: Enough lewdness. Up Francis! Up!

ALENÇON: I am up, believe me.

ELIZABETH: I mean, rise.

ALENÇON: I am risen. Try me.

ELIZABETH: If you have so much appetite . . . drink your soup.

ALENÇON: I need thicker nourishment than that.

ELIZABETH: I will not listen to any more of this wantonness. Simier . . . persuade him to make himself . . decent. We need him in the council chamber. (*She goes.*)

ALENÇON: I talk about love and she gives me soup!

SIMIER: It's the first course of the marriage breakfast. What else? And do get up, my Lord.

39

Exterior, courtyard. Day.

Leicester is with Elizabeth.

LEICESTER: You must not do these things!

ELIZABETH: I shall do what I choose.

LEICESTER: But visiting him in bed! Taking him soup! Do you realize what people are saying?

ELIZABETH: I do not distress myself with common gossip, and nor should you.

LEICESTER: They're asking . . . are you a maid? Or a woman?

ELIZABETH: Then they're fools.

LEICESTER: Am I a fool? Because you make me wonder.

ELIZABETH: Well, cease wondering. I am a maid . . . as you seem determined I shall remain. (*Relenting.*) Robin, how can you doubt me?

LEICESTER: You make even more of him than you did last time. You laugh and dally with him like a . . . like a . . .

ELIZABETH: Like myself. You know me well enough. Am I like anyone?

LEICESTER: No.

ELIZABETH: Then trust me. As I trust you.

(*She leads the way to the privy chamber.*)

40

Interior, privy chamber. Day.

The councillors rise as Elizabeth comes in with Leicester. Present are Burghley, Walsingham, Hatton, and Sussex. Elizabeth takes her place and they all sit.

ELIZABETH: Well, my Lords? Is there anything to say before we see the French Ambassador?

BURGHLEY: I believe not, ma'am.

SUSSEX: He brings very good news.

ELIZABETH: Then let us hear it.

(*Enter Alençon, Simier, and Fenelon, who bow then take their seats.*)

ELIZABETH: You are welcome, my Lords. What does the French King say, Fenelon?

FENELON: He sends his warmest greetings to your Majesty, and gladly agrees to all your terms. He will support the Duke in the Netherlands to the same extent as you do yourself.

BURGHLEY: The alliance will be offensive and defensive?

FENELON: It will, my Lord. We are eager to see the Spanish expelled once and for all.

BURGHLEY: Then I believe we are in harmony at last, ma'am.

WALSINGHAM: There are no new conditions?

FENELON: None. His Majesty wants only what he has always wanted . . . the happiness of calling the Queen of England his sister, and the perfect agreement of our two countries and peoples.

ALENÇON: When shall it be? Let us fix the day here and now.

LEICESTER: One moment. The French King still requires his guarantee . . . the marriage?

FENELON: Naturally, my Lord.

LEICESTER: What guarantee does he offer us in return?

FENELON: The marriage is an equal guarantee for us both, my Lord. It is the bond of flesh between country and country.

LEICESTER: The French King may repudiate his brother. What then?

SUSSEX: My Lord, this is too much!

LEICESTER: He has never shown himself very friendly up to now. Why are we supposed to think he has changed?

FENELON: But the question of any further guarantee has never arisen!

LEICESTER: It has now.

FENELON: But . . . your Majesty . . . what do you want?

LEICESTER: I suggest . . . since your Majesty's sister, Queen Mary, had the misfortune to lose Calais, we have had no foothold in France . . . no port which is ours to come and go in at our will. I suggest, in return for all you are giving, that you ask for Calais as your dowry.

(*There is a stunned silence. Elizabeth is as amazed as anyone.*)

ALENÇON: But that's preposterous!

LEICESTER: Do you rate the Queen so low that you will not even surrender a small port, which is, in any case, ours by right?

ELIZABETH: My Lord! You have spoken enough!

LEICESTER: I have only said what was in my heart.

SUSSEX: You have never said it in the council. It's . . . it's . . .

SIMIER: The Earl of Leicester does not believe in speaking his heart except for his own advantage.

LEICESTER: There is no advantage to me in this. I am only saying what I believe is best for England.

SIMIER: There is more in your heart, I think. Tell us all.

LEICESTER: No, there is nothing more.

SIMIER: You lie.

LEICESTER (*leaping to his feet*): You dare to challenge me . . . you . . . you minion!

ELIZABETH: My Lords . . .

SIMIER: Yes.

ALENÇON: Simier!

SIMIER: It's time the whole of the noble and gallant earl's heart was known. Her Majesty will be interested. I think.

ELIZABETH: What? What is this?

SIMIER: The Earl of Leicester is not what he seems.

ELIZABETH: Well?

SIMIER: For instance . . . he is married, your Majesty.

ELIZABETH: What!

SIMIER: Oh, yes, for the past year and more. To your cousin, ma'am. To Lettice Knollys. Is it not so, my Lord?

(*In the long pause which follows Elizabeth slowly rises. So does everyone else. She is pale with fury.*)

ELIZABETH: Is it true?

LEICESTER: Your Majesty . . .

ELIZABETH: *Is it true?*

LEICESTER: Yes.

(*Another long pause. Everyone is holding his breath.*)

ELIZABETH: Lord Burghley.

BURGHLEY: Ma'am?

ELIZABETH: Convey the Earl of Leicester to the Tower.

LEICESTER: Your Majesty . . .

ELIZABETH: My lord Duke.

(*Alençon advances. Elizabeth waits for him to reach*

her. When he gets there, she suddenly and violently kisses him on the mouth.)

ELIZABETH: My Lords . . . I present you with the next King of England.

(She throws her arms round him and bursts into a storm of tears.)

41

Interior, long gallery. Day.

Burghley, Sussex and Walsingham are waiting for Hatton in an otherwise deserted long gallery.

BURGHLEY: Well, God be thanked! Her Majesty has done her part, now Parliament must do theirs.

WALSINGHAM: Oh, they will . . . they'll refuse to permit it.

BURGHLEY: Precisely.

SUSSEX: Oh, but she means it.

BURGHLEY: I think not.

SUSSEX: But you saw her!

BURGHLEY: The kiss was for Leicester, not Alençon.

WALSINGHAM: I wish I thought so.

SUSSEX: No, no, Burghley. It was a public gesture. There was only one way to take it.

BURGHLEY: Only one way for the French. She has sealed the Duke to her. But there will have to be many sessions of Parliament before it goes any further.

ELIZABETH R

(*Enter Hatton from presence chamber. A torrent of Elizabethan oaths follow him.*)

BURGHLEY: Have you dissuaded her?

HATTON: No.

WALSINGHAM: He can't go to the Tower!

HATTON: I rather think he'll have to. I've tried everything . . . reason, flattery . . . I wept, Walsingham. I shed real tears.

SUSSEX: There was no need to go that far.

HATTON: I have heard her speak roughly before, but this time she passed all bounds. I don't know where she learned such language.

WALSINGHAM: Simier couldn't have chosen a worse moment.

BURGHLEY: Or a better one, from his point of view.

SUSSEX: It had to come out some time. We should be grateful . . . he's spared us the burden of telling her.

HATTON: She says we've betrayed her. And as for Leicester . . . the marriage was high treason.

BURGHLEY: It was hardly that—ill-judged, yes, and guilty in its secrecy, but not treason.

HATTON: Well, tell her. You'll probably end up in the Tower yourself.

BURGHLEY: Someone must take the risk. The whole negotiation could founder on Leicester's imprisonment.

WALSINGHAM: I'm surprised the streets aren't full of people already.

266

HATTON: They will be, as soon as they hear.

SUSSEX: The Earl of Leicester is not so much loved as that.

HATTON: You don't know much about your countrymen, Sussex. Leicester is an Englishman and a Protestant jailed so that a French Catholic can make free with the Queen.

WALSINGHAM: Alençon's life won't be worth a halfpenny once the mob is up.

BURGHLEY: I'm afraid not—she will have to be told, Sussex.

SUSSEX: I? But I make no secret of it. I cannot think of a better place for Leicester to be.

BURGHLEY: That is why it will come so much better from you than from any of us. It will be clear that you have no personal reason for pleading for him . . . that you act solely in the interest of the safety of the state.

SUSSEX: I cannot.

BURGHLEY: Well . . . Hatton has tried and failed. Walsingham is not likely to do any better. And I . . . I would rather not. I think you're the unanimous choice.

42

Interior, bedchamber. Day.

Elizabeth looks exhausted and miserable. Sussex is with her.

ELIZABETH: I have given my order, and I expect to be obeyed.

SUSSEX: I must ask you to hear me, ma'am.

ELIZABETH: I am tired of hearing people.

SUSSEX: I understand that, ma'am, but ...

ELIZABETH: I will hear no one else.

(*Sussex slowly and painfully gets on his knees.*)

SUSSEX: Your Majesty, though I say it with pride, I have spent my best years in your service. You have never made me beg from you before.

ELIZABETH: Get up. This does no good.

SUSSEX: Please let me speak.

ELIZABETH: Get up, I say.

SUSSEX: I do not kneel for myself. You know me well enough for that.

ELIZABETH (*more gently*): Get up. If I know you, you know me. I will not pardon him because ... I cannot.

SUSSEX: You can.

ELIZABETH: If you knew what my feelings were ...

SUSSEX: I do know. But ... you will let me say this because I love you better than any Duke of France ... you are the Queen. And you must let the Queen rule you in this, not the woman.

ELIZABETH (*pause*): Very well. (*She helps him rise.*) Say what you must.

SUSSEX: The Earl of Leicester ...

ELIZABETH: Is a traitor!

SUSSEX: You know I do not like him. I think he is

headstrong, violent . . . often foolish. There is hardly anything in all these years on which we have agreed. But he has served you, in his own fashion, as loyally as I.

ELIZABETH: You call it loyal to marry that—that odious—that—

SUSSEX: It was not unlawful. Marriage is an honourable estate, or I would not have urged you to it.

ELIZABETH: Honourable, to go and do it like that, in secrecy, with . . .

SUSSEX: I do not defend him. I cannot. But the marriage was properly conducted. He has committed no legal offence.

ELIZABETH: He has offended me!

SUSSEX: Of course. And grievously. And you have the right and the power to commit to the Tower whomsoever you please. You may commit me, if you wish, for telling you you mustn't. The damage it would do to you . . . and to your own marriage . . . would be irreparable.

(*There is a long pause.*)

ELIZABETH: That is your advice to the Queen. What is your advice to the woman?

SUSSEX: To marry, as you mean to.

(*Elizabeth bursts into tears again.*)

ELIZABETH: Oh, no, no! The Queen is the one who means to marry, not I!

SUSSEX: But, your Majesty—

ELIZABETH: Help me, Sussex. You have always helped me. I'm afraid.

SUSSEX: But what of? (*He is dreadfully taken aback.*)

ELIZABETH: Of dying. I don't want to marry him or anyone.

SUSSEX: But you will not die!

ELIZABETH: I hate the very idea of marriage. I can't do it. Every day, I'm more and more afraid.

SUSSEX: But—but—

ELIZABETH: I have my reasons.

(*She talks almost feverishly.*)

You must believe me—I would not tell anyone what they are—but they are good reasons, true reasons. And now—I have gone too far—I cannot turn back—because of Robin—of the Earl of Leicester—he— (*She pulls herself up and turns pleadingly to him.*) Help me. Help me retrieve myself.

SUSSEX: I had always thought you wanted to marry.

ELIZABETH: I know. I have wanted and not wanted and made your life a misery. But I tell you the truth now. I shall not marry. Ever.

43

Interior, Simier's apartments. Day.

Alençon is with Simier. Alençon pulls the ring Elizabeth sent him from his finger and throws it on the floor.

ALENÇON: Well, God damn all women and islanders,

and may all Englishwomen go to hell and burn there for all eternity!

SIMIER: I thought we were home.

ALENÇON: Home? What kind of home have I ever had? My mother's a murderess, Elizabeth's a coquette, the Dutch are bigots and drunken sots—I shall wander the face of the earth before I ever find a home!

SIMIER: Well, it is better to do it in comfort and style than as a beggar. They will have to buy you off.

ALENÇON: Like a mercenary!

SIMIER: This raises your price. You can always threaten them with Spain. They need the alliance as much as ever. And there are plenty of other women in the world—prettier, too, and younger.

ALENÇON: Women!

SIMIER: You can have an heir, my Lord.

ALENÇON: But he won't be King of England.

SIMIER: He will be of the Netherlands. And . . . France?

ALENÇON: You told me not to count crowns before the coronations.

SIMIER: Well, you hoped for five, and I said that was too much. But the Netherlands is yours for the fighting, and your brother still shows no sign of begetting—

ALENÇON: What will my mother say?

SIMIER: It doesn't matter, my Lord—so long as she says it with gold.

271

Interior, privy chamber. Day.

Simier and Burghley are sitting at the table.

SIMIER: It's not enough.

BURGHLEY: But, Simier—

SIMIER: My master has been humiliated.

BURGHLEY: Not at all. As far as the world is concerned, he is still betrothed to the Queen. He is leaving England solely to continue his campaign in Flanders, and will return in due course to marry her.

SIMIER: You and I and a hundred others know he will not. Soon everyone will know.

BURGHLEY: I hope not. For all our sakes, the pretence must be kept up. The alliance, as you can see from the support we are offering, is a very real one, and the longer the Spanish believe in the possibility of the marriage the better.

SIMIER: Very subtle, my Lord, no doubt. But if the alliance is to be as real as you say, we require much more substantial evidence than you have so far suggested.

BURGHLEY: How much do you want?

SIMIER: Sixty thousand pounds.

BURGHLEY: Sixty! But . . .

SIMIER: And half of it in cash before the Duke sails.

BURGHLEY: It is out of the question. There is not that amount in the treasury.

SIMIER: How much have you?

BURGHLEY: I suggest—thirty thousand to be paid fifteen days after the Duke's departure, the rest fifty days after that.

SIMIER: We won't stir without something down.

BURGHLEY: Very well. I think we could manage ten thousand—the rest as I have said.

SIMIER: Done! Thank you, my Lord. The Duke will leave within the next three days. Good day.

BURGHLEY: Good day, Simier.

(*Simier goes. At once Walsingham comes in from the bedchamber.*)

WALSINGHAM: How much?

BURGHLEY: Not bad. Sixty. I thought we'd have to settle for seventy-five.

45

Interior, presence chamber. Day.

Alençon and Simier are saying good-bye to Elizabeth. Also present are Burghley, Hatton, Sussex and Walsingham, with Lady Cobham and the Queen's ladies.

ALENÇON: Sooner than leave you, I would rather we both perished.

ELIZABETH: Oh, you must not threaten a poor old woman in her own kingdom, my Lord! That is not the language of a lover.

ALENÇON: You mistake me. I meant no hurt to your

blessed person, only that I would sooner be cut to pieces than not marry you, and so be laughed at by the world.

(*He affects tears. Elizabeth gives him her handkerchief.*)

ELIZABETH: No one shall laugh at you, my Lord. Dry your eyes. You make me weep myself.

(*She begins to do so. Rather more convincingly than he. Simier and the councillors watch stoney-eyed.*)

ALENÇON: I shall return before those tears are dry.

ELIZABETH: I would give a million pounds to have my frog swimming in the Thames instead of those stagnant marshes of the Netherlands.

(*Simier looks suddenly as though he realizes he could have got more out of Burghley than he did. Burghley looks as though he is having some difficulty in suppressing a smile.*)

ALENÇON: I shall stir them up, and before the ripples have reached the bank, I shall be back to marry you.

(*He bows low and kisses her hand. Then he turns to go. Move in on Elizabeth.*)

ELIZABETH (*voice over*): I grieve, and dare not show my discontent.
I love, and yet am forced to seem to hate.
I do, yet dare not say I ever meant.
I seem stark mute, but inwardly do prate.
I am, and not: I freeze and yet am burned
Since from myself, my other self I turned.

(*While she says the poem, she is looking straight ahead, watching Alençon go down the long gallery.*)

46

Interior, long gallery. Day.

Cross cut this scene with the previous scene. Alençon is stopping to talk to the courtiers, who are assembled as in the opening scene of the play for Fenelon ... only this time they are dressed normally, and are smiling and chatting. Among the courtiers is Leicester. When Alençon sees him, he stops. Leicester gives him a mocking look. Alençon hesitates, then moves on.

ELIZABETH (*voice over*): My care is like my shadow in the sun,
Follows me flying, flies when I pursue it:
Stands and lies by me, doth what I have done:
This too familiar care doth make me rue it.
Nor means I find to rid him from my breast
Till by the end of things it be suppressed.
Or let me live with some more sweet content
Or die, and so forget what love e'er meant.

(By the time Elizabeth has whispered the last lines of the poem, Alençon has gone and the door of the long gallery has closed upon him.)

47

Interior, presence chamber. Day.

Close up of Elizabeth, her face expressionless. Standing in the doorway is Leicester. He hesitates, then comes forward and kneels in front of her.

ELIZABETH: Welcome to court, my Lord. You see your policy has triumphed. What advice have you for me now?

LEICESTER: I would not dare to offer you advice, ma'am.

275

ELIZABETH (*slight smile*): Why not?

LEICESTER: The philosophers teach us that beauty is wisdom, and so you are the wisest woman in the world.

ELIZABETH (*slight frown*): You will not speak to me like that. It is not fit. You are a married man. And I ... We will deal with each other more honestly from now on.

(*She rises from her throne and comes down the steps. She goes slowly, like an old woman, towards the privy chamber. She pauses.*)

ELIZABETH: My Lord Sussex.

SUSSEX: Ma'am?

ELIZABETH: I am tired. I will lean on your arm, if I may.

(*Sussex gives her his arm. She leans on him. They go towards the privy chamber. Hold on Leicester watching them. Fade out.*)

6. Leicester with Lettice Knollys (Angela Thorne), later to become the Countess of Leicester (*Shadow in the Sun*).

7. The Queen in Council with Leicester (left) and the now older Sussex (John Shrapnel) (*Shadow in the Sun*).

8. Elizabeth with the Duke of Alençon (Michael Williams) and (centre) his servant, Jean Simier (John Hughes) (*Shadow in the Sun*).

HORRIBLE
CONSPIRACIES

by
HUGH WHITEMORE

Horrible Conspiracies was first shown on BBC Television on March 10 1971, as the fourth play in the series, *Elizabeth R*, with the following cast:

ELIZABETH I	*Glenda Jackson*
MARY, QUEEN OF SCOTS	*Vivian Pickles*
SIR FRANCIS WALSINGHAM	*Stephen Murray*
SIR AMYAS PAULET	*Hamilton Dyce*
SIR ANTONY BABINGTON	*David Collings*
GILBERT GIFFORD	*Bernard Holley*
THOMAS PHELIPPES	*David Nettheim*
WILLIAM DAVISON	*John Graham*
JOHN BALLARD	*David Garfield*
RICHARD TOPCLIFFE	*Brian Wilde*
JOHN SAVAGE	*James Culliford*
SIR EDWARD KELLEY	*Malcolm Hayes*
DR DEE	*Raf de la Torre*
JOHN WHITGIFT, ARCHBISHOP OF CANTERBURY	*John Ruddock*
RICHARD TARLTON	*Barry Irwin*

Non-speaking

COURTIERS	*Tony Chantel, Donald Sinclair, Eden Fox, Cy Town, Hal Collins*
CLERGYMAN	*Anthony Nash*
SINGER	*Martin Chamberlain*
LADY-IN-WAITING	*Pat Gerrard*
LADIES-IN-WAITING	*Madaline Oakley, Linda Oxer, Jean Woolard, Carol Hoffman*
RED GUARDS	*Trevor Lawrence, Andrew Dempsey*
BLACK GUARDS	*Peter Wilson-Holmes, Alan Granville, Roger Oakley, Martin Grant, Lionel Sansby*
EXECUTIONERS	*Paul Freemont, Harry Tierney, Eric Kent*
LADIES-IN-WAITING	*Melanie Fraser-Gill, Margaret Pilleau*
PRIEST	*James Mellen*
PRISONER	*David Hilton*

Producer and Director Roderick Graham
Designer Richard Henry

CHARACTERS

ELIZABETH, QUEEN OF ENGLAND

MARY, QUEEN OF SCOTS

SIR FRANCIS WALSINGHAM

SIR AMYAS PAULET

SIR ANTONY BABINGTON

GILBERT GIFFORD

JOHN SAVAGE

JOHN BALLARD

THOMAS PHELIPPES

WILLIAM DAVISON

RICHARD TOPCLIFFE

SIR EDWARD KELLEY

DR JOHN DEE

JOHN WHITGIFT, ARCHBISHOP OF CANTERBURY

AN ACTOR

RICHARD TARLTON (*clown*), *non-speaking*

AN EXECUTIONER, *non-speaking*

COURTIERS, ATTENDANTS, MUSICIANS, AND SERVANTS

INTERIORS

Presence chamber, privy chamber, bedchamber
A dungeon
A room at Chartley, corridor outside (part)
Walsingham's room, adjoining ante-chamber (part)
Babington's room
Fotheringay: Mary's room
Fotheringay: Hall
Phelippes' room (part)
Limbo, for exterior night scene

TIME

1586–1587

1

Interior, presence chamber. Night.

Elizabeth and the court are watching a masque. Sub-dued lighting; flickering shadows. An actor steps forward, black-robed and gaunt, holding a mask before his face. He bows, and addresses the Queen.

ACTOR:
Great England's Emp'ress, Brave Albion's Queen,
Of matchless grace and stately mien;
To whom the Gods bow down before,
So prais'd in Peace, so skilled in War!
No living thing, no nymph so fair
Can with her beauty hold compare.
She reigns supreme o'er all she sees:
O'er rustic banks and swelling seas,
O'er man and woman, Duke and Lord,
O'er farm and castle, beast and sword.
For she has conquer'd all, sweet Beth;
See, I am vanquish'd, too . . . old Death!

(*The actor removes his mask; his face is painted to represent a skull. The courtiers gasp. Close reaction shot of Elizabeth.*)

2

Main Titles

Superimpose title captions:
Horrible Conspiracies by Hugh Whitemore

Under the titles, a reverberating clap of thunder.

3

Interior, privy chamber. Day.

Elizabeth and Walsingham. Walsingham is fifty-six; a serious and sombre-looking man.

WALSINGHAM: Following her various marriages, Darnley's murder, and the rising against Bothwell, your royal cousin, Mary Stuart, fled to this country, and threw herself upon your great mercy. She rewarded your Majesty's protective kindness by inspiring number-less plots, encouraging hellish priests, Popish conspiracies, and all manner of dangerous wickedness. For well-nigh twenty years, she has infected this realm, while her son, James, sits upon the Scottish throne. And yet, madam, you refuse to recognize her as your enemy, and do nothing to rid yourself and your kingdom of this bosom serpent.

ELIZABETH: Caution I can understand, Walsingham —none better—but your great fears go beyond the bounds of reason. You see danger in every shadow.

WALSINGHAM: By no means . . .

ELIZABETH: The coils of your brain must be writhing with anxiety; like a pit of vipers.

WALSINGHAM: It is merely a proper concern for your Majesty's safety.

ELIZABETH: Oh no, it is more than that. It lies deep within you, Sir Francis: a melancholy humour. I advise purgatives.

WALSINGHAM: Purgatives, madam?

ELIZABETH: Quickbeme, borage and white wine. They will rid your body of its corrupting blood.

WALSINGHAM: Even so, and with respect, my anxiety will still remain.

ELIZABETH: Because of my cousin?

WALSINGHAM: Mary of Scotland is a constant threat—

ELIZABETH: Come now, how can that be? Safely stowed at Chartley, with Sir Amyas Paulet in charge of her keeping close. My cousin is a threat to no one.

WALSINGHAM: Her very presence in England is a threat to your life.

ELIZABETH: My life . . . ?

WALSINGHAM: Men will conspire, assassins will be found.

ELIZABETH: You tire me, old moor.

WALSINGHAM: The matter drags its feet, and something must be done.

ELIZABETH: Later, then—tomorrow. I am in no mood for this sombre business.

WALSINGHAM: But, madam—

ELIZABETH: Besides, I am quite content with the present arrangement. She is watched day and night, correspondence is forbidden her, all contact with her friends is prevented. She can do me no harm.

WALSINGHAM: Remember, she is no stranger to cunning devices. Ways can be found to deceive the most watchful gaoler.

ELIZABETH: Sir Amyas is a faithful servant; he will not fail me.

WALSINGHAM: I can but repeat, ma'am: her very

283

presence endangers your life. Only by your death can she hope for full freedom and a restoration of her estate.

ELIZABETH: Yet she is still a sovereign princess.

(*She turns away from Walsingham.*)

I wish no further discussion on this matter, Sir Francis. My cousin shall remain at Chartley.

4

Interior, room at Chartley. Day.

Sunshine; birdsong. Mary is standing by the window. Although still an impressive woman, she has lost her youthful beauty. She is corpulent, round-shouldered, and crippled with rheumatism. Her hair is bright auburn. Sir Amyas Paulet enters. He is fifty-one; a stern-faced puritan.

MARY: I did not call, Sir Amyas.

PAULET: Your pardon, madam; I came only to inquire for your health.

MARY: More like you came to spy on me; to make sure that I was not engaged on some unlawful act. Conspiring with the birds, perhaps—or bribing the rats for means of escape.

(*Paulet permits himself a modest smile.*)

Even your smile strikes chill into my heart. Great Elizabeth could not have chosen a better guard-dog. Your work is your pleasure, is it not?

PAULET: It is certainly a pleasure to serve her Majesty in whatever way she chooses.

MARY: And does she choose that I be denied converse with my servants?

PAULET: I fail to understand you, madam. No such denial has been enforced.

MARY: Why, then, was my laundress questioned this morning?

PAULET: A sensible precaution, nothing more. I wanted reassurance that she was not employed in secret matters on your behalf.

MARY: A laundress employed on secret matters . . . ?

PAULET: She might have been carrying letters.

MARY: Ah yes, she might indeed. The possibility had not occurred to me. (*She gazes at Paulet.*) I think, Sir Amyas, that you are the strangest man I have ever known. You profess a devotion to religion, but your life seems based on cruelty.

PAULET: Not cruelty, madam: strictness. A close observance of her Majesty's command.

MARY: Was it not cruelty that prompted you to burn my embroideries and other harmless gifts because you thought they might bring me comfort?

PAULET: The embroideries, as you call them, were nothing but symbols of Catholic blasphemy. Besides, I am instructed to ensure that you receive no gifts, harmless or otherwise. I was merely carrying out my duties.

MARY: How many great sins are committed in the name of duty.

(*Paulet turns to go.*)

One thing more, Sir Amyas: why am I now prevented from offering charity to the village people?

PAULET: I considered it unnecessary.

MARY: *Unnecessary . . . ?* Many of them are poor, and deserve our charity!

PAULET: If they are poor, it is because of their own lewdness. No virtuous man requires charity. Likewise, ma'am, I propose to stop any further payments from yourself to your servants.

MARY: Upon what grounds?

PAULET: The distinction between reward and bribe is uncomfortably narrow. I wish there to be no misunderstandings.

MARY: I have no doubt that these restrictions spring not from Elizabeth, but from your own hatred towards me.

PAULET: If that is your opinion, then may you cling to it for comfort.

MARY: It is opinion well based! Why, even at Tutbury —when I was grievous sick—even then you showed me no kindness.

PAULET: Your immediate needs were taken care of.

MARY: My bed sheets were never changed!

PAULET: Indeed they were, madam.

MARY: Not until I complained most vigorously.

PAULET: Then perhaps you would have been wise to complain sooner.

MARY: You did nothing for my comfort in that wretched house! Small wonder I fell ill. Every corner was a pissing place, the middens bred vermin, the damp knotted my bones, and the bad air mortified my spirits.

PAULET: That was Tutbury, ma'am. Surely you are more content now that you have removed?

MARY: How can I be content in a prison?

(*Close shot of Mary, as she turns to face Paulet.*)

There is a place in England, I am told—a wood at Saint Leonard's—where nightingales never sing. Some unseen evil drives them away. They sing all around, but never in that wood. It is the same with me, I fear. In this house, I think only on death.

5

Interior, dungeon. Day.

A man is lying on the rack, his naked body covered by a rough blanket. The door opens, and Richard Topcliffe enters. He bows to the prisoner.

TOPCLIFFE: God give you comfort, sir. (*He goes to the rack, and removes the blanket.*) Such white nakedness. So soon to be torn apart. (*He tosses the blanket into a corner, and smiles at the prisoner.*) I am Richard Topcliffe, faithful servant of Her Glorious Majesty, Queen Elizabeth. Rack Master. (*He goes to the door, and bolts it shut.*) Her Glorious Majesty has entrusted me with the careful destruction of her enemies. Oh, I am very close to the throne, sir priest . . . I have seen her bare above the knee! She trusts me well. I am to rid her of the Catholic scourge. My life's work. (*He approaches the rack, and gazes down at the prisoner.*) From whence, I wonder, have you sprung? From the English College at Rheims, perhaps? Or the Seminary at Douai? (*He smiles.*) Yes, you have a Jesuit look about you. No doubt you believed you would convert the whole of England with your Popish tricks. Alas, but you were sadly mistaken. (*The smile fades from Topcliffe's face; he leans towards the prisoner.*) Where

287

have you said mass? In whose house? How came you hither?

(*The prisoner does not reply. Topcliffe smiles.*)

You'll not be silent long, traitor priest. No man is silent on the rack.

(*Topcliffe tightens the rack. The man screams.*)

6

Interior, presence chamber. Day.

Music. Elizabeth is talking informally to groups of assembled courtiers. Camera pans to the main door. Two men are standing beside the door: Dr John Dee, a handsome, white-bearded man of sixty, and Sir Edward Kelley. Kelley is thirty-two, and exceptionally tall. He wears a long black cloak, and a black skull-cap. Sir Antony Babington enters the presence chamber, almost colliding with Kelley. Babington is an attractive, richly-dressed young man of twenty-five.

BABINGTON: Forgive me, sir.

(*Kelley grasps Babington and swings him round.*)

KELLEY: Who are you?

BABINGTON (*frowning*): Who am I . . . ?

KELLEY: I wish to know your name.

BABINGTON: There is no need for this, sir; I meant no offence.

KELLEY: I believe your name is Babington.

BABINGTON: Then you have no cause to ask it.

KELLEY: Sir Antony Babington.

(*Kelley smiles: Babington stares at him, puzzled.*)

BABINGTON: Why do you smile at me, thus?

KELLEY: One day you will understand. Take care, Sir Antony. Take great care . . .

(*Camera pans across the room as Babington walks away from Kelley and Dee. Elizabeth is seen entering the privy chamber.*)

7

Interior, privy chamber. Day.

Walsingham and his secretary, William Davison, are waiting in the privy chamber. Davison is a pleasant-looking man of forty-five. The two men bow as Elizabeth enters.

ELIZABETH: So . . . what is your news, Sir Francis?

WALSINGHAM: Letters from Paris, ma'am. From them I learn that Bernardino Mendoza is urging warlike action against your Majesty.

ELIZABETH: Mendoza?

WALSINGHAM: The Spanish Ambassador: he was dismissed on your instructions.

ELIZABETH: Ah, yes . . . the sour-tempered Mendoza.

WALSINGHAM: He now represents Spain at King Henry's court.

ELIZABETH: Then I pity the French.

WALSINGHAM: One of my men intercepted a letter

written by Mendoza, and addressed to Secretary Idriaquez. Davison, will you read?

DAVISON (*reading*): 'The insolence of these people so exasperates me that I desire to live only to be revenged upon them.'

WALSINGHAM: He refers, of course, to England.

DAVISON (*reading*): 'I hope to God that time will soon come, and that I may be an instrument in their punishment. I will walk barefoot over Europe to compass it.'

WALSINGHAM: And there is much more in the same vein.

ELIZABETH: The rantings of a Spanish courtier do not interest me greatly.

WALSINGHAM: Nonetheless, Catholic tempers are running high throughout Europe. Mendoza represents a very general opinion.

ELIZABETH: In *your* opinion, Sir Francis. His opinion, your opinion. In *my* opinion, Mendoza is suffering from injured pride. Besides, he is scarcely a man of influence. You waste your time in this matter.

WALSINGHAM: By himself, Mendoza is unimportant, I agree; but, taken in proper context . . .

ELIZABETH: Well?

(*Walsingham dismisses Davison with a nod of his head. Davison bows, and withdraws.*)

WALSINGHAM: I feel I should tell you, ma'am, that I have been reflecting upon our recent conversation about Mary of Scotland.

ELIZABETH: Yes, I am sure you have, Walsingham. Your mind revolves around that particular problem.

WALSINGHAM: And with good reason.

ELIZABETH: Indeed?

WALSINGHAM: The situation with regard to your cousin has changed of late.

ELIZABETH: I am not aware of any change.

WALSINGHAM: I refer to Catholic Europe.

(*Elizabeth turns and stares at Walsingham. Brief pause.*)

Ten, twenty years ago, your royal cousin was held in some disrepute. The Bothwell marriage angered Pope Pius, and many believed that Mary had betrayed the Catholic cause. More recently, though, she has been viewed quite differently. Indeed, some have described her as a martyr. Her youthful errors are forgotten—forgiven, at least—and she is now revered as the shining glory of English Catholicism. It has even been suggested that she renounced your throne for the sake of her faith.

ELIZABETH: Is this true?

WALSINGHAM: Most assuredly. Hence my concern over the Mendoza letter; it is just one example of a growing opposition to your Majesty.

ELIZABETH: In Europe.

WALSINGHAM: In Europe, yes. But such men would find allies here with no great difficulty. It requires just one spark. The net must be tightened. Around her, and around the whole Catholic rabble.

8

Interior, room at Chartley. Day.

Mary, Paulet, and an attendant. Mary is gazing at the rain, as it beats against the window. She removes her riding cloak, and gives it to the attendant.

291

MARY: No, the rain is too heavy. I shall not ride today.

(*The attendant goes out.*)

No doubt that pleases you, Sir Amyas.

PAULET: Pleases me?

MARY: To know that I shall be shut away for another twenty hours. At least it spares your men the trouble of riding with me.

PAULET: Perhaps tomorrow the rain will clear.

MARY: Perhaps. Leave me, Sir Amyas. Your company is more cheerless than the storm.

PAULET: Madam.

(*Paulet bows, and goes to the door.*)

I almost forgot, ma'am, there is a gentleman present.

MARY: A gentleman . . . ?

PAULET: Sent here on matters of state. It occurred to me that he might fulfil your desire for some conversation.

MARY: And what of your duties?

PAULET: Madam?

MARY: I thought I was forbidden such quiet luxuries.

PAULET: He is well-trusted. Besides, I have no wish to be your tormentor, lady.

(*Mary goes to the centre of the room. She pauses briefly.*)

MARY: Very well, Sir Amyas. I shall be pleased to receive this 'well-trusted' gentleman.

(*Paulet bows, and goes out. Mary smooths her dress, and pats her hair into place. Paulet returns with Gilbert Gifford, a good-looking young man of about thirty.*)

PAULET: Gilbert Gifford, ma'am.

MARY: Good morning, Gifford.

GIFFORD (*bowing*): Madam.

MARY: Thank you, Paulet; you may go.

(*Paulet bows, and goes out. Mary turns and smiles at Gifford.*)

This is your first visit to Chartley, is it not?

(*As a reply, Gifford goes to Mary, kneels, and kisses her hand.*)

GIFFORD: Majesty . . . !

(*Mary stares incredulously at him.*)

MARY: Gifford . . . you are a Catholic!

GIFFORD: Son of a loyal Catholic family, ma'am. Our seat is in Stafford. I am a gentleman and love the Virgin Mary.

MARY: Then you are in the greatest danger.

(*Gifford rises to his feet.*)

GIFFORD: No, not I. The path has been carefully prepared. I have crept into favour with the mighty Walsingham and through him, Sir Amyas Paulet.

293

MARY: Gifford, you are very welcome!

GIFFORD: And with your gracious consent I will do all I can to help your Majesty.

MARY: In what way?

GIFFORD: In whatever way you command.

MARY: I must have news.

GIFFORD: Of your friends?

MARY: Is that possible?

GIFFORD: There are letters from France—secret letters; I shall devise a plan to bring them here.

MARY: Take care, I am closely watched. By day and by night, with much cunning. What's more, Sir Amyas has acquired a new lieutenant; a man whom I mistrust and dislike above all others. His beard stinks of vomit.

GIFFORD: And his name?

MARY: Phelippes.

GIFFORD: Thomas Phelippes.

MARY: You know him?

GIFFORD: You are right to fear him, ma'am; deceit and false-dealing are his greatest virtues.

MARY: Then what hope is there for my delivery? You face an impossible task, brave Gifford.

GIFFORD: No task is impossible, Majesty. Remember, you have many friends—both abroad and in this country—who desire only your deliverance from this place. We shall not fail!

9

Interior, Walsingham's room. Night.

Walsingham and Phelippes are standing by a table which is covered with documents. Thomas Phelippes is about forty: yellow-haired, shortsighted, and disfigured by pock-marks.

WALSINGHAM: You have done well, Phelippes. I am reassured.

PHELIPPES: The lady grumbles much, but Sir Amyas will not yield.

WALSINGHAM: His heart is hardened against her.

PHELIPPES: More than that, he regards her present discomforts as just reward for her former licence. I suspect that he believes himself to be an agent for the Almighty.

WALSINGHAM (*smiling*): Yes, that would please him well.

PHELIPPES: It is, for him, a sacred trust.

WALSINGHAM: And for us, a constant anxiety.

PHELIPPES: Her Majesty has not consented to further action?

WALSINGHAM: No, alas, she has not. I have warned her in the strongest possible terms; she listens with obvious reluctance, and then insists that the situation be left without change.

PHELIPPES: Cousinly love, perhaps?

WALSINGHAM: Fear, most probably. Fear of revenge by Mary's supporters. If one Queen is killed, then why not another?

PHELIPPES: Well, there is some truth in that, no doubt.

WALSINGHAM: The problem is: wherein lies the greater danger—Mary alive, or Mary dead?

PHELIPPES: That is your problem, Sir Francis: I thank the Lord it is not mine.

(*Walsingham grimaces with pain, and leans against the table for support.*)

The pain has returned, sir?

WALSINGHAM: It seldom leaves me these days; indeed, I am growing used to it.

PHELIPPES: Shall I call the physician?

WALSINGHAM: No, no, no . . . just help me to a chair.

PHELIPPES: You should rest more, sir; seek proper advice.

WALSINGHAM: The spasms are short. I shall be well again soon. (*He sits down.*) Thank you . . . thank you, Thomas.

(*Walsingham is silent for a moment, recovering his composure. He smiles up at Phelippes.*)

So . . . was there anything more?

PHELIPPES: One small item of intelligence has come my way, sir. The priest Ballard has returned to this country.

WALSINGHAM: He is in London?

PHELIPPES: Swathed in a cloak of secrecy. Calling himself Captain Fortescue and dressed as a soldier, I am told.

10

Interior, Babington's room. Night.

A single candle illumines John Ballard, as he sits wait-ing in a corner of the room. He is a man of about forty, heavily-built, and wearing a military cloak. Ballard rises to his feet as Babington enters.

BABINGTON: Captain Fortescue?

BALLARD: Sir Antony Babington . . . I am honoured, sir.

BABINGTON: My man said you wished to see me?

BALLARD: Yes, sir, that is correct.

BABINGTON: It is very late; I am not used to receiving visitors at this hour.

BALLARD: My business cannot be delayed.

BABINGTON: Business? Have we then business together?

BALLARD: Oh yes, sir—and of the greatest moment.

BABINGTON: Forgive me, Captain, but I am not aware . . .

BALLARD (*interrupting*): You may regard *me* as a stranger, Sir Antony . . . but I know you like a friend.

BABINGTON (*echoing his words*): Like a friend . . . ?

BALLARD: A close and trusted friend, sir. I know, for example, that you are Squire of Dethick, twenty-five years old, rich, and acquainted with many brave young gentlemen. You attend Elizabeth's court, and are well-favoured there. Furthermore, sir, I know that you are of the Catholic Faith, and have much love for our graci-ous lady, Mary of Scotland.

297

(*Babington stares at Ballard, but says nothing.*)

Are these not true facts?

BABINGTON: I am not obliged to answer you, Captain.

(*Ballard removes the military cloak.*)

BALLARD: See . . . I am no Captain. My name is John Ballard; I am a priest ordained. This— (*Throwing the cloak onto a chair*) was merely a device to deceive your servants.

(*Babington goes to him.*)

BABINGTON: Then you are welcome, Father . . . most welcome to my house!

BALLARD: Thank you, sir; I thank you.

BABINGTON: Will you take some wine?

BALLARD: Later, perhaps; when we have talked.

BABINGTON: Very well.

(*Babington gestures Ballard to a chair.*)

Tell me, Father, what is this business you have come to discuss?

BALLARD: Briefly, it is for the drawing-up of plans to despatch the English Queen, and to place our gracious Mary upon her lawful throne.

BABINGTON: To despatch the English Queen . . .?

BALLARD: Only by her death can this realm hope for rightful monarchy and true religion.

BABINGTON: And for this you come to me?

BALLARD: It is known that you are gallant and adventurous. Moreover, your friends hold you in the highest regard; already, you are their leader.

BABINGTON: Even so ...

BALLARD: You are afraid?

BABINGTON: I know not what I am! I need to think ...

BALLARD: Then think on this: Recently, I have been in Paris, and there I talked with Bernardino Mendoza, the Spanish ambassador. He knows of our plan, and promises armed troops for our assistance.

BABINGTON: Will he honour his promise?

BALLARD: Without any doubt. A Catholic league of sixty thousand men is being prepared for this very purpose. Elizabeth shall be killed, then Walsingham and his crew. The armies will invade to put down any opposition, and Mary shall be set upon the throne.

(*Babington stares at Ballard: brief pause.*)

BABINGTON: This is a lofty scheme, John Ballard.

BALLARD: You fear it will not work?

BABINGTON: How can I tell?

BALLARD: Believe me, sir, all Europe is waiting for you to act.

BABINGTON: For *me*?

BALLARD: Gather your friends together, discuss the plan with them.

BABINGTON: But what exactly do you expect us to achieve?

299

BALLARD: First, the assassination of Elizabeth; second, the rescue of Queen Mary from Chartley, wherein she is so cruelly enclosed.

BABINGTON: When is this to be?

BALLARD: As soon as you can prepare yourselves. The hour is ripe, Sir Antony, you should act without delay.

BABINGTON: It is a heavy burden you cast upon my shoulders.

BALLARD: A heavy burden, but a rich reward.

BABINGTON: Yes ... yes, that is true.

(*Babington sits. Brief pause.*)

If it were only Queen Mary's escape ... then I would not hesitate.

BALLARD: It is the killing of Elizabeth that gives you pause?

BABINGTON: I wish her dead, as well you must know; but to find a man both willing and trustworthy for the act ...

BALLARD: Have you forgotten John Savage?

BABINGTON: Savage?

BALLARD: A young Catholic soldier who hates the Queen; you met him last year, I believe. He has sworn to be the means of her death, and will subscribe to any plans you may devise.

BABINGTON: Yes, he would do it.

BALLARD: Meet him, Sir Antony, talk, confer.

BABINGTON: And should I not also talk with the Spaniard Mendoza?

BALLARD: For what purpose?

BABINGTON: To ensure that we shall strike together; that his armies are prepared.

BALLARD: If you so wish, but it will require travelling to France.

BABINGTON: That is no problem.

BALLARD: Your passport . . . ?

BABINGTON: Walsingham thinks I am loyal. He has no reason to deny me a passport.

BALLARD: Then you are agreed?

BABINGTON: Give me two days; I must have time to consider.

BALLARD: Two days is two days too long.

(*Babington turns, and crosses to the window.*)

BABINGTON: Has Queen Mary been told?

BALLARD: As yet, she knows nothing. Sir Amyas Paulet keeps her very close; correspondence is impossible.

BABINGTON: Then a way must be found to inform her of this plan.

BALLARD: So . . . you will do it?

BABINGTON: I will.

(*Ballard goes to Babington, and grasps him by the hand.*)

301

BALLARD: God give you strength and courage, my son; God preserve you from our enemies.

BABINGTON: God save Queen Mary.

BALLARD: Amen!

11

Interior, bedchamber. Night.

Elizabeth, Dee, and Kelley.

ELIZABETH: Omens? What omens?

DEE: Signs of death, Majesty; visions of ghostly apparitions.

ELIZABETH: You have seen them yourself?

DEE: Not I, but Sir Edward Kelley, through his great gifts . . .

ELIZABETH: Sir Edward . . .?

KELLEY: A man dressed all in tattered robes . . . his face, hideous to behold . . . ravaged and split open, like the head of a corpse long buried . . . I saw him walk abroad, outstretching his arms and crying with the voice of a mighty beast . . . around his head flew carrion crows, and wolves followed at his heels.

ELIZABETH: What means this vision, Dr Dee?

DEE: I cannot say with any exactness, ma'am; but it foreshadows death.

ELIZABETH: Death . . . you speak to me only of death.

(*Kelley laughs softly.*)

Oh, I have lived long in its dark shadow, yet still I fear it above all else. More and more, as I grow older.

DEE: All mortals are afraid of dying, whether they be Queen or commoner.

ELIZABETH: Cannot you interpret these signs more precisely?

KELLEY: To question the dead requires much time and skill and courage. It is necessary to feed a black cat with human flesh, to slice off its head, and prepare from it an incense with blood and herbs. But such things are forbidden, Majesty, and men who practise the craft run the risk of losing their ears.

ELIZABETH: But I must know *whose* death is pronounced!

DEE: Some great personage, no doubt.

ELIZABETH: A queen, perhaps? Or the cousin of a queen?

KELLEY: It could be either, Majesty.

12

Interior, room at Chartley. Day.

Mary and Gifford.

GIFFORD: The news is good, ma'am; all is arranged.

MARY: Tell me, Gifford.

GIFFORD: As you may know, there is no private brewery in this house. Thus, all supplies of beer are procured from a man in Burton. It is brought here—once every week—in large kegs. This same brewer has been bribed, and will act on my instructions. I will make a leather wallet—small enough to slip into the barrel—and into this wallet, you will place your letters.

MARY: Good . . . this is excellent.

GIFFORD: Once away from the house, the wallet can be removed, and the letters sent to the French Embassy in London, and from thence—to Paris. Likewise, you will be able to receive correspondence from your friends abroad.

MARY: When, Gifford? When can this traffic begin?

GIFFORD: The brewer comes tomorrow; have letters ready, and I will ensure that they are despatched.

MARY: Gifford, you have served me well in this.

GIFFORD: There is still much danger, madam. Remember, 'God may send a man good meat, but the Devil sendeth an evil cook'.

(*Paulet enters.*)

PAULET: Forgive me, madam; I thought you were alone.

GIFFORD: I was on the point of taking my leave.

MARY: Farewell, then, Gifford. I have enjoyed our conversation.

GIFFORD: It is my honour, ma'am. I shall see you tomorrow, I hope.

MARY: Yes, tomorrow.

(*Gifford goes to the door, saluting Paulet with a nod of his head.*)

GIFFORD: Sir Amyas . . .

PAULET: Good-bye, Mr Gifford.

(*Gifford goes out.*)

You seem much cheered by his company, madam.

MARY: Does that surprise you?

PAULET: Yes, I confess I am somewhat surprised that you have matters of mutual interest that deserve such earnest discussion.

MARY: There has been no 'earnest discussion', Sir Amyas; we conversed generally.

PAULET: Indeed . . .

MARY: Though I could scarcely expect you to appreciate such simple human pleasures.

PAULET: You think not?

MARY: Since you are so devoid of simple humanity.

(*Paulet smiles.*)

MARY: See . . . even at that, you smile. As if proud of your chill humour.

PAULET: I am not ashamed of it, madam.

MARY: Then I am truly sorry for you. A warm spirit and greatness of heart are qualities I prize above all others; they spring from a joy in living, which, even in the confines of prison, can lift a man from despair into hope.

PAULET: 'Can lift a man', you say; why not a woman?

MARY: Aye, and woman too, Sir Amyas.

(*Paulet smiles again.*)

13

Interior, Babington's room. Day.

Babington, Ballard, and John Savage. Savage is a professional soldier in his late twenties.

BALLARD: And their names . . .?

BABINGTON: Edward Abington, Robert Barnwell, Chidiock Tichbourne, Edward Charnock, Sir Thomas Gerrard, Thomas Salisbury—of these I am sure.

BALLARD: You have conferred together?

BABINGTON: We have, and we are agreed.

BALLARD: And you, John Savage, you are prepared to play your part in this venture?

SAVAGE: I have sworn an oath that I shall be the means of her death; I have sworn, and I will act.

BALLARD: Good! (*Smiling at Babington.*) I knew we had chosen well.

BABINGTON: Two things must be done, though, before we can proceed.

BALLARD: They are?

BABINGTON: A meeting with Mendoza, and correspondence with Queen Mary.

BALLARD: The first I leave to you, Sir Antony; the second is already under way.

BABINGTON: How so?

BALLARD: A good, faithful Catholic— (*To Savage.*) — and a man known to you, I believe: Gilbert Gifford . . .

SAVAGE: Gifford, aye! I knew him at Rheims, when we were together at the college.

BALLARD: Gifford has devised a plan whereby letters may be safely exchanged with Chartley.

BABINGTON: The plan has been tried?

BALLARD: Not yet, but Gifford says it will work.

BABINGTON: And if it does?

BALLARD: There will be no further obstacles. We shall move with all haste.

14

Interior, room at Chartley. Day.

Music. Mary is about to go riding; Servants and attendants bustle about her. Gifford enters.

MARY (*to attendant*): My gloves. (*As she leaves, she passes a letter to Gifford.*)

15

Interior, Walsingham's room. Day.

Walsingham and Phelippes.

WALSINGHAM: So . . . Priest Ballard has been visiting Sir Antony Babington. The young gentleman should choose his friends with greater care.

PHELIPPES: What's more, sir, Ballard was not alone: John Savage kept him company.

WALSINGHAM: Savage? Not the soldier who swears brave oaths?

PHELIPPES: Aye, and shuns brave action.

WALSINGHAM: The coward from Rheims.

PHELIPPES: The very same, sir.

WALSINGHAM: Well, Sir Antony must have an inclination for rogues.

PHELIPPES: They flatter him, no doubt. His head is easily turned.

WALSINGHAM: Were these meetings prolonged?

PHELIPPES: An hour, two hours, then they would disperse.

WALSINGHAM: Time enough, Thomas. They must be carefully watched.

PHELIPPES: There is no difficulty in that. Like all fools, they believe they are safe from discovery.

(*There is a knock on the door.*)

WALSINGHAM: Enter!

(*Gifford enters. Walsingham hurries to him.*)

Gifford! ... what news?

GIFFORD: It works, Sir Francis; Mary of Scotland has written to France.

WALSINGHAM: Let me see, let me see ... (*He takes the letter from Gifford and gently opens it.*) Yes ... as you said, Thomas, it is written in code.

PHELIPPES: If I may, sir ... (*He takes the letter, and examines it.*) Thank you.

WALSINGHAM: Well?

9. Mary, Queen of Scots (Vivian Pickles), with Gilbert Gifford (Bernard Holley), Walsingham's spy (*Horrible Conspiracies*).

10. John Ballard (David Garfield) and Sir Antony Babington (David Collings) writing to Mary of their plans for her rescue (*Horrible Conspiracies*).

11. The execution of Mary, Queen of Scots, with Sir Amyas Paulet (Hamilton Dyce) looking on (right foreground) (*Horrible Conspiracies*).

PHELIPPES: A simple matter, sir: substitution. A few hours, and we shall know all.

WALSINGHAM: Good!

(*Phelippes takes the letter across to the table; Walsingham turns to Gifford.*)

So, she believed you Gifford?

GIFFORD: And praises God for my ingenuity.

WALSINGHAM: There were no problems?

GIFFORD: None, sir.

WALSINGHAM: The brewer played his part?

GIFFORD: And with enthusiasm; he is being paid twice, after all: once by Queen Mary, and once by you.

WALSINGHAM: When the letter has been decoded, you must take it straight to the Embassy of France.

GIFFORD: With all speed, sir.

WALSINGHAM: Make it known that you act as courier, and that all communications for the Scottish Queen are to be delivered into your hands.

GIFFORD: And then brought here?

WALSINGHAM: Brought here while Master Phelippes translates the code, and then carried back to Chartley.

GIFFORD: You can rely on me, Sir Francis, to do all that you require.

WALSINGHAM: Indeed I can, as you value your life.

GIFFORD: My life, sir . . .?

WALSINGHAM: Remember under what circumstances

you were brought to me: a Catholic house-rat, squeaking for mercy. I could have ordered your hanging twelve months ago.

GIFFORD: Yes, sir, I am truly grateful.

(*Walsingham gazes at Gifford for a moment.*)

WALSINGHAM: I can find it in my heart to pity Mary of Scots for placing her trust in a man like you.

GIFFORD: Yes, sir. (*He bows, and edges towards the door.*)

WALSINGHAM: One thing more, Gifford: No man is to know that the letters pass this way. If this is discovered, then you shall carry the blame.

GIFFORD: No one shall know, sir; not one soul.

WALSINGHAM: Very well, that is all.

GIFFORD: Thank you, sir.

(*Gifford goes out. Walsingham crosses to a table, and pours some wine.*)

WALSINGHAM: Now we shall learn all, Thomas. Her very mind is opened to us.

16

Interior, dungeon. Day.

Topcliffe picks up some chains from the dungeon floor, and stows them in a corner. He rinses his hands in a bowl of water, and glances towards the door. Walsingham is standing in the shadows.

WALSINGHAM: Good day, Master Topcliffe.

TOPCLIFFE: Why, Sir Francis! I am honoured.

(Walsingham enters the dungeon; he smiles at Topcliffe.)

WALSINGHAM: Are you still tearing limbs from Jesuits?

TOPCLIFFE: Whenever I have the good fortune, sir.

WALSINGHAM: No doubt they cry aloud, Rack Master?

TOPCLIFFE: Oh yes, sir, most piteously.

WALSINGHAM: Do any of them cry of conspiracy?

TOPCLIFFE: Sir . . . ?

WALSINGHAM: Have you any word, a whisper, of men plotting her Majesty's overthrow?

TOPCLIFFE: No, sir; not even the most secret whisper.

(Brief pause; Topcliffe approaches Walsingham.)

Is there, then, some new suspicion?

WALSINGHAM: I have good cause to think so. The principals are already in my sight; I look to you to entrap the lesser people.

TOPCLIFFE: I will do all that I can, sir.

WALSINGHAM: Indeed, I am sure you will.

TOPCLIFFE: But it would be helpful, sir, if the flow of priests from Europe to this country could be stemmed a little. At present, they cross the channel with comfortable ease, and I fear many of them go unrecognized.

WALSINGHAM: Sterner restrictions would require the consent of the Queen.

TOPCLIFFE: Such consent she would surely not withhold. You have her ear, Sir Francis. She loves you well.

WALSINGHAM: May be so.

17

Interior, bedchamber. Day.

Elizabeth is lying on a crumpled bed. Nervous attend-ants stand by the door. Walsingham is standing at the bedside. Pull back from initial close shot of Elizabeth.

ELIZABETH: No, Walsingham, no! I do not favour these extreme measures.

WALSINGHAM: They are traitors, madam, and the men who shield them are traitors also.

ELIZABETH: We cannot enforce too rigid a law. Only by moderation will this realm be united.

WALSINGHAM: The risk is great ...

ELIZABETH: Are you so afraid of a few fugitive priests?

WALSINGHAM: I am sore afraid of the power of Rome. Our country must be cleansed of this Catholic infec-tion; I would give my life to achieve it.

ELIZABETH: Yes, yes, Sir Francis, I do not doubt your zeal.

(Elizabeth groans, and sways forward. Walsingham steps towards her.)

WALSINGHAM: May I ... ?

ELIZABETH: No, stand off! You cannot aid me.

(Elizabeth regains her composure as the pain passes; she leans back on her pillows.)

God's death! First teeth, now stomach. My belly croaks like yours, old moor.

(Walsingham manages a wan smile; Elizabeth glances up at him.)

I have no love for Rome, as well you may know. Nonetheless, we must exercise great care and circumspection. Religious observance is a personal matter, and spiritual needs vary from person to person. I have no wish to open windows in men's souls. Besides, I am well protected; by you, and by Richard Topcliffe.

(*Elizabeth smiles at Walsingham.*)

18

Interior, dungeon. Night.

Moonlight illumines the instruments of torture.

19

Interior, room at Chartley. Day.

Long shot: Mary is standing by the window, a ray of sun shines upon her face. She looks young and beautiful and vulnerable.

20

Interior, Walsingham's room. Day.

Walsingham and Phelippes are examining letters.

WALSINGHAM: All these are from France?

PHELIPPES: Remember, sir, that Mary has been forbidden letters for many months. Much of it is now outdated.

WALSINGHAM: But they have all been kept by the French Ambassador?

PHELIPPES: Yes, de L'Aubespine has been a faithful

friend. These two are from the Spaniard, Mendoza, promising arms and assistance. They alone are evidence enough.

WALSINGHAM: We shall have more, Thomas. If we wait, we shall have much more. And these? They are from Thomas Morgan?

PHELIPPES: Mostly, sir. As Mary's agent in Paris, he gives her any items of intelligence that might be of interest. In these, there is little or nothing that we do not know already. Apart, perhaps, from . . . this letter: Morgan speaks highly of Sir Anthony Babington. He recommends the young gentleman to Queen Mary, saying he would doubtless prove a good and tireless servant.

WALSINGHAM: Well, let us send it on, Thomas. Who knows, it may lead to some greater design.

PHELIPPES: You wish me to give everything to Gifford?

WALSINGHAM: Yes, and with firm instructions to carry the letters forthwith to Chartley. We must not keep the lady waiting.

(*Davison enters.*)

WALSINGHAM: I am not to be disturbed, Davison.

DAVISON: A gentleman is asking to see you, Sir Francis.

WALSINGHAM: Then send him away.

DAVISON: It is Sir Antony Babington.

WALSINGHAM (*turning to Davison*): He is *here* . . .?

DAVISON: And wishes to apply for a passport.

WALSINGHAM: Indeed?

PHELIPPES: Shall I go in there, sir?

314

WALSINGHAM: Yes, and leave the door partly open. I want you to hear.

(*Phelippes picks up the letters, and goes into an adjoining room.*)

Very well, Davison.

(*Davison goes to the door.*)

DAVISON (*speaking off*): This way, if you please.

(*Babington enters.*)

BABINGTON: This is most kind of you, Sir Francis.

WALSINGHAM: No, no, my pleasure.

(*Walsingham gestures Babington to a chair.*)

I am sorry you were kept waiting.

BABINGTON: Only for a few minutes.

WALSINGHAM: My secretary tells me that you are planning a journey?

BABINGTON: Yes, sir.

WALSINGHAM: And for this, you now require a licence?

BABINGTON: That is correct, yes.

WALSINGHAM: Where will you travel, Sir Antony?

BABINGTON: To France.

WALSINGHAM: To Paris?

BABINGTON: Yes, sir.

WALSINGHAM: Yes, I see. For what purpose, may I know?

315

BABINGTON: To visit friends, nothing more.

WALSINGHAM: You have many friends in Paris?

BABINGTON: Not many.

WALSINGHAM: But some ...

BABINGTON: Yes, some. You will remember, Sir Francis, I am of the Catholic Faith.

WALSINGHAM: Ah yes, of course.

BABINGTON: I enjoy visiting my Catholic friends from time to time.

WALSINGHAM: Yes, I understand that. (*Brief pause.*) The journey is urgent?

BABINGTON: Not urgent, no.

WALSINGHAM: Good. You see, there might be some delay in this.

BABINGTON: Delay?

WALSINGHAM: With the licence. Regrettable, alas, but unavoidable.

BABINGTON: Not too great a delay, I hope.

WALSINGHAM: That depends.

BABINGTON: On what?

WALSINGHAM: Administrative details. Again, unavoidable.

(*Babington rises to his feet.*)

BABINGTON: Sir Francis ... I may be able to help you in France.

WALSINGHAM: Help me?

BABINGTON: I have friends.

WALSINGHAM: So you said.

BABINGTON: And they have friends. One hears many things.

WALSINGHAM: Do I understand you, Sir Antony; are you offering your services to spy for me?

BABINGTON: If I could be of assistance, I will gladly do all I can.

WALSINGHAM: To be frank, I had not expected this.

BABINGTON: I would not disappoint you.

WALSINGHAM: No, no, that is not my fear.

BABINGTON: We are agreed, then?

WALSINGHAM: I must consider . . . consider what you can most profitably achieve.

BABINGTON: And my passport?

WALSINGHAM: You will be informed.

BABINGTON: I am grateful, Sir Francis.

WALSINGHAM: No, it is I who owe you gratitude . . . it has been a—most interesting—conversation.

BABINGTON: Thank you, sir.

WALSINGHAM (*dismissing Sir Anthony*): We shall meet again, and discuss this thing further.

(*Babington goes out, and Walsingham closes the door. Phelippes enters from the adjoining room.*)

PHELIPPES: What scheme is this, do you suppose?

WALSINGHAM: Self-protection, most probably. He seeks to worm himself into my favour.

PHELIPPES: Will you employ him in France?

WALSINGHAM: Sir Antony is not going to France, Thomas, I shall see to that.

21

Interior, room at Chartley. Night.

Mary is seated. Gifford enters.

GIFFORD: Madam . . .

MARY: Close the door, Gifford. (*He does so.*) Much news from France. My friends are eager to assist me out of this place.

GIFFORD: There are plans?

MARY: Not yet, but I am urged to trust a gentleman called Babington.

GIFFORD: Yes, yes, I know him.

MARY: And like him?

GIFFORD: Sir Antony is a good man, and your devoted servant.

MARY: Is he indeed?

GIFFORD: He was, I believe, page to Shrewsbury when you were committed into the Earl's care. He often speaks of his profoundest admiration for you.

MARY: Yes . . . yes, I partly remember him.

GIFFORD: What's more, he is accepted at Court, and has a wide circle of brave Catholic friends.

MARY: You think I should write to him?

GIFFORD: With all haste, madam. I have no doubt that he will serve you well.

22

Interior, Phelippes' room. Night.

By the light of a flickering candle, Phelippes carefully unseals Mary's letter. He begins to decode it.

23

Interior, Babington's room. Day.

Babington and Ballard.

BABINGTON: She is, I think, the noblest woman I have ever seen. Beauty of spirit and dignity of form so wonderfully fused! I tell you, Father, ever since the day I first saw her, I have dreamed of serving her; and now, it is within our grasp to make her Queen of England!

BALLARD: There is still much to be done.

BABINGTON: Details are easily accomplished, especially with God on our side. Remember, by placing her upon the throne, we restore proper faith to this country of ours. It is a great cause, Father ... a crusade!

BALLARD: It is also an enterprise that carries much danger in its wake. 'Let a wise man look e'er he leap!' We must be ever cautious.

BABINGTON: Aye, and so it shall be; though with Gifford as our firm ally, there can be little to fear.

(*He offers wine to Ballard*.)

BALLARD: Thank you, no.

BABINGTON (*pouring wine for himself*): So . . . this letter. We must tell her all, every particular. First, that an invading force is being prepared abroad; second, that there are many Englishmen who will join that company, and fight on her behalf; third, that she will be delivered from Chartley—this, by myself, and a band of friends. Fourth, Elizabeth's death. The despatch of the usurping competitor. (*He glances across at Ballard*.) That is all, is it not?

BALLARD: All, yes . . . everything.

BABINGTON: Good! Now . . . pen and paper. At last, the business begins!

24

Interior, Walsingham's room. Day.

Walsingham and Phelippes. Phelippes is reading Babington's letter.

PHELIPPES: . . . he then goes on to assure the Scottish Queen that Elizabeth will be put to death by 'six noble gentlemen'—his own trusted friends—while he himself promises to take her from Chartley—'with a band of an hundred faithful followers'. Finally, he asks that suitable rewards should be forthcoming when the mission is complete.

(*Phelippes folds the letter, and turns to Walsingham*.)

We could not ask for more than that.

WALSINGHAM: Indeed not. It is very full and comprehensive. More than I had expected, I do confess.

PHELIPPES: Shall I close the seals?

WALSINGHAM: You have copies?

PHELIPPES: Oh, yes.

WALSINGHAM: Then despatch it this day to Chartley.

PHELIPPES: It shall go within the hour, sir.

(*Close shot of Phelippes, as he smiles across at Walsingham.*)

We await her very heart in the next.

25

Interior, room at Chartley. Day.

Camera tracks slowly towards Mary, as she sits by the window reading Babington's letter. Silence, save for a summer birdsong.

26

Interior, privy chamber. Night.

Music: courtiers are dancing. There is much laughter as Richard Tarlton, the Queen's favourite clown, begins to dance in the centre of the room. Camera tracks slowly towards the door of the privy chamber.

27

Interior, privy chamber. Night.

Elizabeth and Walsingham.

ELIZABETH: It is, of course, possible that my cousin will reject his scheme.

WALSINGHAM: Possible, yes; but most unlikely.

ELIZABETH: Then she is a fool! Worse, she degrades the high office to which she was born.

(*Pause.*)

(*Turning to Walsingham.*) These men—these friends of Babington's—are they dangerous?

WALSINGHAM: Scarcely more than boys, madam; callow youths spurred on by misplaced dreams of glory. Why I am told that they have commissioned a portrait to be painted, so that their likenesses may be admired by posterity. They invite discovery with every move.

ELIZABETH: Should they not be arrested?

WALSINGHAM: I counsel delay, ma'am. It is of the utmost importance that we see how the Scottish Queen replies. We must be sure of her deep complicity.

ELIZABETH: A delay would mean danger.

WALSINGHAM: Yes.

ELIZABETH: To me. You are putting my life at risk, Sir Francis. (*She smiles.*) You are quite right, old moor. I will abide by your decision.

WALSINGHAM: Have no fear, madam. You are surrounded by your loyal and loving subjects.

28

Interior, presence chamber. Night.

Babington enters and walks past the assembled courtiers.

29

Interior, privy chamber. Night.

Elizabeth and Walsingham.

ELIZABETH: Alas, my life has been o'er-shadowed by conspiracy. The axe, the dagger, the block . . . they are as common to me as spring flowers to a countryman. Fears and doubts encircle my head, like black crows around a copse. Yet, every time a new treachery is revealed, I am strangely surprised. Foolishly, I expect good in a world where men pursue evil.

WALSINGHAM: All will be resolved, ma'am. Your enemies never prosper.

ELIZABETH: Not yet, but one day . . . (*She glances across at Walsingham.*) Who knows what end awaits me?

WALSINGHAM: Be comforted, madam.

ELIZABETH: No, let me live out this humour. Leave me to my melancholy.

WALSINGHAM: Shall I return to bid you good night?

ELIZABETH: As you please, Sir Francis.

(*Walsingham bows, and goes out.*)

30

Interior, presence chamber. Night.

Walsingham emerges from the privy chamber, and stands watching the dancers. Babington approaches him.

BABINGTON: Good evening, Sir Francis, how fares the Queen?

WALSINGHAM: Much over-burdened with matters of
of state.

BABINGTON (*confidentially*): I trust you have not forgotten our talk of France?

WALSINGHAM: By no means, Sir Antony. You are forever in my thoughts.

31

Interior, bedchamber. Night.

Elizabeth enters, and dismisses her attendants.

ELIZABETH: Leave me!

(*The attendants withdraw. Elizabeth stands in the
centre of the room.*)

May they all perish in great agony! May their bodies
be torn apart, and their souls be damned to everlasting
torment!

32

Interior, presence chamber. Night.

*The courtiers have dispersed and the great room is
almost empty. Only Richard Tarlton remains, sitting
in one corner, idly tapping a tabor.*

33

Interior, Babington's room. Night.

Ballard is waiting. Babington enters.

BALLARD: Good Sir Antony, you have my message?

BABINGTON: Aye.

BALLARD: I am discovered.

BABINGTON: *Discovered . . . ?*

BALLARD: As I guess.

BABINGTON: But how?

BALLARD: One of my servants—a man I trusted—he is in Walsingham's pay.

BABINGTON: Is this certain?

BALLARD: Almost without doubt.

BABINGTON: Then we are finished!

BALLARD: Not so . . .

BABINGTON: We are finished, Ballard!

BALLARD: I have been discreet; your name has not been spoken.

BABINGTON: There is still great risk.

BALLARD: Not if you act now! Despatch Queen Bess, and we shall all be saved.

BABINGTON: What of you?

BALLARD: I can hide in safety for a day or two. Kill the Queen, and kill her now!

34

Interior, privy chamber. Day.

Courtiers are assembled: among them, Dee and Kelley. The bedchamber doors open, and the courtiers bow as Elizabeth enters. She goes to Dee and Kelley.

ELIZABETH: Well, Sir Edward—do wicked spirits still surround us?

KELLEY: The clouds thicken, Majesty; the storm approaches.

ELIZABETH: And death . . . ?

KELLEY: The Great Spectre sharpens his sword. Be always ready to die.

35

Interior, Babington's room. Day.

Babington and Savage.

SAVAGE: So Ballard is fled?

BABINGTON: Aye, for his life.

SAVAGE: This is bad indeed. What remedy now?

BABINGTON: None, but to kill her presently. Go you to the Court tomorrow and execute the fact.

SAVAGE: Nay, not tomorrow, Sir Antony.

BABINGTON: Why not?

SAVAGE: My apparel is unready.

BABINGTON: Your *apparel* . . . !

SAVAGE: I cannot go to Court in this.

(*Babington takes some coins, and hurls them onto the table*.)

BABINGTON: Then get clothes this day, and do as you are bid!

326

SAVAGE: But Sir Ant—

BABINGTON (*cutting in*): If the Queen be not killed, we are all of us dead men!

36

Interior, Phelippes' room. Day.

WALSINGHAM: What news, Thomas?

PHELIPPES: None, I fear. The Scottish Queen maintains her silence.

WALSINGHAM: How much longer will she wait?

PHELIPPES: Have patience, sir; she must reply soon.

WALSINGHAM: Reply yes, but what? That is the centre of my concern. What if she deals lightly with young Babington, and dismisses the plan?

PHELIPPES: We still have enough to condemn her.

WALSINGHAM: My good Phelippes, it needs a direct acceptance before Elizabeth will act. She will seize any excuse to postpone the matter.

PHELIPPES: Perhaps you are mistaken.

WALSINGHAM: No, not I. The Queen fears that Europe will descend on us if Mary is brought to justice. Above all else, she wishes to preserve her Catholic cousin.

PHELIPPES: Then there is nothing we can do.

WALSINGHAM: Save wait.

PHELIPPES: Therefore, have patience, Sir Francis.

WALSINGHAM: Yes, I will try. (*He sighs, and picks up*

ELIZABETH R

the documents from the table.) Here . . . take these to
Davison, if you will. They have all been approved.

PHELIPPES: Yes, sir. (*He takes the documents and his
cloak, and crosses to the door.*) Oh, I meant to tell you,
sir—Babington is waiting next door.

WALSINGHAM: Yes, and has been for these two days,
from time to time.

PHELIPPES: Will you not see him?

WALSINGHAM: An anxious man is more likely to act
in foolish haste. Let the fears grow in his mind.

(*Phelippes smiles, and goes out.*)

37

Interior, Walsingham's ante-chamber. Day.

*Babington rises as Phelippes enters. Davison is sitting
at a desk.*

BABINGTON: What says Sir Francis, will he see me now?

PHELIPPES: Perhaps later. He is too busy at present.

BABINGTON: It is urgent that we talk; most urgent!

DAVISON: Calm yourself, Sir Antony.

BABINGTON: Cannot you tell him?

DAVISON: Tell him what?

BABINGTON: That I am here!

PHELIPPES: He knows that already.

BABINGTON: Then why does he refuse me?

DAVISON: Is it matters of state that you wish to discuss?

BABINGTON: Davison—it is a plot against our Sovereign Lady!

DAVISON: Indeed?

BABINGTON: I have names, full knowledge of all the conspirators.

PHELIPPES: Most likely just a rumour.

BABINGTON: It is more, much more! They scheme her death!

PHELIPPES: Is that so?

BABINGTON: These men—they must be captured!

DAVISON: Do you hope for reward, Sir Antony?

BABINGTON: I hope for nothing!

PHELIPPES: Then you are wise.

DAVISON: Very well, give me their names.

BABINGTON: One is Ballard; John Ballard. A priest.

PHELIPPES: Your urgent news is news no longer. John Ballard is taken and already lodges in the Tower.

38

Interior, Chartley: a corridor. Day.

Gifford and Paulet.

GIFFORD: You look tired, Sir Amyas.

PAULET: Weary of this delay, that is all. She sits and

thinks, and stands and ponders, and then she sits again. There is no end to it.

GIFFORD: If it is tiresome for you, then consider Sir Francis; he must be truly on the rack.

PAULET: Aye he must indeed. Babington is flown, did you know?

GIFFORD: I did not.

PAULET: Learning of Ballard's arrest, he fled the city, taking with him a trembling band of fellow traitors. Even now they are in hiding.

GIFFORD: Soon it will be over.

PAULET: Yes, I think so too. The hunt is closing; the kill cannot be far away.

(*Gifford nods to a nearby door.*)

GIFFORD: Perhaps the fox needs company?

PAULET: I offered conversation but was curtly dismissed.

GIFFORD: Ah yes, but you are a foe, Sir Amyas; you forget that I am a friend.

PAULET: God preserve me from friends like you. I would sooner entertain a legion of enemies.

(*Gifford smiles, and goes towards the door. He knocks, and enters the room.*)

39

Interior, room at Chartley. Day.

Mary is sitting by the window: Gifford goes to her.

GIFFORD: Good day, madam. Are you well?

MARY: Well enough, Gifford.

GIFFORD: The weather is fine; the flowers bloom in glory. It is a rare summer.

MARY: I would it were dark winter, and I was free.

GIFFORD: Aye, yes, that must be so. But be cheerful, madam; you are not without loving servants.

MARY: No, and it brings me great comfort.

(*Mary turns, and looks up at Gifford.*)

I have been reviewing my life, Gifford; considering the steps that have brought me to this place. Wondering what else I should have done to prevent it.

GIFFORD: That is a melancholy past-time, madam; I do not recommend it.

MARY: No, you mistake me. I regret nothing. I know my faults and my virtues: I know that I am a creature of impulse, seldom thinking before I act, driven on by passions, delighting in the unexpected, bored by sensible caution, and disliking all who are not of my humour. This is my alchemy, and I rejoice in it; even though it has brought me much unhappiness, even though it has led me here, I would not have been created differently. This is not self-love, Gifford, merely the acceptance of what I am and what I shall ever be. God made me thus, and I am glad he did so. (*She smiles.*) Consider, if you will, the consequences of being born a thing like Sir Amyas. Are you surprised that I give thanks?

GIFFORD (*also smiling*): Yes, and so do we all.

MARY: You do not condemn me, then?

GIFFORD: For what?

MARY: All those failings that others rebuke so loudly.

GIFFORD: Madam, I am too aware of my own vices to censure others.

MARY: Gentle Gifford . . . I am always glad of your company.

GIFFORD: It is my honour to serve you, Majesty.

(*Pause. Mary turns, and gazes out of the window.*)

MARY: When I awoke this morning, I was curiously happy. It was as though I had forgotten . . . where I am, and what I am. I sang like a bumblebee in the fresh sunlight. Those few minutes were like a living memory. A glimpse of life as it used to be.

GIFFORD: And shall be again.

MARY: Aye, God willing. (*Brief pause. She gives a letter to Gifford, whispering.*) Gifford, take this. Send it straight to my friends in London.

GIFFORD: Madam, I will.

MARY: Keep it safe, I beg you, for it contains my life and freedom.

GIFFORD: Madam.

40

Interior, Phelippes' room. Night.

Phelippes has just finished deciphering Mary's letter. He folds the letter and the 'translation' together, and seals them. He takes a pen and addresses the letter to Sir Francis Walsingham. He draws a gallows on the letter.

41

Interior, bedchamber. Night.

Elizabeth and Walsingham.

WALSINGHAM (*reading the letter*): 'Trusty and well beloved', that is how she begins. She then questions Babington as to the manner of her rescue, making emphatic note that it will be necessary to employ 'a good army, or some very good strength' to free her from Chartley. She further demands that she be immediately informed of the progress of the conspiracy, for fear that Paulet might learn of the plan, and transport her elsewhere, or otherwise reinforce the house with soldiers and fortifications. She further writes, 'Orders must be given that when the design has been carried out, I can be got out of here'. The design in question being your Majesty's death. Following more detailed instructions concerning her rescue and flight, your cousin concludes: 'Consider and consult together if, as it is possible, you cannot execute this particular purpose'—her escape from Chartley, that is—'it will then be expedient to proceed with the rest of the enterprise. If the difficulty be only with myself, if you cannot manage my rescue because I am in the Tower or some other place too strong for you, do not hesitate on that account. Go on for the honour of God.' (*He folds the letter, and places it upon a table.*) There she ends it, madam.

(*Elizabeth does not move. Silence. Elizabeth goes to the table, picks up the letter, looks at it, and then replaces it. She turns to Walsingham.*)

ELIZABETH: Murderess! Vile, plotting, murderess! She seeks my death! I who have been the saviour of her life many a year, to the intolerable peril of my own! *May God forgive her!*

(*Silence.*)

WALSINGHAM: It is as I said, Majesty. As I foretold.

(*Elizabeth gazes at Walsingham. Brief pause.*)

ELIZABETH: Yes . . . you get great joy from this, Walsingham, do you not?

WALSINGHAM: No joy, madam, from such wickedness.

ELIZABETH: Oh yes, I know you well . . .

(*Elizabeth approaches Walsingham.*)

God's death, you sicken me, Walsingham! A piss bowl of self-righteousness! Thin-blooded, like a maid. Why am I served by men such as you?

WALSINGHAM: I meant no offence, Majesty.

ELIZABETH: Yes, yes, yes, humble yourself, bow low. I am surprised this news did not disturb your feeble stomach. No doubt the flux will strike later, gushing forth in triumph. Walsingham's fountain of glory.

(*Walsingham does not move. Elizabeth walks away from him, and sits down. Pause.*)

Some move must now be made against my treacherous cousin. What do you advise?

WALSINGHAM: I shall consult with Paulet, Majesty. The lady should be removed from Chartley for a spell while her personal papers are examined; this to be done with all secrecy, for fear that necessary proofs be destroyed. She should then be charged with conspiring your Majesty's death, and brought to justice on that account.

ELIZABETH: I will leave this matter in your hands for the moment.

(*Elizabeth rises to her feet, and walks to the bed-*

chamber door. She pauses, looking back at Walsingham.)

What of the man Babington: is he still at liberty?

WALSINGHAM: No, no, he is taken, ma'am. He was found at Saint John's Wood, hiding in a forester's hut.

ELIZABETH: Let him be well punished for his sins.

WALSINGHAM: The punishment prescribed by law is terrible indeed, if the executioner takes care to extract the extremity of pain.

ELIZABETH: He is no ordinary traitor. Tell Richard Topcliffe to create some new device.

42

Interior, dungeon. Day.

Babington is chained to the wall. Topcliffe enters.

TOPCLIFFE: You know me, do you not, Sir Antony? You know my business here.

BABINGTON: I am to die this morning.

TOPCLIFFE: Indeed you are, brave Sir Antony. (*He approaches Babington.*) Death is no mystery, be assured of that. Indeed, it is quicker to end life than to engender it. Reflect: it takes longer for a man to thrust his seed into a woman's belly than to plunge a dagger through his enemy's heart.

BABINGTON: It will be quick then?

TOPCLIFFE: Death is always quick; it is the path to dying that can be tedious slow.

BABINGTON: Tell me, I pray you, what has been arranged?

335

TOPCLIFFE: Through the City to Holborn and thence to the fields of Saint Giles; that will be your last road. Yoked with John Savage, you will be led in solemn procession. Many will have gathered anxious to hear the last words of a—(*Venomously*.)—traitor!

BABINGTON: I am no traitor, I swear it! It was not my doing. I was led on by others—I am not guilty, Topcliffe!

(*Topcliffe smiles.*)

TOPCLIFFE: Peace, Sir Antony . . . peace! Save your cries for the gallows; you will need breath enough later.

(*Topcliffe draws near to Babington.*)

Recall my words concerning conception and death. There are men, I am told, such skilled lovers, who can prolong the divine moment for a full half-hour. So in death. Either the soul can be shot from the body with abrupt suddenness, or it can be—enticed—forth. In such matters, I have the delicacy of a practised seducer. (*He draws his sword.*) As in conception, so in death . . . the business begins here. (*Topcliffe's sword touches Babington's groin.*) . . . with the privities. Castrated, ripped up . . . bowelled alive, brave Sir Antony . . . quartered, yet still living. So many wonders await you in Saint Giles' field.

BABINGTON: Almighty God, have you no mercy?

TOPCLIFFE: None, I fear, for the Queen's enemies.

(*Babington slumps forward in his chains.*)

BABINGTON: *Parce mihi, Domine Jesu . . . Parce mihi!*

(*Jubilant church bells drown Babington's agonized cries.*)

43

Exterior. Limbo. Day.

Sir Edward Kelley turns to camera, and smiles. Big close shot. The church bells continue, very loud.

44

Exterior. Limbo. Day.

Close shot: a crucifix lying in a pool of blood. The church bells continue very loud.

45

Interior, room at Chartley. Day.

Paulet and Phelippes. Phelippes is standing by the door.

PHELIPPES: She is coming, and in her best draperies.

(*Mary enters.*)

MARY: Why, you are not ready, Sir Amyas.

PAULET: Go you on, madam; I have business with Master Phelippes.

MARY: Will you not ride?

PAULET: Later, perhaps, when our talk is over.

MARY: Do not waste the August sun; it is a fine morning.

PHELIPPES: You will be hunting the buck, ma'am, so I am told.

MARY: Hunting—and killing—in Walter Aston's Park.

337

ELIZABETH R

PHELIPPES: God send you good sport.

MARY: Thank you, Phelippes.

PAULET: In truth, ma'am, I have never seen you more richly apparelled.

MARY: I must not disappoint the local gentry. Some lords are riding with us, are they not?

PAULET: Oh yes, ma'am, you will not be alone.

MARY: Take care, Sir Amyas.

PAULET: Madam?

MARY: You are growing too civil. First, you suggest I go hunting, then you admire my dress. What has happened to the stern gaoler of Chartley?

PAULET: Perhaps he has gone into summer retirement.

MARY (*with a smile*): Then I hope never to see him again.

(*Mary goes out. Phelippes moves to the door.*)

PAULET: Wait! Wait till she has ridden off.

(*Phelippes pauses by the door.*)

PHELIPPES: Now?

PAULET: Now, yes.

(*Phelippes opens the door.*)

PHELIPPES (*calling*): Bring down the Queen's casket.

(*He turns to Paulet.*)

It is well-planned, Sir Amyas, I give you credit.

338

PAULET: Yes, the scheme is not without pleasing ingenuities. Nor indeed without some irony.

PHELIPPES: How so?

PAULET: She will be seized near Tixall, that is the plan. Sir Thomas Gorges and his men will ride towards her across the moor. Thus, the irony: Will she not hesitate as she sees the horsemen approach? Might she not think it is Babington and his band of rescuers? Her heart will beat fast for those few seconds. Her final moments of happiness, I suspect.

PHELIPPES: Will she be imprisoned long?

PAULET: At Tixall? That I do not know. Much depends on Great Bess, and upon Sir Francis, of course.

PHELIPPES: Yes, there is much to be done in London: evidence to be sorted and gathered. It will all take several weeks.

PAULET: No doubt.

(*An attendant enters, carrying an ornamental casket.*)

Yes, put the casket here . . . upon the table.

(*The attendant places the casket on the table, and withdraws. Paulet smiles across at Phelippes: he takes a dagger, and breaks the delicate lock. He lifts the lid.*)

Look at this, Thomas: Popish trinkets . . . the lady's toys.

(*Paulet throws some small devotional objects onto the table.*)

And here . . . yes, here we have it! (*Picking up some documents.*) Letters, ciphers, her very closest secrets!

46

Interior, privy chamber. Day.

Davison is transcribing a letter. He sands it, gets up and knocks at door of bedchamber.

ELIZABETH (*voice off*): Come in.

Interior, bedchamber. Day.

DAVISON: Your letter to Queen Mary, Majesty.

ELIZABETH: Thank you. (*She reads.*) You have in various ways and manners attempted to take my life and to bring my kingdom to destruction by bloodshed. I have never proceeded so harshly against you, but have, on the contrary protected and maintained you like myself. These treasons will be proved to you and all made manifest. Yet it is my will that you answer the nobles and peers of the kingdom as if I were myself present. I therefore require, charge and command that you make answer for I have been well informed of your arrogance. Act plainly without reserve, and you will sooner be able to obtain favour of me. Good! See that it be delivered with all haste. Tell Paulet.

47

Interior, Fotheringay: room. Day.

Mary is reading a book. Paulet enters. Mary stares at him.

MARY: I had not thought to see your face again.

PAULET: There are things you must know, madam.

MARY: Having deceived me so shamefully, I had imagined that you would shun my presence; but I was forgetting that you are without such delicate feelings.

PAULET: The deception was not mine, lady. You conspired and planned to escape, did you not?

MARY: I do not deny that I have earnestly wished for liberty and done my utmost to procure it for myself. In this, I acted from a very natural wish.

PAULET: And the conspiracy?

MARY: What of it?

PAULET: Was it not deceiving thus to conspire with Babington and his friends?

MARY: I cannot be held responsible for the criminal projects of a few desperate men, which they planned without my knowledge or participation.

PAULET (*he smiles*): 'Without your knowledge' . . .! Madam, we have much evidence that you wholeheartedly approved of their plan to set you upon the English throne.

MARY: I do not aspire to public position, Sir Amyas; advancing age and bodily weakness prevent me from such a wish, and I have no desire to hold high office in a world so full of crime and troubles.

(*Paulet gazes at Mary; he says nothing. Brief pause.*)

So . . . what are these things I must know?

PAULET: You have been brought here to Fotheringay to be examined by certain lords; and you are required to make answer to the grave charges that you did conspire to displace our Sovereign Lady, Elizabeth of England, and to ruin her kingdom by the shedding of blood.

MARY: Does Bess acknowledge me as close kin, and rightful heir to her throne?

M

PAULET: No, ma'am, she does not.

MARY: Then she has no claim on me. I am no subject, Paulet, but a queen. I owe England nothing.

PAULET: You would be wise, madam, to confess your grievous faults and crimes before you are brought to trial.

MARY: I am not a child to be advised thus. Keep your counsel, for I will have none of it.

PAULET: Pray remember that the matter is treason.

MARY: Who calls it so?

PAULET: The Commons have thus named it.

MARY: I care nothing for the Commons; they have always hated me. And as for the charge of treason, it is groundless. I have merely sought protection from Catholic princes, since my position here is so vulnerable.

PAULET: You deny the charges, then?

MARY: I do most certainly. They are devices by which means I may be put to death, nothing more.

PAULET: We have firm proof, Madam.

MARY: Assembled by Walsingham, no doubt. He would stop at nothing to see me speedily removed.

PAULET: It is not a personal matter, but law. Since you are in England, madam, you are bound by the laws of our country.

MARY: Who says this?

PAULET: My instructions come from her Majesty the Queen.

MARY: I am myself a queen, Paulet, the daughter of a king, a stranger, and the true kinswoman of the Queen of England. As an absolute monarch, I cannot submit to orders, nor can I submit to the laws of the land without injury to myself and other Sovereign princes. For myself, I do not recognize the laws of England, nor do I know or understand them. I came here on my cousin's promise of assistance, and was at once imprisoned. I am now alone, without counsel, or anyone to speak on my behalf. My papers and notes have been taken from me, and I am destitute of all aid. How, then, can you expect me to stand before a court that I do not recognize, and which has been assembled only to connive at my death?

PAULET: We shall proceed tomorrow, madam, and we shall proceed even though you be absent and continue contumacious.

(*Mary gazes at Paulet without speaking. Brief pause.*)

MARY: Who sits in judgment upon me?

PAULET: The Chancellor, nine earls, thirteen barons, the Privy Councillors, and Chief Justices Wray and Anderson.

MARY: In such company, I am condemned unheard.

(*Mary crosses to the window. Pause. She turns to Paulet.*)

Tell your masters I shall attend. But remember this, Paulet: the theatre of the world is wider than this realm of England. My death, should it presently occur, will blaze wide and dangerously.

PAULET: Madam I am commanded by her Majesty to deliver this letter to you. (*He goes.*)

(*Mary takes the letter, and begins to read.*)

MARY (*voice over*): You have in various ways and man-

ners attempted to take my life and to bring my
kingdom to destruction by bloodshed. I have never
proceeded too harshly against you but have on the
contrary . . . (*Fade.*)

48

Interior, presence chamber. Night.

*The doors are flung open, and Davison strides through
the deserted chamber. He goes to the privy chamber,
and an attendant opens the door for him.*

49

Interior, privy chamber. Night.

*Davison enters, and bows to Elizabeth. The attendant
closes the door.*

ELIZABETH: Davison, come in. You have made good
speed.

DAVISON: The messenger spoke of great urgency.

ELIZABETH: Indeed that is so. (*Going to him.*) Think
you the Commissioners at Fotheringay have reached
an end of their business?

DAVISON: Most likely, madam. If not this day, then
tomorrow without fail.

ELIZABETH: Then write a letter and despatch it straight.
The sentence on my cousin must be stayed. Write a
few lines saying this is my command.

(*Davison starts to move, but hesitates.*)

Quickly, Davison; do not delay!

DAVISON: As you wish, madam.

ELIZABETH: Say they must adjourn their meeting until I have considered further.

50

Interior, Fotheringay: hall. Day.

Paulet and Gifford: in the background, servants are removing chairs and tables that were used at the trial. Paulet is holding a letter.

PAULET: This is madness, Gifford! She has been publicly charged and found guilty; and now we are told to stop all proceedings!

GIFFORD: Only the execution is delayed.

PAULET: Even for this, there is no cause. Mary Stuart had no defence but denial, and you yourself know the plainness and evidence of the proofs against her.

GIFFORD: Nevertheless, I am told she spoke well.

PAULET: Not so, by no means! It was all sham; long, artificial speeches, blaming Elizabeth and the Council, protesting her innocence, wringing tears from her eyes—counterfeit acting from start to end! Fortunately the Court was wise enough to hear her case with proper indifference.

GIFFORD: You seem quite distressed that the lady is not to die.

PAULET: It is a mark of weakness! Traitors should die, and with all haste, so that good men may live in safety.

GIFFORD: Take comfort, Sir Amyas, her death cannot be far away.

345

51

Interior, Fotheringay: room. Day.

Long shot. Mary is sitting by the window, working at her embroidery.

52

Interior, presence chamber. Day.

Courtiers are assembled, among them: Walsingham and Archbishop Whitgift. Ceremonial. Elizabeth enters, and addresses the assembly.

ELIZABETH: As I came to the throne with the willing hearts of my subjects, so do I now, after twenty-eight years' reign, perceive in you no diminution of good will. And although I find that my life has been full dangerously sought, yet still am I clear from malice. I have had good experience and trial of this world; I know what it is to be a subject, what to be a Sovereign, what to have good neighbours, and sometimes evil-willers. I have found treason in trust, seen great benefits little regarded. In this late Act of Parliament, you have laid a hard hand upon me: that I must give direction for my cousin's death, which cannot but be most grievous and an irksome burden to me. I, who in my time have pardoned so many rebels, winked at so many treasons, am now required to proceed thus against such a person. If I should say unto you that I mean not to grant your petition, by my faith, I should say unto you more than perhaps I mean. And if I should say unto you that I mean to grant your petition, I should then tell you more than is fit for you to know. Your judgment I condemn not, neither do I mislike your reasons; but pray accept my thankfulness, excuse my doubtfulness, and take in good part my answer answerless.

(*Ceremonial. Elizabeth withdraws to the privy chamber.*

As the courtiers disperse, camera closes on Walsingham. Whitgift approaches him.)

WHITGIFT: Her Majesty's words clearly displeased you, Sir Francis.

WALSINGHAM: I had hoped for a firm decision, my Lord Archbishop.

WHITGIFT: So had we all.

WALSINGHAM: Some days I fear the Scottish Queen will outlive us all, and laugh upon our graves.

WHITGIFT: There is still one path open to us; as yet, unexplored.

WALSINGHAM: Indeed?

WHITGIFT: Indeed so. I have spoken to Robert Leicester, and he well approves the plan.

WALSINGHAM: What plan is this?

(Whitgift takes Walsingham by the arm, and leads him away from the throng of courtiers.)

WHITGIFT: The lady could be removed in secret.

WALSINGHAM: In secret . . .?

WHITGIFT: A phial of poison . . . a soft pillow; such means would spare her the torment of the axe. There is mercy as well as convenience in this method.

(Walsingham stares at Whitgift, but says nothing.)

A man called Wingfield would perform the deed. He is well experienced and reliable.

WALSINGHAM: I think not, my Lord.

WHITGIFT: Your reasons?

347

WALSINGHAM: The act should be legal, publicly performed. Otherwise, she will be more dangerous dead than alive.

WHITGIFT: Very well, Walsingham, whatever you please. But let me know if you change your mind, and I will contact the man Wingfield on your behalf.

WALSINGHAM: Thank you, my Lord Archbishop—

(*We detect the irony.*)

—I am grateful for your offer of assistance.

53

Interior, Fotheringay: room. Day.

Mary is working at her embroidery. Paulet enters.

PAULET: You wished to see me, madam?

MARY: Yes, I did.

(*Mary puts down her embroidery, and turns to face Paulet.*)

I am much displeased that you have removed the royal cloth of state from my chair.

PAULET: You are now only a dead woman, without the dignity and honours of a queen.

(*Mary smiles.*)

MARY: How your mind hovers around death! You are a true Englishman, Paulet, for the history of your country is a bloody business indeed.

PAULET: Blood runs through all countries in times of peril.

MARY: There can be no peril at this time, surely? For I am safely locked away.

PAULET: You threaten us all, lady, until your head be off.

MARY (*with a smile*): There are those who think otherwise; even among *your* friends.

PAULET: That I doubt.

MARY: Oh yes, I observed them at my trial. The Lords Rutland and Warwick, for example; they look kindly upon me.

PAULET: You deceive yourself, madam. Not one of them is favourable to your cause.

MARY: You think not ... ?

PAULET: And everyone else is astonished to see you so calm under the circumstances in which you find yourself. No living person has ever been accused of crimes so frightful and odious as yours.

MARY: Is it, then, a crime to stand by the truth?

PAULET: Your truth is not mine, madam.

MARY: No, indeed, for mine is the truth of the Catholic Faith.

PAULET: You parry words and shift their meaning!

MARY: And you are angry because I ever outwit you. (*She laughs.*) See, you stand there, like a fish, gaping for a reply!

PAULET: I do not desire to see you, madam. Your presence disturbs me.

MARY: Then go, Sir Amyas, I have no need of your company; with death at my side, I have much to think on.

349

Interior, privy chamber. Day.

Elizabeth and Walsingham. Elizabeth is holding a lengthy document.

ELIZABETH: And you expect me to read *all* of this?

WALSINGHAM: It is but an argument . . . or rather, several arguments . . . for the immediate execution of the Scottish Queen.

ELIZABETH: In other words, your arguments.

WALSINGHAM: Yes, ma'am, but sound nonetheless.

ELIZABETH: All men believe their arguments to be sound.

WALSINGHAM: Perhaps if I could explain madam . . .

ELIZABETH: If you must, Sir Francis.

WALSINGHAM: The longer your cousin lives, the more your Majesty's life is endangered.

ELIZABETH: You have said this before. Many times.

WALSINGHAM: It cannot be overemphasized. Remember the Papists, Atheists, malcontents and Jesuits who all live in hope that the crown shall come to the Scottish Queen.

ELIZABETH: And what of the Scottish King if his mother is done to death?

WALSINGHAM: James? Surely there is no cause to fear him?

ELIZABETH: I did not say I feared him, Walsingham.

WALSINGHAM: He has no love for Mary Stuart; he cares not whether she lives or dies.

ELIZABETH: His subjects might care, though. Have you thought of that?

WALSINGHAM: James can manage his subjects.

ELIZABETH: Then there is France; will they smile on her beheading?

WALSINGHAM: That is impossible to foretell.

ELIZABETH: But important to foresee. With a Spanish war becoming increasingly probable, we cannot afford to antagonize France. Without them, we would be alone in Europe. And for what purpose? The early death of a weak, fragile, sickly woman, who has already been a prisoner for almost twenty years.

WALSINGHAM: What of your own feelings, madam? You wish her to live?

ELIZABETH: I wish her dead, old moor, but it is the doing thereof. Oh, it is easy enough for you, Sir Francis—you can draw-up your plans, advise, persuade, argue . . . but it is not you who decides. It is not you who carries the burden of responsibility. If Mary dies, it will be because of me. My word. My act. Her blood will stain my soul, Sir Francis. Not yours.

55

Exterior. Limbo. Day.

Blackness. An owl hoots. Big close shot of Kelley: His face is suddenly illuminated by a strange, shimmering light.

56

Interior, Mary's bedchamber. Night.

Close shot of Mary, asleep: she twists and turns upon her pillow.

57

Interior, bedchamber. Night.

Close shot of Elizabeth, as she stands gazing out of the bedchamber window. She, too, is illumined by a shifting glowing light.

58

Sky (through window). Night.

The strange shimmering light of the Aurora Borealis is seen in the night sky.

59

Exterior. Limbo. Night.

Kelley looks at sky.

KELLEY: Fire and Flames! The heavens are ablaze with anger!

60

Interior, Mary's bedchamber. Night.

Close shot of Mary, as before. She awakes, as if from a nightmare, and stares directly into camera.

61

Interior, presence chamber. Day.

A number of courtiers are waiting for an audience. Davison is standing near the privy chamber, carrying a bundle of official documents. Paulet enters, and goes to Davison.

DAVISON: Sir Amyas!

PAULET: Good morrow, Davison.

DAVISON: What brings you to London?

PAULET: An urgent summons from her Majesty, no less. I have ridden many hours.

DAVISON: Sir Francis will be sorry not to have seen you.

PAULET: And I, him. Is he still unwell?

DAVISON: Indeed he is.

PAULET: What is the cause of his sickness?

DAVISON: The doctors have many theories but I suspect that it springs from the anxiety of these past months.

PAULET: No doubt, no doubt.

DAVISON (*confidentially*): But, Sir Amyas, the remedy is close at hand.

PAULET: How so?

DAVISON: This very morning her Majesty has agreed to sign the warrant.

PAULET: *This morning . . . .!*

DAVISON: Even now, I await her pleasure.

PAULET: This is the best news I could have hoped for! The matter has become an embarrassment to us all.

DAVISON: It can scarcely have pleased the Scottish Queen.

PAULET: No, but she has borne herself with remarkable courage. Even I have been forced to admire her for it.

(*A courtier emerges from the privy chamber, and walks past Paulet and Davison.*)

But why this change of heart, do you know?

DAVISON: There have been many rumours of a French conspiracy, but I think it is because of Edward Kelley. Great lights were seen in the sky three nights ago, and Kelley pronounced omens of certain death. Our Sovereign Lady pays much heed to such ghostly apparitions.

PAULET: Well, whatever the cause, I am grateful for it.

DAVISON: She is still the most reluctant at heart, of that I am sure. (*Confidentially.*) I was instructed to place the warrant with other papers to be signed, so that it shall not be unduly prominent.

PAULET: This is not true?

DAVISON: It is, most assuredly.

(*An attendant opens the privy chamber doors.*)

ATTENDANT (*off*): Her Majesty is ready, Mr Davison.

DAVISON (*to Paulet*): And thus the game commences.

PAULET: May it conclude successfully.

DAVISON: Thank you, Sir Amyas.

62

Interior, privy chamber. Day.

Elizabeth is sitting at a table. Davison enters.

ELIZABETH: Good morning, Davison. How is Sir Francis today?

DAVISON: Somewhat better, Majesty, I thank you.

ELIZABETH: But still in his bed?

DAVISON: I fear so.

ELIZABETH: Give him my good wishes.

DAVISON: I will, madam.

ELIZABETH: Now . . . those are to be signed I believe?

DAVISON: Yes, madam.

(*Davison gives the documents to Elizabeth. She begins to sign them.*)

ELIZABETH: The weather is kind to us this February.

DAVISON: Indeed it is, ma'am.

ELIZABETH: I was delighted to feel the strength of the sun upon my face this morning. Perhaps we shall enjoy an early spring.

DAVISON: That, certainly, is to be hoped.

ELIZABETH: Do you often travel abroad, Davison?

DAVISON: Abroad, ma'am?

ELIZABETH: To the country.

DAVISON: As often as I am able. Town dwelling is not to my taste.

ELIZABETH: Very wise. Bright air comforts the brain, does it not?

DAVISON: So I believe.

ELIZABETH: Oh, yes. All evil humours spring from the town. 'Bad air doth putrify and corrupt the blood of man.'

DAVISON: Yes, ma'am.

ELIZABETH: May God send us fresh spring sunshine.

DAVISON: Amen to that.

(*Elizabeth lays down her pen, and pushes the documents across the table.*)

ELIZABETH: Here, Davison . . . All is done.

DAVISON (*picking up the papers*): Thank you, ma'am. (*He goes to the door.*)

ELIZABETH: Davison.

DAVISON: Madam?

ELIZABETH: You know what has occurred.

DAVISON: Yes, madam, I do.

ELIZABETH: Does it not affect you in any way?

DAVISON: Affect me?

ELIZABETH: Distress you.

DAVISON: I prefer to see the death of a guilty person to the death of one who is innocent.

ELIZABETH: Yes, and so would all good men. You will tell Walsingham of this, will you not?

DAVISON: I will, madam.

ELIZABETH: But take care. I fear the grief thereof will go near to kill him outright.

(*Elizabeth smiles at Davison: he smiles in return.*)

Send Paulet to me.

DAVISON: Yes, madam.

ELIZABETH: And Davison . . . I want to hear no more of this matter until it is all quite finished.

DAVISON: Yes, madam. (*He bows, and goes out.*)

(*There is a brief pause. Paulet enters.*)

ELIZABETH: Faithful Amyas, I am glad to see you.

PAULET: Majesty.

ELIZABETH: Great business has been done here this morning, did you know that?

PAULET: Yes, ma'am, and I am much relieved at the news.

ELIZABETH: Yet still there will be delay before the matter is concluded. The warrant goes now to the Council. There will be discussion, argument.

PAULET: It is always so in such business, madam.

ELIZABETH: But I am in deadly peril while Mary still lives! Hourly, I am in peril. There have been signs of death in the heavens, Paulet.

PAULET: You are well guarded, madam; there is nothing to fear.

357

ELIZABETH: It is not just my person that concerns me; it is my country and the preservation of our true religion. This, too, is in great danger . . .

PAULET (*puzzled*): Madam . . .?

(*Elizabeth gazes at Paulet, she sighs: and walks away from him.*)

ELIZABETH: I am disappointed in you, Amyas. I thought you loved me well.

PAULET: And so I do, Majesty . . . no man more! My good livings and life are at your disposition.

ELIZABETH: Then why have you found no way to shorten the life of this captive Queen?

PAULET: To shorten the life . . .? Madam, I cannot answer this!

ELIZABETH: Surely you knew of my reluctance to shed blood.

PAULET: I knew you were in doubt.

ELIZABETH: And yet you did nothing?

PAULET: I was not aware that such action was expected of me.

ELIZABETH: There is still time, Sir Amyas.

PAULET: Time?

ELIZABETH: To do it privily.

(*Paulet stares at the Queen, aghast.*)

PAULET: Forgive me, madam . . .

ELIZABETH: You will not do it?

PAULET: God forbid that I should make so foul a ship-wreck of my conscience, or leave so great a blot to my posterity!

ELIZABETH: You fail me, then.

PAULET: I will do anything to serve you, Majesty—

ELIZABETH: You fail me, nonetheless!

(*Pause. Elizabeth approaches Paulet.*)

I should have guessed that yours would be a dainty conscience. Brave words, but little else, Sir Amyas. Although you profess great zeal for my safe-keeping, you will perform nothing. Like all great matters, the act is my burden. No one will aid me.

(*Pause. Silence.*)

You are dismissed, Paulet.

63

Interior, Walsingham's room. Day.

Walsingham is lying on a couch, swathed in blankets. Phelippes is standing at his side.

WALSINGHAM: You must make sure that they act before the Queen changes her mind yet again.

PHELIPPES: Davison has already carried the warrant to the Lord Chancellor, who has affixed the Great Seal. The Privy Council is resolved to end the business without delay.

WALSINGHAM: Good. See to it that the axeman is well paid. Ten pounds should be enough for his labour.

PHELIPPES: Very well, sir.

WALSINGHAM: And Thomas. Let no word be buzzed abroad till the head be off. It must be done in secret.

PHELIPPES: Trust me, Sir Francis; it shall be as you say.

WALSINGHAM: So . . . the bosom serpent will now be crushed.

64

Interior, Fotheringay: room. Day.

Mary is kneeling at a priedieu. She holds a crucifix in her hands.

MARY: Even as thy arms, O Jesus, were spread here upon the cross, so receive me into Thy arms of mercy, and forgive me all my sins.

(*A violent knocking on the door. Mary rises slowly to her feet.*)

The end of Mary Stuart's troubles is now done.

65

Interior, Fotheringay: hall. Day.

People have gathered for the execution, and are waiting for the arrival of Mary. A low wooden platform has been erected in the centre of the hall: it is draped in black. The executioner is standing on the platform, beside the block. A great blaze has been lit in the fireplace, and the flames flicker across the faces of the people who have come to watch the beheading. Camera pans slowly across the faces of the silent spectators.

Music begins.

66

Interior, bedchamber. Day.

Long shot. Elizabeth is sitting up in bed, with the blankets pulled high around her. Camera tracks slowly into close shot. Music continues.

67

Interior, Fotheringay: hall. Day.

Mary enters the hall. She is dressed entirely in black, save for a long white veil, which flows down her back like a bride's. She holds a Prayer Book and a crucifix. Mary goes to the platform steps, and kneels in prayer. Reaction shots of the spectators, most of whom are visibly moved. Mary rises to her feet. Her attendants help her to remove the black cloak. Under it, she is wearing a red petticoat and a red satin bodice, with long sleeves. The executioner steps forward, and takes Mary's jewels. One of Mary's attendants binds her mistress's eyes with a white cloth. The attendants withdraw from the platform. Mary kneels at the block. Music ends as Mary stretches out her arms, and cries aloud.

MARY : *In manus tuas, Domine, confide spiritum meum!*

(Camera closes on Paulet as the axe descends. The axe falls again. Pull-back as the executioner reaches down to lift up the head. He grasps the auburn hair; it comes away in his hand. A wig.)

68

Interior, privy chamber. Night.

Elizabeth, Paulet, courtiers, and attendants. Dee and Kelley are among those present.

ELIZABETH: Who despatched the warrant of execution to Fotheringay?

PAULET: William Davison, ma'am.

ELIZABETH: I gave no instructions that the warrant was to be delivered.

PAULET: It was signed, Majesty.

ELIZABETH: For safety's sake, Paulet. I gave no further instructions! You have all acted against my most earnest desires!

(*To an attendant.*) Seize Davison this night, and commit him to the Tower. I am innocent of her death, as God Himself may judge! (*Pause.*) Continue Paulet.

PAULET: And thus, she departed this miserable world. The blazing hair was false, madam. It was a wig. In truth, she was grey and ageing, her beauty gone. The executioner raised up the severed head, and cried aloud, 'God save the Queen;', whereupon, the Dean of Peterborough pronounced, '*So perish all the Queen's enemies!*' . . . his voice echoing around the hall. And still, the dead woman's lips moved, trembling, as if trying to speak. They continued to move thus for a full fifteen minutes. As the body was lifted, the Queen's terrier dog crept from beneath the skirts, where it had been hiding, and lay down beside the displaced head. Women bore the animal away, and washed the blood from its hair. The book was burned. Her clothes and few possessions were cleaned or burned. No trace of her blood remains. She is quite removed from this earth, madam.

(*Pause. Silence. Nobody moves.*)

69

Interior, presence chamber. Day.

**Walsingham enters, and walks towards the bedchamber.
Dee and Kelley bow to him as he passes. An attendant
opens the door to the bedchamber.**

70

Interior, bedchamber. Day.

**Elizabeth is standing by the bed, wrapped in shawls.
Walsingham enters. The door closes behind him.**

ELIZABETH: You are recovered, then, Sir Francis?

WALSINGHAM: Thank you, ma'am, the pain is less
severe.

ELIZABETH: And the deed is done. Your work is
accomplished. (*She goes to Walsingham.*) The dog died,
did you know? The terrier. It refused food, grew thin,
and died. The dog and its mistress. Both dead.

WALSINGHAM: There was no other path, Majesty. You
acted with great wisdom.

ELIZABETH: You think there is great wisdom in killing
a queen?

WALSINGHAM: She is at rest, madam. With God's good
grace, she will find eternal peace.

ELIZABETH: Peace? Ah no, you are much mistaken.
There is no peace for the dead, Sir Francis; it is a busy
time for my royal cousin. See, already the creatures
are at work, crawling between her lips, entering her
nose, burrowing beneath her eyes. Worms cluster in
her belly, competing with foul maggots for the tastiest

morsel. Even now, she is being invaded by a legion of grey flesh-eaters. Now the body writhes and moves with the activities of countless parasites. There is no peace for my cousin, Walsingham, and will be none until she is consumed and rotten; only then will her white bones be at rest.

(*Walsingham says nothing. Elizabeth draws close to him.*)

This is our common end, old moor; picked clean by worms, flesh curdling with corruption, stinking like a blocked midden. So do not talk to me of 'peace' and 'God's good grace'; dying is a fearful process.

(*Elizabeth turns, and walks away from Walsingham.*)

I have known Death since I was a child; I have stared long into his white, unseeing eyes. I know him. When you are lying on your last bed, remember my words, cry out for mercy, bite deep into your lips, and recall how you plotted my cousin's most terrible end.

(*Pause. Silence. Walsingham bows, and goes out of the room. Elizabeth remains motionless for a moment. She then utters a great cry of grief and remorse. The cry subsides into a choking sob of despair. Elizabeth sinks onto the bed. Camera cranes up into high long shot.*)

THE ENTERPRISE
OF ENGLAND

by
JOHN PREBBLE

© *John Prebble, 1971*

The Enterprise of England was first shown on BBC Television on March 17 1971 as the fifth play in the series *Elizabeth R*, with the following cast:

ELIZABETH I	*Glenda Jackson*
THE EARL OF LEICESTER	*Robert Hardy*
LORD BURGHLEY	*Ronald Hines*
SIR FRANCIS WALSINGHAM	*Stephen Murray*
PHILIP II	*Peter Jeffrey*
SIR FRANCIS DRAKE	*John Woodvine*
THE EARL OF ESSEX	*Robert Ellis*
IDIAQUEZ	*Christopher Hancock*
SANTA CRUZ	*Geoffrey Wincott*
MEDINA SIDONIA	*Gordon Gostelow*
FATHER ROBERT PARSONS	*Paul Hardwick*
JOHN TREGANNON	*Michael Culver*
HOWARD	*Peter Howell*
CORDOBA	*Ian Ricketts*
SPEAKER	*Robert Sansom*
DUTCH ENVOY	*Bill Horsley*
OLD SOLDIER	*Derek Hardwick*
YOUNG SOLDIER	*Malcolm McFee*
PHILIP'S SON	*David Parfitt*

Non-speaking artists

SEAMAN (JACOB)	*Patrick Milner*
NURSE TO PHILIP'S SON	*Sally Lewis*
FATHER CHAVEZ	*Stanley Jacomb*
ASTROLOGER	*David J. Graham*
LADIES-IN-WAITING }	*Joy Hope, Sonya Petri, Maureen Nelson*
DUTCH ENVOYS	*Sonnie Willis, Bill Matthews*
HALBERDIERS	*Pat Gorman. Ronald Mayer*

Producer Roderick Graham

Director Donald McWhinnie

Designer Peter Seddon

CHARACTERS

ELIZABETH I

THE EARL OF LEICESTER

LORD BURGHLEY

SIR FRANCIS WALSINGHAM

PHILIP II

SIR FRANCIS DRAKE

THE EARL OF ESSEX

IDIAQUEZ

SANTA CRUZ

MEDINA SIDONIA

FATHER ROBERT PARSONS

JOHN TREGANNON

HOWARD

CORDOBA

SPEAKER

DUTCH ENVOY

OLD SOLDIER

YOUNG SOLDIER

PHILIP'S SON

INTERIORS

Walsingham's room
King's rooms, Escurial, Spain
Gallery, palace, England
Burghley's bedchamber
Castle of Sagres, Portugal
Corridor, Escurial, Spain
Audience chamber, palace, England
Santa Cruz's chamber, Spain
Privy chamber, England
Leicester's tent, Tilbury, England
Inn room at Plymouth

EXTERIOR

Leicester's tent, Tilbury

Brief outline of plot

The Catholic Queen, Mary of Scotland, has been executed in England. Philip of Spain, determined to avenge her death, is preparing to launch a fleet against England. He calls this the Enterprise of England. Elizabeth is afraid of war, and of its cost. She and Burghley hope for the success of the peace talks with Spain in the Netherlands: even though Walsingham assures her the talks are just a device to give the Spaniards more time to prepare the Armada.

It is now May and Philip orders his Captain General, Santa Cruz, to be ready to sail in October. Meanwhile Drake has sacked Cadiz and sunk several Spanish ships. Elizabeth is furious for she had ordered Drake's recall. Philip urges Santa Cruz to leave immediately in spite of the losses to the Armada, but he is now very ill and the fleet is still not ready. Walsingham presses Elizabeth to mobilize her forces against a Spanish invasion, but she still does not believe Philip will attack. She finally agrees when the Spaniards withdraw from the peace talks in the Netherlands, and when her astrologer prophesies a major disaster for the year 1588. Santa Cruz dies and Philip gives the command to the Duke of Medina Sidonia, who is not even a sailor. Elizabeth's forces have waited for three months and still the Armada has not arrived. She blames Walsingham for misinforming her. But then she sees a tract by a fervent Catholic, Cardinal Allen, denouncing her in extreme terms. Philip has approved this document and Elizabeth is finally convinced that he does mean to attack. The Armada sails but is much delayed by bad weather. Elizabeth goes to Tilbury to see her troops. While she is there news is brought that the Armada has been scattered and England is victorious. Back in London, Burghley tells her that the Earl of Leicester is dead. She reads his last letter in despair.

1

Interior, the Escurial, Spain. Day. Spring, 1587.

The tolling of a funeral bell out of view. Philip kneeling at a confessional. As camera tracks back slowly it takes in his confessor, Chavez, and the bleak interior of the bedchamber. Keeping Philip in shot, camera retreats through the doorway into the outer room and at low angle holds on a boy, the Infante Philip. He too is kneeling, but not in prayer. A listless, insipid child, he is idly playing with the model of a galleon, riding it across the pages of a large open book. Pan from him and take in Idiaquez, writing at his desk by the window. He is a thin, dry man in black, almost an extension of the quill he holds. There is a knock at the door and Idiaquez looks up above the wall of documents before him. Robert Parsons enters cautiously. He is an English exile, a Jesuit, a stocky man, swarthy and coarse in appearance. Idiaquez rises, placing a finger on his lips and goes to the door to the inner room, closing it. He then crosses to the open window and closes that too, shutting out the sound of the bell. Meanwhile Parsons has advanced into the room, bowing clumsily to the boy, who ignores him. When Idiaquez returns to the desk, Parsons, glancing back at the boy with an uncertain frown, sits beside the secretary.

PARSONS (*a whisper*): Is it true? There was no word of it when I left Madrid.

IDIAQUEZ: You need not whisper. The Prince hears nothing when he is playing.

PARSONS (*clearing his throat*): There was no word when I . . .

IDIAQUEZ: Letters from Paris reached his Majesty last night.

PARSONS: The English have truly murdered her?

IDIAQUEZ: Your countrymen have truly murdered her.

PARSONS (*crosses himself*): May God receive her innocent soul.

IDIAQUEZ: Amen.

PARSONS: And translate her to celestial bliss.

IDIAQUEZ (*a slight, weary beat*): Amen.

PARSONS: Now may He call upon us His avenging servants . . .

(*When Idiaquez says nothing.*)

You do not agree?

IDIAQUEZ: Your pardon, Father Robert. I did not realize you had finished.

PARSONS: Finished?

IDIAQUEZ: Your prayer.

PARSONS: Do you mock me, Idiaquez?

IDIAQUEZ: No. But why have you come? Is it to tell the King of Spain that he must avenge the Queen of Scots?

PARSONS: God's will demands it.

IDIAQUEZ: Though the King's exchequer may not yet permit it.

PARSONS: There is no richer prince in Christendom!

IDIAQUEZ: You have forgotten the Pope, Father Robert.

PARSONS: His Holiness has many calls upon his purse, but he will bless the armies that destroy Elizabeth.

IDIAQUEZ: Has he not said that were she not a heretic she would be the most perfect and accomplished prince in the world?

PARSONS: Now you mock the Holy Father.

IDIAQUEZ: You are a good man, Robert Parsons. I would protect myself from your dangerous simplicity, that is all.

PARSONS: You are a clerk. And you are afraid of war.

IDIAQUEZ: So is my royal master. Remember that he fears war as a burned child dreads the fire. He'll not be long at the confessional. Meanwhile . . . with your permission . . .

(*He lifts a quill and gestures toward the papers before him. As he begins to write, cut to:*)

2

Interior, Walsingham's room, England. Day. Spring, 1587.

Walsingham is at his desk. Drake enters, approaching the table with a triumphant grin on his face.

WALSINGHAM: You carry your news on your face, Francis.

DRAKE: Sweet Jesus! Were Elizabeth only a man . . .

WALSINGHAM: We might all be headless by now. But you have your commission at last?

DRAKE: Aye. At last. But God save me from another campaign like this. There have been days when she granted me an audience nine times before supper. And then weeks when she looked through me as if I were made of glass.

WALSINGHAM: How far will the commission carry you?

DRAKE (*slyly*): She warned me against talking to 'that rogue Walsingham'.

WALSINGHAM: No doubt. Since Mary Stuart was relieved of her head Burghley and I have both been rogues. But I can be patient. I am accustomed to the burden of the Queen's conscience. What did you say to her?

DRAKE: What we've all been saying for three years. That Philip will send a fleet against us. This much more . . . That we must now strangle the Anti-christ on his own doorstep before he takes a pace beyond it.

WALSINGHAM: Not that Drake's war with Spain should become England's?

DRAKE: My war, as you call it, has given your purse a golden lining, as well as the Queen's.

WALSINGHAM: Or your own, my friend. But she has truly given you a warrant for an assault on Philip's ships in their harbours?

DRAKE: I'll tell you the wording of it. 'To impeach the purpose of the Spanish fleet.' How that may be done is left to my taste, even to 'distressing their ships within their havens'.

WALSINGHAM: Then I advise you to set upon the venture without delay.

DRAKE: I leave Gravesend for Plymouth tonight. In a week I'll be under sail for Cadiz.

WALSINGHAM: Write to me from Plymouth. And Francis . . . I pray you earnestly, do not delay.

DRAKE: She'll not change her mind now.

WALSINGHAM: As easily as she would a gown. You know that. And persuade us that we are chameleons not she. Get you gone, Francis.

DRAKE: I would sup with you.

WALSINGHAM: God speed you, but be gone now.

(*Close on Drake as he rises.*)

DRAKE: I'll bring you a golden hair from Philip's beard. (*A grin.*) If I can find one that I've not already turned grey.

(*Cut to:*)

3

Interior, the King's rooms, Escurial. Day. Spring, 1587.

As the door to the inner room opens and Philip comes out. He is sick and old, his once yellow beard now white. He walks with the help of a stick, and he carries a handkerchief which he occasionally holds to an eye afflicted with a cataract. When he is not doing this, he gently kneads hands that are painful with gout. He pauses for a moment by the Prince and places a hand momentarily on the boy's head. The Prince looks up with an empty face. Philip moves to his chair by the desk. Idiaquez remains seated, but Parsons has risen and is bowing awkwardly.

PHILIP: I did not know that you were to have an audience, Father Robert. But you are welcome.

(*The door to the inner room remains open, and Chavez can be seen preparing himself and the altar table for the administration of the sacrament.*)

PARSONS: Your Majesty, I've come to impl . . .

375

PHILIP (*to Idiaquez*): I've not slept since I read the letters from Paris. Call the physician to bleed me tonight. (*To Parsons*.) Your countrymen are brutes, Father Robert.

PARSONS: No, your Majesty, not all of them. Many pray that you will free them from the tyranny of that heretical bastard, Elizabeth.

PHILIP: I would be grateful to hear that they prayed less for my help and more for the courage to free themselves. Is it not true that English Catholics are among those who seize my ships in the Indies, and fight my soldiers in the Netherlands?

PARSONS: If so, they are thereby deposed and excommunicated! But Sire, I have told you . . .

PHILIP (*gently*): You tell me what Doctor Allen writes to you. But neither of you are in England. You are here, and he is in Rome. (*He turns to Idiaquez*.) I will write to Rome.

IDIAQUEZ: Sire.

PHILIP: I will tell the Curia that I grieve for the Queen's death, for she would have been the most suitable instrument to bring both Scotland and England back to the Church. Is that not so, Father Robert?

PARSONS: Most assuredly, Sire.

PHILIP: Although, having done so, she would have made both the allies of France. Idiaquez, I will say nothing of that to Rome.

(*Idiaquez smiles briefly, but Parsons is puzzled.*)

PARSONS: I do not understand your Majesty.

PHILIP (*to Idiaquez*): I will tell the Curia that as God

in his wisdom ordained that Elizabeth should take the
life of Mary, so He will raise up another for the
triumph of His Church.

PARSONS: Amen!

PHILIP: Then may we not leave it to him, Father
Robert? What would you have me do?

PARSONS: Avenge her death!

PHILIP: Yet if she is a saint, as we agree, should I
punish those who have been God's instruments, translating her immortal soul to Heaven?

PARSONS: Majesty, I do not dispute God's purpose in
ordaining her murder. But by that foul deed He also
revealed the obscene heresy of the usurper Elizabeth.

PHILIP: Father Robert, are you suggesting that God
lags behind His Holiness the Pope, who has already
excommunicated her?

PARSONS: Majesty . . . I am saying that now is the time
for the Enterprise of England!

PHILIP: I ask your pardon, Father Robert. I see it is
statecraft not theology you would debate with me.

(*He lifts a hand as Parsons opens his mouth to protest
a denial.*)

For twenty years men have urged this Enterprise upon
me. Yet I had no ships for the purpose until I conquered Portugal. That was a terrible war, Father
Robert. I am still at war in the Netherlands, and I
cannot yet trust France. How can I send an army and
a fleet against England?

PARSONS: Majesty . . . for four years the Marquis of
Santa Cruz has been gathering your ships at Cadiz and
Lisbon . . .

PHILIP (*deadpan*): To protect the Indies and to reinforce my armies in the Netherlands. All men know that.

(*Chavez has appeared at the doorway to the inner room, wearing vestments for the administration of the sacrament. Philip looks at him and nods. He rises painfully and moves towards the doorway.*)

Pray excuse me.

(*Parsons rises too.*)

PARSONS: Sire . . . what may I write to Doctor Allen? What comfort can we send to the faithful in England?

PHILIP (*pausing*): Tell them that I will be guided by God.

PARSONS: Majesty . . . there is need of haste.

PHILIP: Then we must walk with feet of lead, lest we stumble. (*He moves slowly toward the inner room.*)

PARSONS: Sire . . .

(*Philip halts again, his lips tightening with impatience.*)

Majesty . . . If it has been God's will to take the soul of that murdered Queen, it is also his obvious design to bestow upon you the crowns of England and Scotland.

PHILIP (*a beat*): Pray for me, Father Robert.

(*Hold on him as he turns away and enters the inner room. As he kneels before the little altar, Chavez turns to it and raises the Host. Cut to:*)

4

Interior, gallery, the royal palace, England. Day.

In the foreground a halberdier comes to attention as Elizabeth and her lady-in-waiting round the corner and approach camera. The Queen is dressed in mourning, and although middle-aged, she walks briskly like a younger woman. Pan them by to a door at the end of the gallery, where the lady-in-waiting fumbles with the handle. Elizabeth seizes it, turns it, and enters the room. Cut to:

5

Interior, Burghley's bedchamber. Day.

Elizabeth entering, the lady-in-waiting closing the door behind them. Burghley lies sick in his bed, and Sir Francis Walsingham, who is sitting beside him, rises quickly, bowing. A beat, as Elizabeth looks at them both imperiously, then she walks to the bedside and sits in the chair Walsingham has vacated. Burghley struggles to sit upright in the bed.

BURGHLEY: Madam . . .

ELIZABETH: Rest you still, old man.

(*As he still struggles.*)

God's death, Burghley! I command you. Rest you still!

(*In a gentler tone, as he subsides.*)

They did not tell me that you were ill . . . not until this morning.

BURGHLEY: Gout, madam, gout. I suffer more from your displeasure.

379

ELIZABETH: And so you should. You are a wicked wretch.

BURGHLEY: As your Majesty pleases.

ELIZABETH: A false dissembler.

BURGHLEY: Nay, madam, not that.

ELIZABETH: Old and doting.

BURGHLEY: Indeed, I have passed too long on this . . .

ELIZABETH: And a traitor.

BURGHLEY: Madam, I protest I have not . . .

ELIZABETH: How is it with you, Walsingham? Does the stone still plague you?

WALSINGHAM: Aye, madam.

ELIZABETH: You swallow too much bad physic and arrest too many good physicians. God's death, I am almost your age, Walsingham, yet I can dance six galliards in a morning and enjoy a healthful sweat.

WALSINGHAM: Your Majesty's continuing good health is a joy to her people.

ELIZABETH: Nay, I, too, am sometimes sick. In another body no great a matter, but much in a princess. (*To Burghley.*) What says your physician?

BURGHLEY: That I am close to three score years and ten, and may expect the flesh to weaken.

ELIZABETH: Old man, I fear I have used you grievously.

BURGHLEY: Since your Majesty dismissed me from your council I have indeed been . . .

ELIZABETH: Yet you tricked me, both of you. I did not desire that wretched woman's death.

(*Burghley and Walsingham glance at each other.*)

Aye, I know your impudent thoughts! (*Plucks at her dress.*) Could I wear these weeds a month if I had desired her death?

WALSINGHAM (*imperceptible irony*): Your Majesty's grief is a model to Europe. The King of France is astonished that you still weep for her.

ELIZABETH: Little good his astonishment will do me. Not while you empty England's purse into the greedy palms of his Huguenots.

WALSINGHAM: Madam, I would have the Protestant cause triumphant, and you its greatest prince.

ELIZABETH: There is only one Jesus Christ, one Faith, all else is a dispute over titles.

WALSINGHAM: The King of Spain would not have your...

ELIZABETH: I'm not afraid of Philip! God's death I fear a mistake in my Latin more than I do him.

WALSINGHAM: Your Majesty's Latin is without fault.

ELIZABETH: How could you know? You've a poor hand for it. (*To Burghley.*) My Lord, you see I've come in penitence. To you, my spirit . . . (*To Walsingham.*) . . . and to you, my Moor. To ask you to sit in council again.

BURGHLEY: Madam, my legs are weak . . .

ELIZABETH: It's your good head I need, not your bad legs. Have your servants carry you, if they must. But

381

mark this, both of you, I have not forgotten that you contrived the death of that woman. (*Then innocently to Walsingham.*) You have received letters from Drake.

WALSINGHAM: Aye, madam. From the *Elizabeth Bonaventure* which he boarded at Plymouth last week.

ELIZABETH: Well?

WALSINGHAM: He said that the wind commanded him away, with six of your ships and four of his own.

ELIZABETH: Recall him.

WALSINGHAM: Madam, it is too late. He is at sea.

BURGHLEY: And upon your commission, madam.

WALSINGHAM: To work what malice he could upon the Spanish ships at Cadiz and Lisbon.

ELIZABETH: That was not my commission.

(*Burghley and Walsingham are too astonished to speak.*)

Am I not to be obeyed? Jesus, my father would have had your heads!

WALSINGHAM: Madam, the King of Spain is resolved to set his Enterprise against us this year. The only way to bridle his ambition is to strike at his ships before they sail.

ELIZABETH: You will recall Drake. I command you.

BURGHLEY: Madam, your Majesty knows that I have ever been your servant in your desire for peace. But the King of Spain must now come against us.

ELIZABETH: He has talked of his Enterprise for twenty years. Crowing cocks lay no eggs. Nothing is changed.

BURGHLEY: Madam, the death of the Queen of Scots has changed all.

WALSINGHAM: Majesty, Mary of Scotland bequeathed her crown to the King of Spain. And her false claim to yours.

ELIZABETH: Recall Francis Drake!

WALSINGHAM: Once at sea, your Majesty, he respects no orders but his own.

ELIZABETH: Then I'll hang the rogue above his own deck. If he sets foot on Spain we shall most assuredly have war.

BURGHLEY: Your Majesty's soldiers have been fighting in the Spanish Netherlands for two years.

ELIZABETH: Aye! It costs me a hundred thousand pounds a year to maintain Leicester's army there. And with that I must also stomach his impudent title of Governor. But no more. I've ordered him back to England I'm determined upon a truce with Parma and peace in the Netherlands.

WALSINGHAM: The Duke of Parma is a great captain, madam, and the Spanish cause prospers from his victories in the Low Countries. It's not his nature to think of peace while he's winning. Nor will he agree to anything that his uncle the King of Spain does not sanction.

ELIZABETH: Then you are confounded, Master Spy! For he's agreed to meet my emissaries at Bourbourg.

WALSINGHAM: He plays you for a dupe.

ELIZABETH (rising): Guard your tongue, sirrah!

WALSINGHAM: Madam, will you abandon the Dutch?

ELIZABETH: They'll meet Parma's emissaries with mine. I'll give them peace. And send them good English cloth instead of soldiers. (*To Burghley*.) My Lord, come soon to my council.

BURGHLEY: Your Majesty, I fear Walsingham is right. They'll deceive you if they can.

ELIZABETH: If we're honest with them, their deception will soon be exposed. So be my friend again.

BURGHLEY: God keep me to serve your Majesty.

ELIZABETH: Amen to that. (*Moves to the door and pauses*.) Touching the matter of Francis Drake, I know that even my command will not bring him back. But charge him upon his life . . . he's to enter no port of Spain, nor land a man upon it . . . Yet . . . if at sea he should chance upon an Indies fleet . . .

(*Walsingham bows, hiding a smile.*)

I would have him shed as little blood as the venture permits.

(*Elizabeth goes out with the lady-in-waiting. Walsingham stares at the closed door.*)

WALSINGHAM: Drake will be a week gone before the Privy Council signs the countermand. The fastest pinnace will not come up with him until he has done the work.

BURGHLEY (*a sigh*): This time I fear she will hang the fellow.

WALSINGHAM (*turning to him*): She will put her hand upon her heart honestly, and protest to Spain that he acted without her orders.

BURGHLEY: You suspect her of too much duplicity.

WALSINGHAM: No, my Lord, I charge her with stupidity. For she is set upon this peace with Parma.

BURGHLEY: There is a good sense in it, sir. The war has been a heavy burden upon our treasury.

WALSINGHAM: A war against the papists is a burden true men must gladly bear.

BURGHLEY: If your friend Drake burns Philip's ships we shall have papists enough about our ears.

WALSINGHAM: You were warm enough for the venture until she came this night. My Lord, I believe your value to the Queen has ever been that you follow her wandering wits like a faithful dog.

BURGHLEY: Take care, Walsingham, I am not yet a dotard.

WALSINGHAM: And I have been threatened by princes. (*Then a smile.*) My Lord, I would not quarrel with you. I would have you understand. To repair the hurt that Drake will do, Philip must purchase time by deluding the Queen with this mummery of peace in the Netherlands. And in that time we may woo her from it and persuade her to assemble her power on sea and land.

(*Cut to:*)

6

Interior, corridor, the Escurial. Day. May 1587.

Close up of the toy ship held in the hand of the boy prince. Pull back to see boy and nurse. She is holding his hand, as they walk down the corridor. They stop at the door to the King's rooms.

(*Cut to:*)

7

Interior, King's rooms, the Escurial. Day. May 1587.

The door opens and the nurse enters with the Prince. The three men already in the room look toward the door. Philip is sitting in his chair, papers in hand. Idiaquez is at the desk. Before them stands the Marquis of Santa Cruz, the King's Captain-General. Though an old, bald-headed man, his bearing is upright and military. His gentle eyes contradict the ferocity of his white, pointed beard, the upturned spikes of his full moustache. He bows stiffly to the Prince. When the nurse curtseys and leaves, the Prince walks across to his father. Philip holds him by the shoulders and kisses his forehead.

PHILIP: Good morning, my son. Sit with us. Listen. And remember what you may.

(Pan the Prince across to his stool. He sits on it, places the galleon on his knees and fingers its yards and rigging. He does not look at the men again. Cut to the three men looking into camera at the Prince. Philip is the first to take his eyes away.)

The boy is pleased with your gift, Santa Cruz. Nothing else has so occupied his mind.

(Santa Cruz bows shortly.)

I want one-hundred-and-fifty great ships. No more.

SANTA CRUZ: It is not enough, Sire.

PHILIP: With as many auxiliaries, dispatch-boats, picket-boats, zabras and fregatas.

SANTA CRUZ: Your Majesty, I could have such a fleet at sea within a month. But it would be ill-manned and ill-supplied.

(*A beat, then stubbornly.*)

And too little.

PHILIP: It may yet be too much for my purse.

SANTA CRUZ: Two years ago, Sire, when I proposed that your ships should invade England immediately . . . (*Stops.*)

PHILIP: Yes?

SANTA CRUZ: I received no reply from your Majesty.

(*Philip picks up paper from desk.*)

PHILIP: You asked for five hundred ships and two hundred barges. A hundred-thousand soldiers and seamen. Two million pounds of cheese, seventy thousand bushels of beans and rice, five million gallons of wine . . . et cetera, et cetera. I was perhaps struck dumb by the magnitude of your proposal, Don Alvaro. And do you remember the cost?

SANTA CRUZ: Four million ducats, your Majesty.

PHILIP: It was impossible.

SANTA CRUZ: Since the cost may now be twice that sum, and for half the force originally stated, may I suggest your Majesty abandons the Enterprise?

PHILIP: Don Alvaro, I do not think you are a coward . . .

(*Santa Cruz stiffens and places a hand on the hilt of his sword.*)

But you have been ill.

SANTA CRUZ: A fever. It is of no consequence, your Majesty.

387

PHILIP: Do you wish to surrender your commission as my Captain-General?

SANTA CRUZ: Your Majesty knows that if he so ordered I would sail against England with a single galleas.

PHILIP: Santa Cruz, do not debase yourself with such foolish bravado.

(*Santa Cruz bows an apology.*)

And be of good heart. I have accepted your proposals.

(*Santa Cruz brightens.*)

With some modifications, of course.

SANTA CRUZ (*heavily*): Yes, Sire.

PHILIP: My nephew Parma was of the same cautious mind as yourself, but I have persuaded him to take an army of thirty thousand men from the Netherlands to Kent, supported by your fleet. Since we may thus send less soldiers from Spain, we shall need no barges and fewer transports.

SANTA CRUZ: With your Majesty's permission . . .

PHILIP (*holding up a hand*): We may also rely upon the armed assistance of those English Catholics who are . . .

IDIAQUEZ: Your Majesty . . .

PHILIP: Do not interrupt me, Idiaquez. Doctor Allen tells me that a third, if not more, of Elizabeth's subjects will rise against her. We may expect them to supply us with provisions as well as men, and we can reduce our own supplies accordingly, from eight months to three.

SANTA CRUZ: Your Majesty is wrong.

PHILIP (*a long beat*): Wrong, Don Alvaro?

SANTA CRUZ: Mistaken, Sire. Your Majesty cannot

understand the great risk . . . the many difficulties that must attend a rendezvous between a land force and a fleet in enemy seas. A contrary wind . . . a lost day . . .

PHILIP: Yet you once proposed such a rendezvous with a French army. Why not now with Parma?

SANTA CRUZ: I asked for five hundred great vessels, Sire, and a seaborne army to make a landing should the French be unable to . . .

PHILIP: Have I not shown you that one hundred and fifty will suffice?

(*When Santa Cruz says nothing.*)

Of course I have. When may they sail?

SANTA CRUZ: After so many years of indecision, your Majesty's impatience is . . .

PHILIP: God is impatient, Don Alvaro, and we may not be his laggard servants. I've told the Pope that I shall be master of England by the end of October.

SANTA CRUZ (*a beat*): As your Majesty pleases.

PHILIP: Go then. Write to me daily. Count me ever your friend, Don Alvaro, but be gentle with my purse.

(*Santa Cruz takes a pace back, and bows stiffly.*)

SANTA CRUZ: God guard the Catholic person of your Majesty.

(*He leaves with his back straight. The King now contracts in his chair, his strength drained from him. He lowers his head and holds the handkerchief to his weeping eye.*)

IDIAQUEZ (*uneasily*): Majesty . . .?

PHILIP (*lifting his head*): It is nothing but the affliction in my eye. Tell the physician that he may bleed and purge me again this evening. (*And then.*) Idiaquez, do you know that my father warned me never to lose the friendship of England?

IDIAQUEZ: So you have told me, Sire.

PHILIP (*turning to the Prince*): My son!

(*The Prince looks up sharply from his toy, his face suddenly attentive. Cut back to Philip and Idiaquez.*)

(*Looking off to Prince.*) Because of the love I owe to my father I have patiently endured the insults and heresies of that island. I was once its King. I have always been its friend and have suffered its unkindness with humility. (*Looks away from the boy.*) I have always deserved the gratitude of Elizabeth. But for me, her sister would have taken her life. When I was urged to destroy her, I refused. Yet I may not boast of my tolerance, for Christ has asked no less of me.

(*Holds the handkerchief painfully to his eye again.*)

IDIAQUEZ: Sire, may I call the physician to you now?

PHILIP: His bleeding weakens me, and the purges cloud my mind. I must not waste the rest of the day upon my bed. You wished to speak when Santa Cruz was here?

IDIAQUEZ: Upon the matter of the English Catholics, Sire.

(*From now on the King does not look at Idiaquez, and he speaks his thoughts aloud.*)

PHILIP: His Holiness always writes of her with admiration, even as he urges her death upon me. He sends me a million crowns to drag her from her throne, yet calls her one of the greatest princes in Christendom. He speaks of her courage and my timidity, of her wit and my dull piety. We three are yoked together in love and hate, and my neck is galled with sores.

IDIAQUEZ (*persevering*): Your Majesty must put no trust in the advice given you by Doctor Allen and Father Robert.

PHILIP: I, too, have been dazzled by her brilliance, and I have scourged myself in penance for the sin of envy.

IDIAQUEZ: There can be no substantial help from the English Catholics.

PHILIP: God has scaled my poor eye with this affliction, yet he has revealed my duty and put an end to my cowardly patience. (*Turns slowly to Idiaquez.*) You are wrong, Idiaquez.

IDIAQUEZ: Your Majesty knows how strongly abhorrent an alien government is to the English. It unites all men in opposition, whatever their faith.

PHILIP: Idiaquez, we must look to God for favour in an enterprise so entirely his own.

IDIAQUEZ: Then we should acknowledge that favour. Your Majesty, where it is most evident. It is my opinion that it would be better to suspend the invasion of England and employ both the fleet and the army in the reduction of the Netherlands.

PHILIP: It is not the Dutch who rob my treasure fleets . . .

(*The door is abruptly opened and Santa Cruz enters woodenly, a paper tightly gripped in his hand.*)

Don Alvaro . . . ?

SANTA CRUZ (*holding out the paper*): From Cadiz . . . Drake . . .

(*As he drops on one knee before the King, cut to:*)

8

Interior, the castle of Sagres, Portugal. Night. May 1587.

*The door is burst open and John Tregannon and a
seaman, who have put their shoulders against it, half
fall into the small room. They are followed by Sir
Francis Drake. All three are accoutred for war, smoke-
blackened and bloody, swords in their hands. This was
the Governor's room, and floor and table are littered
with discarded papers and clothing. It is lit by the
flames of great fires outside, and there is the noise of
shouting, cheers, and sporadic musketry. Drake
sheathes his sword as he goes to the window, picking
up a wine carafe from the table. He drinks thirstily as
he looks out. The seaman stands guard at the door, and
Tregannon walks about the room, turning over the
litter with his sword.*

TREGANNON: God's blood, here was a Don who
departed in haste. What is this place, Master Francis?

DRAKE (*at window*): You were at the council, Tregannon. It's the castle of Sagres on the lee side of the cape.

TREGANNON: Aye, that I know ... (*Bends, finds a gold
chain among the papers, and quickly thrusts it inside
his doublet.*) But there was more.

DRAKE: It was once a school. Of seamanship. (*Tosses
the wine carafe to Tregannon.*) Founded by old Henry
the Navigator. Your feet are on holy ground, friend
John.

TREGANNON: I'd rather they stood on the streets of
Cadiz. (*Drinks.*)

DRAKE: Man, would you have me take four galleons
in among a hundred? And against shore batteries to
boot? (*To the seaman.*) Get below there, Jacob, and
tell Master Platt he's to burn all that will burn ...
Tregannon, here ...

(*Seaman leaves. When Tregannon reaches the window.*)

You set a torch to those storehouses?

TREGANNON: When we had overcome the Dons who . . .

DRAKE: What was in them?

TREGANNON: Meal, wine. Barrel staves for the most part, piled high as my main truck.

DRAKE: And yonder?

TREGANNON: A great hall of books . . .

DRAKE: Prince Henry's library . . . I'd as lief saved that . . . But no matter. (*Turns away toward the table.*) We've taught them more than they'd find in the old man's books.

(*Sits at the table, finds paper, ink and quill, and begins to write.*)

TREGANNON: They fought like lions to keep us from the barrel staves.

DRAKE: Without casks for biscuits and water, the greatest fleet is nothing. You know that, Tregannon.

TREGANNON: I know we had the Dons by the throat at Cadiz. If we'd set but one ship's company ashore . . .

DRAKE: Nay, John, when the wind dropped we'd have been hares in a gin. Man, you expect too much from the hand of God. In two days off the harbour mouth we sank or burned forty of the ships that came out to meet us, including their flagship.

TREGANNON: I expect the hand of God to have more gold in it.

DRAKE: You're a pirate, Tregannon.

TREGANNON (*a grin*): Then there's two of us in this room, Admiral.

(*As Drake writes on quickly.*)

If you're writing to our noble lady the Queen . . .

DRAKE: To Walsingham.

TREGANNON: Oh, that knave.

DRAKE (*looks up, coldly now*): My friend, Master Tregannon.

TREGANNON: God keep him, then. But tell him John Tregannon says we've lit a great lantern in her Majesty's name, and scotched the Dons forever.

DRAKE: Not yet. But we've made a happy beginning.

TREGANNON: Albeit one with more hard knocks than treasure. We can expect little gratitude from the Queen if we bring her no gold.

DRAKE: We've made her kingdom safe for this summer season. She'll thank us for that.

(*Cut to:*)

9

Interior, royal audience chamber, England. Day. June 1587.

Moving shot of Elizabeth and Essex, advancing into the audience chamber from the door. They pass along a line of bowing men . . . Burghley, Walsingham, Howard, three Dutch envoys and the speaker of the Commons. Essex walks a pace behind the Queen, a gentle smile on his lips. Elizabeth stops at the end of the line, before the Earl of Leicester.

ELIZABETH: My Lord of Leicester, are you afraid to show me your face?

(*Leicester straightens his back and looks at her. He is old and fat, a straggling moustache and beard on a bloated weary face.*)

LEICESTER: Only that I may be blinded by yours, madam.

ELIZABETH: Here's a bold liar!

LEICESTER: Madam, your modesty does not permit you to be ...

ELIZABETH: Don't try to cozen me, sir! And what do you know of modesty, your Excellency?

LEICESTER (*with spirit*): I refused greater titles than Governor which the Dutch would have thrust upon me.

ELIZABETH: And you'll strip yourself of that you accepted.

LEICESTER: Madam, I may not.

ELIZABETH: I command you.

LEICESTER (*a low voice*): Madam ... do not shame me so before these gentlemen.

ELIZABETH (*a beat, and then as she moves*): Burghley! You too, Walsingham!

(*Essex and Leicester: the young man smiles agreeably, almost insolently at the other. Leicester's face and tone are cold.*)

LEICESTER: How fares it with your mother?

ESSEX: Your lady wife is well.

LEICESTER: Commend me to her. (*A glance off.*) The Queen honours you, boy.

ESSEX: Upon your charity, my Lord. You could not have favoured me more had I been your own son.

ELIZABETH (*off*): Essex!

(*Essex bows shortly to Leicester and turns away. Group. The Queen sitting, Burghley and Walsingham standing before her. When Essex arrives he takes a place behind her chair.*)

ELIZABETH (*shaking a sheet of paper*): That rogue Drake has placed this Kingdom in jeopardy.

BURGHLEY: Madam, he did not receive your countermand before he attacked Cadiz.

ELIZABETH: I swore I would hang him and so I shall. Burghley, you will write to Parma and tell him, that upon my heart Drake acted without my authority, and against my wishes. Walsingham?

WALSINGHAM: Madam, if the Duke of Parma is as desirous of peace as your Majesty, and if he believes you to be as honest in intent as you hold him, then he will acquit you of blame in this matter.

ELIZABETH: You stepped through that answer like a barefoot child among nettles. Burghley, speak to me plainly.

BURGHLEY: Your Majesty, Parma will say and do what the King of Spain proposes.

ELIZABETH: That hermit . . . That tortured monk . . . (*She gnaws at the paper.*)

WALSINGHAM: Your Majesty . . . ?

(*As she looks up.*)

By the island of St Michael in the Azores, Drake came upon a great ship from the Indies, the San Felipe. Her treasure, which he brings you, is worth twice the cost of the fleet he took to Cadiz.

ELIZABETH (*the flicker of a smile*): Then I shall hang him with a silken rope instead of hemp.

WALSINGHAM (*encouraged*): He also sends your Majesty a warning.

ELIZABETH: He warns me!

WALSINGHAM: That he has but halted the monstrous power of Spain. That we should build ships and look to the coast of Sussex.

ELIZABETH: When I rode to my coronation an old man cried out from the crowd at the water-gate. He said he remembered King Harry the Eighth. It lifted my heart. But who will be happy to remember me if I challenge Philip and lose?

WALSINGHAM: The challenge has been made by Spain, madam. Who will remember England if you ignore it?

ELIZABETH (*a beat, then*): Are the Dutchmen here?

(*Walsingham turns, lifting a hand. The three Dutch envoys approach. Only one speaks.*)

I have read your petition against my desire to reach a truce with the Duke of Parma.

(*They bow.*)

And your impertinent demand that I should confirm the Earl of Leicester in his title of governor over you. What next, will you make the fellow your Prince?

ENVOY: Our country is a sovereign state, madam, and may surely choose to honour those who serve it well.

ELIZABETH: Your country, sir, is a sieve into which mine has poured much money and sifted little good.

ENVOY: Will your Majesty now surrender us to Spain?

ELIZABETH: Good man, your people are as dear to me as my own, but if I can save them both by peace will you have us fight more bloody battles?

ENVOY: Your Majesty's emissaries have assured Parma's that should he agree to a truce we will admit the authority of Rome.

ELIZABETH: Our Saviour Christ paid his tribute to the Romans.

ENVOY: And was delivered by them to the Cross.

ELIZABETH: God's death! Do Princes now take instruction from common men? You are less than honest with me, sir. You have issued a proclamation in your provinces . . . aye, I know of it . . . ordering no man to talk of peace with Spain. Will you order me so? Is this your gratitude?

ENVOY: Madam, such gratitude has two edges. For while we contest the Spaniards they may not cross the sea to you.

ELIZABETH: You're a bold petitioner, sir.

ENVOY: And I will be bolder, madam. Within a year you may regret the time you waste. Parma laughs at you.

(*Elizabeth rises, steps down and grasps the astonished envoy by the belt.*)

ELIZABETH: God's death, Master Burger, you need a Prince to teach you manners!

(*A beat, then a sudden change of mood and she releases him, she laughs and pets his cheek affectionately.*)

Go to fellow! Were you afraid of me?

ENVOY: Madam, I . . . I . . .

ELIZABETH: Get you gone. Speak your business to my Lord Burghley, but if I'm to see you again let me be treated with honour.

(*Camera returns with her to her chair.*)

Dismiss them all, Burghley, I would be alone.

(*Burghley and Walsingham retire from her, and as all but Essex leave the chamber, bowing:*)

Leicester . . . Stay!

(*Leicester halts by the door. Essex bends forward and, with his eyes on his stepfather, whispers in the Queen's ear. Lifting a hand quickly, but looking at Leicester, she boxes the young man's ear. Essex steps back, hand to the side of his head like a schoolboy.*)

Be off you impudent boy!

(*Essex goes, bowing to his stepfather, with extravagant mockery. Leicester and Elizabeth are alone, looking at each other across the wide chamber. Then he comes towards her quickly dropping on one knee and lifting the hem of her skirt, pressing it to his lips.*)

Get up, greybeard!

(*When he does not move.*)

Sirrah, get up! (*And then.*) Sweet Robin, I entreat you . . . (*But with bitterness as he rises.*) Your Excellency must stand before me as an equal.

399

LEICESTER: Since that title sticks in your throat, madam, you should know that I accepted it for love of you.

ELIZABETH: For love of yourself! And to blind your eyes to your wretched failures.

LEICESTER: Had you sent me the men I needed and the money I asked for, I would not have . . .

ELIZABETH: Jesus, will you dip your hand into my treasury whenever you choose?

LEICESTER: For a year I paid your soldiers from my own revenues!

ELIZABETH: Which you received from me. You whine for money and make widows and orphans!

LEICESTER: Your Majesty has forgotten that I saw my nephew Philip Sidney die at Zutphen.

ELIZABETH (*a beat*): Rob . . . Rob . . .

(*Impulsively she holds out a hand, which he kneels and kisses. And then, sadly.*)

Though all the world forsook me, I thought you'd be true.

LEICESTER: I would die at your feet.

ELIZABETH: What has that to do with it? Get up.

(*He rises, and with her head upon her hand she stares at him for a long beat.*)

It's a hard bargain, my Lord, when both parties are losers. Though I part with your love, you will make open and public resignation of the title given you by the Dutch.

(*He is stubbornly silent.*)

Robin, I am determined upon it.

(*Still he is silent.*)

I cannot treat honestly with Parma if I sustain you in
that office.

LEICESTER: Fore God, if that's all! The man's deluding you. Send me back against him, and I'll ...

ELIZABETH: I'm sending you to Bath.

LEICESTER: Madam ... ?

ELIZABETH: To take the waters. You've been ill.

LEICESTER: A fever. And the gout. But nothing that
may pre ...

ELIZABETH (*mocking*): I'll draw up a diet to reduce
that sagging flesh. Two ounces of meat a day, no more,
though the quality of it I leave to your judgment. On
festival days, the shoulder of a wren at noon, with the
leg for supper ...

LEICESTER: Madam, I beseech you. Assemble your
forces and ships in England, and send me back to the
Low Countries.

ELIZABETH: On Sundays you may have the twentieth
part of a pint of wine, but on ordinary days you will
drink nothing but the healing waters ...

LEICESTER: By God's death, you try my patience!

ELIZABETH (*fiercely*): You will not return to Flanders.

LEICESTER: I'll accept banishment to an Irish bog, if
you order it. But as I love you, do not trust Philip or
Parma ...

ELIZABETH: If I desire Walsingham's advice, I'll hear it from his lips not yours.

LEICESTER: I have not deserved this contempt.

ELIZABETH: Nor I your blustering. You will go where I command, leave me to govern this kingdom.

LEICESTER: How, madam? By playing cards with my pretty stepson?

ELIZABETH (*a controlled calm*): My Lord, do as I command you. Get you well. Your life is dear to me.

LEICESTER: And you destroy it by abandoning me.

ELIZABETH: Robin . . . Much is past. You and I are old . . .

LEICESTER: You are Gloriana. You are ageless.

ELIZABETH: We are mortal. Look in your glass, my Lord.

LEICESTER: Madam . . .

ELIZABETH (*turning her face from him*): You may go.

(*Leicester takes a pace back and bows. He walks away toward the door. Hold on Elizabeth and mix to:*)

10

Interior, King's rooms, Escurial. Day. July 1587.

Prince kneeling on the floor with his toy ship. Pan up from him to Philip, Idiaquez and Santa Cruz beyond. Santa Cruz looks ill and leans heavily on a stick. Philip is reading a paper, holding it close to his one good eye. At last he lowers the paper and dabs a handkerchief to the weeping cataract.

PHILIP: Twenty-four great vessels, the town of Lagos and the Castle of Sagres . . .

SANTA CRUZ: Your Majesty, Drake boasts that he destroyed forty ships.

PHILIP: Am I to be grateful for the difference?

SANTA CRUZ: No, Sire.

PHILIP: Or the loss of two hundred thousand ducats?

SANTA CRUZ: Majesty, we pursued him to the Azores . . .

PHILIP: Where he took the San Felipe.

SANTA CRUZ: Her crew were sick and we . . .

PHILIP: But the daring of the English, Don Alvaro, their daring . . . And that remarkable woman. Idiaquez, surely in all heretics there must be a dread of Heaven's displeasure, for that is the substance of all belief?

IDIAQUEZ: They are English heretics, Sire, with a church and heaven of their own creation.

PHILIP: Not all. How can Elizabeth defy the Church when a third of her people must rise against her?

IDIAQUEZ: If Your Majesty will appeal to the English Catholics, urge them to defend the Church, not to overthrow Elizabeth.

PHILIP: It is illogical to assume that the one does not involve the other.

IDIAQUEZ: Majesty, the English are by definition illogical.

PHILIP: You do not know them as I do. Elizabeth is

403

afraid of her people's discontent. Parma will beguile her with talk of peace. Meanwhile, he urges me to dispatch your fleet at once, Don Alvaro.

SANTA CRUZ: Majesty, it's impossible! The damage done by Drake . . . We have no seasoned wood for barrel staves . . .

PHILIP: My nephew tells me that all you need do is hold the Channel while his army crosses to Kent.

SANTA CRUZ: Sire . . . As it now stands, your fleet may not risk a long voyage.

PHILIP: I have told the Pope that you will reach the Channel before the first day of December.

SANTA CRUZ (*astonished*): In winter, your Majesty?

PHILIP: You've said that you cannot sail at once, and I agree. (*Begins to search among the papers before him.*)

SANTA CRUZ (*an impatient glance at the impassive Idiaquez*): Yet even so, your Majesty underestimates the damage done by Drake.

PHILIP (*finding the paper he wants*): We must take fourteen galleons from the Indies treasure fleets, and ten more from the Portuguese. We are buying merchantmen in Italy and the Baltic which we shall convert to warships.

SANTA CRUZ (*bitterly*): Has your Majesty some scheme for the rapid seasoning of the wood we shall need for new barrels?

PHILIP (*a beat*): Don Alvaro, I recall you once urged haste upon me.

SANTA CRUZ: And with the same devotion to your Majesty I now advise caution.

PHILIP: You are perhaps ill?

SANTA CRUZ: I wish I were in better health to serve you, Sire. But were I thirty years younger I would still advise you against a winter sailing.

PHILIP: Parma will land forty thousand men in Kent, to be supported by a rising of Scots and English Catholics. You wished to close the mouth of the Thames and land an army there.

SANTA CRUZ: I can do so in the spring, Sire. But your Majesty must permit me to carry more soldiers.

PHILIP: My nephew tells me that it will be enough if you seize the Isle of Wight and await his orders.

SANTA CRUZ: With a hundred miles and the English fleet between us.

PHILIP: There is no English fleet. Or are you thinking of the handful of ships that Drake brought to Cadiz?

(*As Santa Cruz says nothing.*)

Your poor health distresses me, Don Alvaro. I will send my physician to you.

(*As Santa Cruz bows mix to:*)

11

Interior, gallery, royal palace, England. Day. November 1587.

Drake advances down the corridor toward the door of the audience chamber, where two halberdiers stand. He pauses by the door, and from inside:

ELIZABETH (*off*): Burghley!

BURGHLEY (*off*): Madam?

ELIZABETH (*off*): Is there word from Ostend?

BURGHLEY (*off*): Aye, madam.

ELIZABETH (*off*): Are you keeping secrets from me, old man?

BURGHLEY (*off*): No, madam.

ELIZABETH (*off*): Then, the dispatch, sir, the dispatch . . .

(*Drake shrugs and moves to the door. A halberdier opens it for him. Cut to:*)

12

Interior audience chamber. Day. November 1587.

In the foreground, Walsingham and Howard turn to Drake as he enters.

Elizabeth stands beyond by the window with Burghley. She is reading a dispatch.

WALSINGHAM (*a whisper to Drake*): What news?

DRAKE: None.

WALSINGHAM: Have you ships at sea?

DRAKE: A pinnace off the Azores, and another by Corunna. But these November gales keep them . . .

(*Elizabeth has moved away from the window toward them. Burghley follows her as quickly as he can.*)

ELIZABETH: What are those rogues doing at Ostend? They've been there since mid-summer. Walsingham, how long does it take honest men to agree?

WALSINGHAM: If all parties are of one mind, your Majesty, an afternoon would be enough.

ELIZABETH: Parma and I are of one mind. Is that not enough?

WALSINGHAM: Unless he mocks your Majesty.

ELIZABETH: By God, I'll suffer no one to mock this poor old woman.

DRAKE: Nor I!

ELIZABETH (*savagely cold*): I thought I'd hanged you, sir.

BURGHLEY (*quickly*): Your Majesty . . . your repeated assurances to the Dutch perplex the Duke of Parma. He asks for time to con . . .

ELIZABETH: Does he expect me to abandon them entirely? God's death, I'll stand by them so long as I have a man left in my Kingdom to fight for me.

(*Drake whispers aside to Howard.*)

DRAKE: Bold talk from a peace-maker.

ELIZABETH: I can hear your quarter-deck whisper.

DRAKE: Will your Majesty hear more?

ELIZABETH: I did not command you hither.

DRAKE: I came upon the Lord Admiral's order.

ELIZABETH: Is the Armada at sea? Has Philip come to devour us?

DRAKE: Will your Majesty wait until he does? Put me to sea again, madam, and let me burn out their rat-holes while their masts are still bare.

407

HOWARD: Madam . . .

(*She turns to him.*)

Sir Francis gives good advice. If we are forced to meet the Armada at sea, it must be at great hazard to this Kingdom. We should prevent the Spanish from sailing.

ELIZABETH: And so says Raleigh. And Hawkins and Frobisher. Only my good spirit . . . (*A hand on Burghley's arm.*) . . . encourages my honest concern for peace.

HOWARD: Madam, there never was, since England was England, such a trick to deceive us as this talk of peace. I pray God we don't curse a white head and grey beard . . .

(*A glance at Burghley.*)

. . . for the mischief it may yet do us.

ELIZABETH: Take care, cousin, that my people do not curse you for a war that destroys them.

DRAKE: Better that than follow a Judas-goat to slaughter!

ELIZABETH: Master Pirate. I know how to distinguish between those who advise me in love and loyalty, and those who follow other fancies.

DRAKE: No man who loves you, madam, may be silent when your ships are unrigged, their guns in the Tower, and their seamen cutting throats for a crust. Aye, and no man would so order it!

ELIZABETH (*a long beat*): I know you'd as lief have a man on my throne. But God gave it to me. I am anointed by Him, and I'm answerable to none but Him. My councillors depend upon me, not I upon them. I hold their lives and heads in my hands. You're dust that I've moulded. You are empty breath without my voice.

(*Pan her away toward the door of her privy chamber. There she pauses and turns.*)

I'm not deceived by Spain. There are men like you who would have Philip set his power against me. But we are princes both, not common soil, and we know that we are bound by the will of God to preserve the peace of our Kingdoms.

(*Elizabeth grasps the door handle.*)

Don't think you can trick me. I've such cunning that if I were turned out of my Kingdom in my petticoat I would prosper anywhere in Christendom!

(*She goes out, slamming the door. Drake and Walsingham.*)

DRAKE: God's mercy, we'll need more than her petticoat! Is the woman bewitched?

WALSINGHAM: If not, we may so contrive it, Francis.

(*And as Drake turns to him in question:*)

Send me word if your watching pinnace sights so much as a Spanish fishing-boat.

(*Hold on his bleak smile and mix to:*)

13

Interior, Santa Cruz's chamber. Spain. Night. December 1587.

Santa Cruz. He lies in bed, his face gaunt with a killing illness. His room is small, a candle on a table by his bed, the sword, morion and breastplate on the floor.

The door is opened by a shadowy figure, Idiaquez. Santa Cruz turns his head weakly.

SANTA CRUZ: Who's there?

IDIAQUEZ: Juan de Idiaquez. (*Advances toward the bed and sits beside Santa Cruz.*) How fares it with your Excellency?

SANTA CRUZ: All is well. I am dying.

IDIAQUEZ: I am sorry to hear that.

SANTA CRUZ: Has spring come?

IDIAQUEZ (*puzzled*): It's not yet Christmas.

SANTA CRUZ: And I am not in London.

IDIAQUEZ: His Majesty sent me. To tell you that his love is constant.

SANTA CRUZ: One thing this day . . . another the next . . . Yet his love is constant.

IDIAQUEZ: You are his greatest captain.

SANTA CRUZ: Of a fleet I cannot get to sea.

IDIAQUEZ: His Majesty understands that your sickness . . .

SANTA CRUZ: The Enterprise is sick. It is doomed with me. (*He struggles to sit up.*)

IDIAQUEZ: Do not disturb yourself, Excellency.

SANTA CRUZ: He instructs me as if I were a cabin boy.

IDIAQUEZ: He is distressed that the fleet has not sailed as he ordered.

SANTA CRUZ: Rope ...

IDIAQUEZ: Excellency?

SANTA CRUZ: ... and canvas ... guns ... green staves ... His contractors cheat him ... His officers are thieves. They take ... they take the pay of deserters ...

IDIAQUEZ: When your Excellency has recovered, no doubt you will be able ...

SANTA CRUZ: Are you a physician?

IDIAQUEZ: What may I say to the King?

SANTA CRUZ: You're a clerk ... base-born ...

IDIAQUEZ: So it pleases men to tell me. (*Takes a sealed letter from inside his doublet and lays it beside the old man's hand.*) His Majesty's further instructions ...

SANTA CRUZ: A winter sailing ... madness ...

IDIAQUEZ: ... upon the storing of supplies, and the proper observance of your Christian duty when you are at sea.

SANTA CRUZ: At sea?

IDIAQUEZ: His Majesty now takes the Sacrament four times daily, in confidence that you will depart before the spring. What may I say to him?

(*Close up of Santa Cruz as he lifts himself weakly and stares, wild-eyed into camera.*)

SANTA CRUZ: Tell him that I have never been more eager to depart.

(*Hold on him and mix to:*)

411

14

Interior, gallery, royal palace, England. Day. December 1587.

Drake and Walsingham are walking together outside the door to the Queen's privy chamber. They are deep in a whispered conversation as they approach camera. As they pass the privy chamber door, it opens, and they turn. A man in a black gown comes out, scrolls of paper beneath his arm. He bobs a bow to them, and hurries away, turning a corner in the background. Drake draws Walsingham into a window alcove.

DRAKE: Who was that black raven?

WALSINGHAM: Her Majesty's astrologer.

DRAKE: We've been waiting upon him? I've seen the fellow before. A sennight ago at your lodgings.

WALSINGHAM: The divinations of Regiomontanus the mathematician, forecast the fall of empires in the coming year. Her Majesty is naturally concerned. Did you not hear the tumult in London?

DRAKE: Aye, a mob shouted at me. Asked me why I wasn't at sea when the Spanish were coming. Is this your doing?

WALSINGHAM: Tell me again. What report did your captain send?

DRAKE: Little enough. A galley out of Lisbon, watching him like a boy over an orchard wall. Will you make an Armada out of that?

WALSINGHAM: Parma has withdrawn his commissioners from Ostend. Upon some dispute over procedure. I'd not counted upon that happy accident, and I'm obliged to him.

DRAKE: I'll not pretend to understand what you're at, but what must I do?

WALSINGHAM: When we see the Queen you must say aye and nay in support of me. No more, but most solemnly.

(*Another angle: taking in the door to the privy chamber beyond. It opens and Burghley steps out.*)

BURGHLEY: Gentlemen . . .

WALSINGHAM: Remember, Francis . . . Most solemnly.

(*They move toward Burghley. Cut to:*)

15

Interior, Queen's privy chamber, England. Day.
December 1587.

Elizabeth is standing by a table upon which there is an astrological globe, and charts of the same. She holds a horoscope, and seems shaken and unnerved.

BURGHLEY (*off*): Madam . . .

(*She turns. Drake and Walsingham enter, bow, and advance. With another frowning glance at the horoscope she drops it on the table.*)

ELIZABETH: Tell me bluntly. Is it true?

WALSINGHAM: Your Majesty, my information is no better than the men who send it to me. But since they do so at the risk of their own lives . . .

ELIZABETH: What men? Where?

WALSINGHAM: In Brussels. And Paris. As to the men, your Majesty will understand . . . (*An apologetic shrug.*)

413

ELIZABETH: The Armada is to sail at Christmas?

WALSINGHAM: If it's not already at sea. One of Drake's captains has sighted vessels under sail from Lisbon.

(*Drake most solemnly as Elizabeth turns to him.*)

DRAKE: Aye, madam.

ELIZABETH: And what was your captain doing there?

WALSINGHAM (*quickly*): Your Majesty has heard that Parma has withdrawn his commissioners from Ostend?

ELIZABETH (*still to Drake*): Could the fellow be mistaken?

DRAKE (*most solemnly*): Nay, madam.

ELIZABETH (*to Walsingham*): They were recalled to receive his instructions.

WALSINGHAM: Aye, madam, but what instructions?

(*Elizabeth half-turns to the table, fingering the papers on it.*)

Your Majesty is aware that since the victory of the Huguenots at Coutras, the French . . .

BURGHLEY (*worried*): Walsingham . . .

WALSINGHAM: My lord?

BURGHLEY: Are you saying that France is also sending an army against us?

WALSINGHAM: That I believe the Duke of Guise will obey his paymaster the King of Spain.

(*Elizabeth turning and reading from a paper she holds.*)

ELIZABETH: '*Octavagesimus octavus mirabilis annus ingruet et secum tristia sata trahet. Si non in totum terra fretumque ruant . . .*'

(*Drake and Walsingham as the former frowns an enquiry.*)

WALSINGHAM (*almost mouthing the word*): Regiomontanus . . .

(*Group.*)

BURGHLEY (*gently*): Madam, the prophecy is cryptic nonsense.

ELIZABETH: Upon which ambitious princes may justify their designs. (*Sharply to Drake*). When can the fleet be mobilized?

DRAKE (*a beat, then quickly*): John Hawkins will get them to sea in fourteen days. That is, men of war. As for provisioning, I cannot say how . . .

ELIZABETH: Let them sail with empty bellies if they must.

DRAKE: Now God be thanked!

ELIZABETH: Is the Speaker here?

BURGHLEY: Aye, madam.

(*Pan Elizabeth away as she strides toward the doors of the audience chamber. The others follow. Cut to:*)

16

Interior, audience chamber, England. Day. December 1587.

Full shot of doors as Elizabeth opens them from beyond with a sweep of both arms. Pan her across to the windows where the Speaker of the Commons is waiting. While he is still bent in a bow.

ELIZABETH: Master Speaker, will the Commons vote me supplies?

(*The Speaker rises, astonished.*)

SPEAKER: Madam, they must decide that in debate. I'm not empowered to . . .

ELIZABETH: They'll waste no time in idle debate, but vote me the supplies I need to defend this realm.

SPEAKER: Madam, may they have no liberty of speech?

ELIZABETH: None that allows every man to release whatever vapours come into his brain.

SPEAKER (*a protest*): No, madam . . .

ELIZABETH: No, sir. Their liberty of speech goes no further than the freedom to say aye or nay.

SPEAKER: Majesty, a bill to vote supp . . .

ELIZABETH: I have power to dissolve parliaments, sir!

SPEAKER: Madam, will you coerce them?

ELIZABETH: God's death, will they coerce me? Burghley!

(*Burghley appears beside them.*)

Tell this malapert fellow his duty.

BURGHLEY: Your Majesty's Commons are her loyal servants . . .

ELIZABETH: Nay . . . (*Turns to Speaker.*) Arrogant! And presumptuous! Hark ye, sir . . . though you know it well enough . . . I'm in parlous debt. I have but £250,000 a year from my revenues, to maintain my dignity and my servants, to support my government and play purse-holder to Protestant Europe. A German prince has more. I've a sovereign's right to call upon you for taxation.

SPEAKER (*unhappily*): Your Majesty knows that such taxation may be levied for her household charges only.

ELIZABETH: Dear man, all England is my household!

BURGHLEY: Madam . . . until today we've been set upon peace, and to your Commons' joy. The Speaker cannot say how matters will go now that we may have war.

(*Elizabeth a sudden change to winning helplessness.*)

ELIZABETH: Good Master Speaker . . . (*Lays a hand on his arm.*) The Spaniards are come against this country and our church. It's not of my choosing, but if the Commons will not support me I shall go out alone to meet my enemies, sword in hand.

SPEAKER: Madam, I did but say that the Commons must debate the matter, not that they would refuse you.

ELIZABETH: Then I am content, my friend. (*A beat, she turns to Burghley sharply, cutting off the smile.*) See to it, my Lord. (*Moves toward the door of the privy chamber, pauses, a beat.*) Send word to Leicester. Tell him to come to London as my Lieutenant-general.

(*She enters the privy chamber. Drake and Walsingham. In the background by the window, Burghley confers with the Speaker.*)

DRAKE: A little magicking with the stars . . . an obedient mob . . . a careful threat and a bold lie. I'm your humble admirer.

WALSINGHAM: Pray the Spanish come, Francis. For if they don't, this time, I doubt we can cry wolf again.

(*Mix to:*)

417

17

Interior, the King's rooms, the Escurial. Day. February 1588.

Philip sits on the edge of his bed in the inner room in his nightshirt, and there is now a bandage over the cataract in his eye. He is reaching for a phial of colourless liquid, he drinks a little of it and grimaces.

IDIAQUEZ (*off*): Your Majesty . . .

(*Philip looks up into camera. Idiaquez stands in the doorway.*)

The Duke of Medina Sidonia, Sire.

(*Philip nods, and Idiaquez turns to the outer room, inclining his head in invitation. Medina Sidonia enters, a middle-sized man, neat and small-boned, with a sensitive and melancholy face. He bows.*)

MEDINA SIDONIA: May God protect the Catholic person of your Majesty.

PHILIP: You've heard that Santa Cruz is dead?

MEDINA SIDONIA: A great loss to your Majesty, and to Spain.

PHILIP: God is merciful. (*As if to himself.*) Always more time . . . more money . . . more ships . . . (*Looks up*). Don Alonso, you will now be my Captain-General of the Ocean sea.

MEDINA SIDONIA (*astonished*): I, your Majesty . . . ?

PHILIP (*to Idiaquez*): Has the physician been called?

IDIAQUEZ: Yes, Sire.

PHILIP: Why are you surprised, Don Alonso?

MEDINA SIDONIA: I'm your Captain-General of Andalusia, Sire. I'm a soldier.

PHILIP: You're not ambitious. Neither headstrong nor quarrelsome.

MEDINA SIDONIA: But most unfit . . .

PHILIP: You've led a blameless life. No man will think you take the office for profit.

MEDINA SIDONIA: Sire, there are many better qualified . . .

PHILIP: You're a devout son of the Church, and your house is the most ancient in Castille. Who can take offence?

MEDINA SIDONIA: Majesty, hear me first.

PHILIP (a gentle sigh): As you will.

MEDINA SIDONIA: My health would not be equal to such a voyage.

PHILIP: One of my physicians will accompany you.

MEDINA SIDONIA: Though I'm a soldier, I've fought no battles. I've no experience of the sea.

PHILIP: God will direct you to victory, Don Alonso, for this is a crusade in His name. As for the sea, it is but a wider road than we travel on land.

MEDINA SIDONIA: I know nothing of what Santa Cruz decided.

PHILIP: I am the architect of the Enterprise. I shall instruct you.

MEDINA SIDONIA (flailing): Majesty, I cannot spend a

419

real of my own in your service. My family is burdened with debt, nine hundred thousand ducats . . .

PHILIP (*chill*): I am not appointing a money-lender.

MEDINA SIDONIA (*wildly now*): Sire . . . The Adelantado Major of Castille is a much better soldier . . . a good Christian, I swear . . .

PHILIP: Your modesty confirms my judgment. An arrogant commander would provoke jealous officers to spiteful indicipline. And your lack of conceit persuades me that you will obey me implicitly.

MEDINA SIDONIA (*a last attempt*): Majesty . . . as your Captain-General of Andalusia I was unable to prevent Drake's landing on . . .

PHILIP: That was the fault of Santa Cruz. You will take the commission, Don Alonso. And for love of me.

(*The interview is over. Medina Sidonia bows in submission. Philip places a hand gently on his bandaged eye.*)

Idiaquez, tell the physician to make haste. And inform Father Diego that I shall take the Sacrament again at noon.

(*Idiaquez and Medina Sidonia retire to the outer room. Cut to outer room as they enter. Idiaquez crosses to his desk, where he brushes a hand across a litter of papers and maps.*)

IDIAQUEZ: Your Excellency may care to begin with these reports from Lisbon and Cadiz.

MEDINA SIDONIA: Why could he not leave me to my orange groves?

IDIAQUEZ: His Majesty wishes the Armada to sail

before mid-summer at the latest. The Duke of Parma believes he'll be able to embark his . . .

MEDINA SIDONIA: I'm always seasick. I always catch cold at sea!

(*Hold on him and mix to:*)

18

Interior, the Queen's privy chamber, England. Day. February 1588

Long shot of Elizabeth and Essex sitting by the window, beyond which snow is falling. They are playing cards, the soft sound of their intimate laughter. Burghley sits anxiously in the foreground by the door, staring at them. He rises as the door opens and Walsingham enters. The Queen looks toward him and lays down her cards. She rises and advances, Essex following leisurely.

ELIZABETH: You've come at last, sir.

WALSINGHAM: Immediately, madam, upon your summons.

ELIZABETH: Which I sent ten days ago.

WALSINGHAM: I've been in the country, your Majesty, and your summ . . .

ELIZABETH: Are we conquered? Are the Spanish in London? You duped me, sir!

WALSINGHAM: No, madam, upon my honour.

ELIZABETH: A plague on your honour! You've not enough to cover a flea. Two months since, upon your information, I mobilized the fleet and the militia. I

421

ordered ship money from my ports and supplies from the Commons. My chested treasure is all but empty, and idle soldiers bully my honest subjects. You've been too clever this time, Master Spy!

(*Essex laughs softly, and Walsingham looks at him coldly.*)

WALSINGHAM: If your Majesty will listen to my . . .

ELIZABETH: Listen to what? More lying tales about a fleet that's still in harbour, and God knows may never sail.

WALSINGHAM (*boldly*): It will sail, madam.

ELIZABETH: Under a dead admiral? Or his successor, that orange-grower, who appears to be more dead than alive?

WALSINGHAM: Madam . . .

ELIZABETH: I'll school you in simple truths, sir. My merchant adventurers wish to use the ports of the New World. My weavers and clothiers want the markets of the Rhine. I'm not only a queen, Walsingham, I'm a tanner and a tinsmith, a collier and a shepherd. How will my trades prosper if you have your war with Spain? (*Turns.*) My Lord . . .

BURGHLEY: Madam?

ELIZABETH: The fleet is to be withdrawn. Hawkins may watch with four ships if he wishes. But no more, the rest will lie up. Remove their guns to the Tower, and dismiss their wasteful crews from my charge.

WALSINGHAM: Madam, I must warn you that Philip . . .

ELIZABETH: No, sir, you must not. You must hold your rattling tongue, lest I have my hangman pluck it out. (*To Burghley.*) Have you written to Parma?

BURGHLEY: Aye, madam. And I've prepared your instructions for new commissioners to meet his agents.

ELIZABETH: Will he agree?

BURGHLEY: I'm confident of it, madam. As I now believe we may trust his good intentions.

WALSINGHAM: My Lord!

BURGHLEY: Sir Francis, a cool head best serves her Majesty at this time.

WALSINGHAM: And none is cooler than mine, for it's chilled by fear for her safety. (*Turns to the Queen.*) Madam, Philip grasps at your crown. All else he proposes is a game of Hoodman Blind.

ELIZABETH: I'll believe that, sir, when I have proof of his malice toward my person. So far, you have discovered none.

(*She moves away toward the card table in background. With an amused smile at Burghley and Walsingham, Essex follows. Mix to:*)

19

Interior, the King's rooms, the Escurial. Night. April 1588.

Philip sits in the outer room. Though he no longer wears the bandage, he dabs frequently at his eye with a handkerchief. He looks weary and ill, more gaunt still in the light of the candle beside him. He is wrapped in a great cloak. As the shot opens he is passing his tongue along his lips, as if his words need moistening before they can be spoken.

PHILIP: What is the title of Doctor Allen's book?

(*Three shot of Philip, Idiaquez and Robert Parsons who stand before them, holding a bound tract. Idiaquez whispers to the King.*)

Of course, he is a Cardinal now.

PARSONS: Yes, your Majesty. He has entitled the work 'An Admonition of the Nobility and People of England'.

(*Philip reaches out a hand and takes the tract from Parsons.*)

PHILIP: Will they be permitted to read it?

PARSONS: It has been printed in Antwerp, your Majesty, but it's already circulating privately in England.

(*Philip opens the tract, squinting at it as he holds it close to his eyes, leaning toward the candle.*)

PHILIP: And its apologia?

PARSONS: That His Holiness has confirmed the declaration by Pius V in respect of Elizabeth's bastardy, and has re-issued the sentence of excommunication upon her as a usurper and an abominable heretic.

PHILIP: You hear, Idiaquez? Go on, Father Robert. What is its argument?

PARSONS: Most cogent, Sire. The deposition of Elizabeth will be right in natural law because she is a tyrant, and in divine law because she is a heretic.

PHILIP: Good. And then?

PARSONS: It sets forth the instructions of his Holiness, that no Englishmen need obey or defend her, but must be ready to join with your Majesty's forces in deposing her and restoring the Catholic Church. Only thus can they save their own and their children's souls.

PHILIP: You've read it, Idiaquez?

IDIAQUEZ: I have, your Majesty. I would not dispute its argument or its theology. But by its gutter vituperation of Elizabeth's person it may have a contrary effect to that which his Eminence intends.

(*Philip shakes his head.*)

PHILIP: You are wrong, Idiaquez. You are always wrong about the English. Father Robert, tell his Eminence that I am pleased with what he has written, and that I wish this to be known in England. (*He holds out the tract to Parsons. Cut to:*)

20

Interior, audience chamber/privy chamber, royal palace, England. Day. May 1588.

Close shot of a hand taking the tract. Two shot Walsingham and Burghley, who is returning the tract to the Secretary of State.

BURGHLEY: Her Majesty has seen this scurrilous work?

(*In the background, closer to the door of the Queen's privy chamber stand Howard, Drake, and Leicester.*)

WALSINGHAM: She is reading it now.

(*Elizabeth shouts from the privy chamber.*)

ELIZABETH (*off*): God's death!

WALSINGHAM: As you can hear.

BURGHLEY: It's a work of poor scholarship. I thought better of William Allen.

ELIZABETH (*off*): Jesu . . . the rogue!

BURGHLEY: Are many copies at large?

WALSINGHAM: Allen's priests carry them like rats transport fleas.

BURGHLEY (*unhappily*): I would I were at home today. First the news that Parma has abandoned the thought of a treaty, and now this ... this ...

WALSINGHAM: My Lord, a cool head will best serve your inflamed choler.

ELIZABETH (*off*): Enough!

(*Something strikes the door inside the privy chamber. It opens and a lady-in-waiting skitters out. As she picks up a copy of the tract, which the Queen threw at the door, Elizabeth follows, snatching it away and waving as she advances on Walsingham.*)

Unjust usurper am I—

(*She swings away before she reaches him, pacing the chamber and beating open the pages of the tract with her hand.*)

Depraved and accursed . . . incestuous bastard . . . begotten in sin . . . unspeakable lusts . . . shame of my sex . . . abuser of my body . . . a poisonous calamity . . . spawn of an infamous courtesan . . .

(*Close shot Walsingham and Burghley.*)

WALSINGHAM (*a whisper*): God be thanked. I'd not hoped for so much passion.

(*Elizabeth finally throws herself into her chair, her face black, her chin on her fist. A long beat while all wait, and then:*)

ELIZABETH: Burghley!

(*As he approaches her cautiously she stares at him. Then the cloud passes and her face is calm, her voice sad and gentle.*)

My Lord, I pray your forgiveness. In my anger with that billingsgate I forgot your wretched grief. Your gentle daughter Anne . . . a sweet lady . . . her death sore wounded me, my spirit.

BURGHLEY (*falling on his knees*): Madam!

ELIZABETH: Nay, old man, get up. All are equal in sorrow.

(*She helps him with a hand, and then clears her mind of the matter, returning to business, but calm.*)

Gentlemen . . .

(*They all come before her.*)

Well, Walsingham, now I have the proof I defied you to discover. Jesu, it could not have been more damnably done had you contrived it yourself.

(*Walsingham bows with an oblique smile.*)

They've played me false. Parma and Philip. So be it. Now my eyes are opened. With God's help, I'll strike those braggarts down.

(*Two shot Drake and Howard.*)

DRAKE (*a whisper*): And with ours.

(*Full group.*)

ELIZABETH: Are there truly men who will obey the Pope in this?

WALSINGHAM: Your Majesty, you have a list of those

recusants you may suspect. Take up their leaders, hang
a few and set others in the Tower.

HOWARD: Madam, it'll be hard for a loyal Englishman
to face your enemies if he fears his house may be
burned behind his back.

BURGHLEY: No, madam, confine some to their houses,
if you wish, and deprive them of horses and arms.

WALSINGHAM: Your Majesty, now's a moment for a
hempen lesson.

BURGHLEY: Madam, that billingsgate as you rightly
name it, could work well in your favour. While Catholic
Englishmen may oppose our church they would not
exchange you for Spanish rule. Tread softly, your
Majesty, and you'll travel well.

ELIZABETH: I'll tread between the pair of you. Take up
those you suspect most, Walsingham, but no hanging.
And let it be known what cruelties the Spanish work.
Have men see that if I fall they will come down with
me and England.

DRAKE: Madam ...

(*As she turns to him.*)

How shall we fight?

ELIZABETH: I must tell *you*?

HOWARD: Your Majesty, it's the opinion of your commanders that you should permit them to take the fleet
to the coast of Spain ...

ELIZABETH: And leave England defenceless?

DRAKE: 'Fore God, against whom? The enemy is there.

ELIZABETH: And in Flanders.

DRAKE: Barges! Your Majesty has been listening to landsmen.

ELIZABETH: I've listened to men who love me as dearly as you, Francis Drake, and who make less noise about their valour.

(*And then:*)

Nay, I'll not be churlish. Fight where you will, though it's against my judgment. (*She rises and moves off stopping by Howard.*) Cousin Howard, you and your officers were born for the preservation of your country. (*She moves to the door of her privy chamber, turns back, and in a resounding voice.*) Set my ships and armies in proper order. See to it, my Lords!

(*Restraining her lady-in-waiting by a touch of her hand, she enters the privy chamber alone. Cut to:*)

21

Interior, Queen's privy chamber, England. Day. May 1588.

Elizabeth enters, closing the door behind her, move with her to the window, which she opens. The sweet noise of spring birds. Sunlight falls into the room. A beat as she looks out, then move with her to a prie-dieu. She kneels. For a moment her head is bent, then move in to close shot as she looks up over clasped hands.

ELIZABETH (*a bold, strong voice*): I acknowledge, oh my King, without Thee my throne is unstable, my Kingdom weak, and my life uncertain. Create therefore in me, oh Lord, a new heart and so renew my spirit. Defend me and my people against all my enemies, who are enemies of truth and exalt themselves against Thy Christ . . .

(*Cut to:*)

429

22

Interior, King's rooms, the Escurial. Day. May 1588.

Philip—his head and shoulders are bent.

PHILIP: . . . in whose blood and passion Thy children are saved. Scourge this sinner for his envious heart, his cowardly spirit and miserable frailty. Give that triumph to my ships and armies which will preserve Thy true Church and glorify Thy name. Comfort me with Thy protection and strengthen me with Thy grace . . .

(Track back slowly to the outer room, fading sound. Philip is seen kneeling on the floor by his bed. Hold, as the sound of his voice fades, on the Infante's toy galleon. It lies on its side on the floor by an open book in the outer room. Cut to Idiaquez, Medina Sidonia, and Luis Cabrera de Cordoba, a young emissary from the Netherlands who is leaning against the wall with his arms folded. Idiaquez is working on papers at his desk. But Medina Sidonia stands apart and erect, nervously fingering the hilt of his sword. Then:)

MEDINA SIDONIA: Idiaquez . . .

(Idiaquez looks up slowly then sharply to his right. Cordoba straightens and bows. Another angle as Philip enters and moves to his chair.)

PHILIP: Don Alonso . . . Don Luis . . . (*He sits, looks at Medina Sidonia.*)

MEDINA SIDONIA: Your Majesty, in two months since I accepted your commission I have come to terms with my conscience and . . .

PHILIP: You answer to God for your conscience, Don Alonso, and to me for my fleet. When will it sail?

MEDINA SIDONIA: Within the week, as your Majesty

commands. One hundred and thirty vessels and twenty-five hundred guns. Thirty thousand seamen and soldiers, of whom two-thirds are Italians and Portuguese . . .

PHILIP: I know the listing, Don Alonso.

MEDINA SIDONIA: Sire, many of the seamen are in fact poor farmers and craftsmen impressed into your . . .

PHILIP: I've chosen the squadron commanders for their skill and experience. It is enough.

MEDINA SIDONIA: Yes, your Majesty, and I fancy that I have myself learnt much about the sea and its . . .

PHILIP: From the highest to the lowest you are to understand the holiness of your mission. I charge you, all men are to abstain from profane oaths . . .

(*Medina Sidonia bows.*)

No common whores are to board the vessels. Each morning at sunrise the ships' boys will sing 'Good morrow' at the foot of the mainmast, and at sunset, Ave Maria. Remember each holy day, and the watchwords, appointed for each day, Jesus, the Holy Ghost, and so on. How many holy friars have you aboard?

MEDINA SIDONIA: Two hundred, Majesty, but the seamen complain . . .

PHILIP: The English will endeavour to engage you at a distance. They have better gunners. So if you must meet them, for love of me do so in close engagement. If you fall in with Drake beyond my coasts ignore him.

MEDINA SIDONIA: Your Majesty told me that I should . . .

PHILIP: Sail straight to Cape Margate, and thence to

431

the mouth of the Thames, and there hold yourself ready for the arrival of the Duke of Parma.

MEDINA SIDONIA: Your Majesty's orders last week told me to seek anchorage off the Flanders coast to escort the Duke ...

CORDOBA: Majesty ...

PHILIP: A moment, Cordoba. Are you confused, Don Alonso?

MEDINA SIDONIA: Indeed, Sire, my poor wits are perhaps ...

CORDOBA: Majesty, I must speak ...

PHILIP (*sharply*): Don Luis!

(*Cordoba bows submissively.*)

Don Alonso, should the Duke of Parma be unable to attack, you may land upon the Isle of Wight.

MEDINA SIDONIA (*his face showing his growing confusion*): Your Majesty expressly forbade me to attack the island.

PHILIP: On the eastward run, but if at Cape Margate you learn that Parma may not come, return from thence to Wight. Idiaquez ...

(*He nods towards a thick pile of papers which Idiaquez hands to Medina Sidonia.*)

Those are your sailing instructions. Mark them well.

(*His arms full of papers, Medina Sidonia bows.*)

The fleet is to sail in six squadrons, under the name of

Portugal, Castille, Andalusia and so on. But when you engage they are to draw into the formation I have devised.

(*Medina Sidonia, another awkward bow.*)

Trust in your commanders Don Pedro de Valdez and Don Juan de Recalde, who are devout and honest men.

MEDINA SIDONIA: Majesty.

PHILIP: There will be a high mass in the Cathedral of Lisbon, and the Archbishop will bless your ships as they leave the Tagus.

MEDINA SIDONIA: Majesty, touching upon these orders . . .

PHILIP: Are they not clear? After twenty years can I have made some mistake, Don Alonso?

MEDINA SIDONIA (*too confused to answer that*): I am your Majesty's servant in all things.

PHILIP: Then go quickly to Lisbon, my good friend. God is with you.

(*Medina Sidonia bows again and backs towards the door. Something crunches beneath his foot. He halts and looks down. High angle, the toy ship crushed beneath his foot. Close up of Medina Sidonia as he looks up into camera, his face full of alarm at what must be an omen. He turns quickly and leaves. Philip rises painfully and picks up the toy. As he returns to his chair holding it:*)

What says my nephew?

CORDOBA: Your Majesty, the Duke of Parma wishes you to know that the enemy is aware of your intentions . . .

PHILIP: Of course.

433

CORDOBA: And earnestly advises your Majesty to make the Armada strong enough to secure landing without his assistance, should that be difficult.

PHILIP: Why should it be difficult, young man?

CORDOBA: Sire, forty English vessels lie off the Low Countries . . .

PHILIP: Don Alonso has instructions to disperse them if necessary, and meet with my nephew at Dunkirk.

CORDOBA: Impossible!

(*A beat.*)

In my opinion, Sire.

PHILIP: Be good enough to tell me why I should consider your opinion.

CORDOBA: Shoal water, Sire.

PHILIP: Shoal water? Idiaquez . . .

(*Idiaquez hands him a map at which he peers.*)

CORDOBA: Several leagues of it in front of Dunkirk. The Armada galleons draw twenty-five or thirty feet, and they'll not get far enough inshore to protect the barges.

PHILIP: It's not marked.

CORDOBA: Yet it's there.

PHILIP: Curb your insolent spirit, Don Luis . . . The Armada will lie off these shoals until the barges come out.

CORDOBA: Or be driven aground by false winds, your Majesty. Or watch English ships of shallow draught get between them and the shore.

PHILIP: I cannot change the instructions I have given to Don Alonso.

CORDOBA: Then since the junction between the Duke's barges and the Armada is the whole point of the Enterprise, and since such a meeting is impossible, your Majesty should abandon the scheme now and save money and lives.

PHILIP (*icy*): Is that your opinion, too, or is it my nephew's advice!

CORDOBA (*stiffly*): Sire, the Duke of Parma instructed me to speak boldly to your Majesty.

PHILIP: And so you have done. Young man, do you know what Don Juan de Recalde replied when he was asked if the Armada would triumph?

CORDOBA: No, Sire.

PHILIP: That however cunning and expert the English may be, and however great their advantage, God is our strength. Therefore he would sail in the confident hope of a miracle.

CORDOBA: Your Majesty, Don Juan is renowned for his wit.

(*As Cordoba bows, cut to:*)

23

Interior, room at a Plymouth inn. Night. Late June 1588.

Drake enters and crosses to the table where Howard is at work by the light of a lantern. Drake sits and pours himself a glass of wine.

DRAKE: Tom Fleming's at sea with the tide in the

Golden Hind. I've known better weather at Plymouth for a sailing.

HOWARD: How far have you ordered his . . .

DRAKE: As far south as the wind takes him. He'll put about when he sights their topsails.

HOWARD: They're long in coming . . . six weeks. God's hand is against them.

DRAKE: Then it's not for us either. The same foul gales that hold them back keep us from attacking them on their own coast.

HOWARD (*passing a sheet of paper*): We match their strength, Francis, in numbers, though we're grievous small in size.

DRAKE (*scarcely looking at the paper*): I've seen puny English hounds pull down a Spanish bull by the nose. (*Laughs.*) That orange grower . . . their commander . . . had never set foot on a ship of war.

HOWARD: Nor had I, sir, until the Queen gave me this office.

DRAKE (*owlishly innocent*): I' faith, that's true! My Lord, what shall we do?

HOWARD: What would you do, if I did not leave so much to you and Hawkins?

DRAKE: Why, my Lord, for the love of England I might pluck you from that chair. Sweet Jesus, there's a treasonable thought.

HOWARD: If they come before the wind, Francis, will they not have the advantage of us?

DRAKE: You're learning seamanship, my Lord. Here's more. We'll weather it out to sea, at dusk God willing,

12. Queen Elizabeth aged 55, on the eve of the Armada against England (*The Enterprise of England*).

13. Elizabeth and the ill and ageing Leicester in his tent at Tilbury (*The Enterprise of England*).

14. Elizabeth with Drake, Vice-Admiral to Lord Howard (John Woodvine); Lord Howard of Effingham, Lord High Admiral (Peter Howell); Leicester, Lieutenant-General; Burghley, Lord Treasurer (Ronald Hines); and Walsingham, Secretary of State (Stephen Murray) planning the defence of England (*The Enterprise of England*).

and come to windward of them at dawn. Hold them against a lee shore, albeit our own. But, my Lord, we must fight as soon as they're sighted, and all the way.

HOWARD : I've no other wish.

DRAKE : God be thanked the Queen has such a kins-man.

(*Cut to:*)

24

Interior, the King's rooms, the Escurial. Day. July 1588.

Two shot. Philip and Idiaquez. The King is reading a letter, holding it close to one eye. The other is covered by the handkerchief he holds.

PHILIP : Don Alonso writes an abominable hand. Where was it written?

IDIAQUEZ : At Corunna, Sire.

PHILIP : This month? July?

IDIAQUEZ : Yes, Sire.

PHILIP : So long? Why is he still there?

IDIAQUEZ : He was driven back by gales, your Majesty, and may not sail until fairer weather.

PHILIP (*passing the letter back, and turning*): Has it come?

(*Cordoba stands before them, travel-stained.*)

CORDOBA : The day I left Corunna, Sire. The twenty-

ELIZABETH R

second. The wind changed, and from the hills I saw
the first squadron under way.

PHILIP (*to Idiaquez*): Is Don Alonso in good heart?

IDIAQUEZ (*looking at the letter*): There are many sick . . .

PHILIP: Queasy stomachs, no more.

IDIAQUEZ: And supplies are . . .

PHILIP: Always supplies!

IDIAQUEZ: They are better than he had hoped, Sire.

PHILIP: Is that all?

IDIAQUEZ (*reading*): 'Your Majesty has embarked all
your resources in this expedition. I can see no way
of redressing any disaster that may befall it.'

PHILIP: He makes too many excuses. But he is a
chivalrous man, and battle will strengthen his heart.
(*Calculating.*) The twenty-second. When will they reach
the Channel?

CORDOBA: Your Majesty, I'm no seaman.

PHILIP: Tut, tut, tut . . . You were eloquent enough
about shoal waters.

CORDOBA: Seven days, your Majesty?

PHILIP: Today is the twenty-ninth. Then tonight . . .
Or tomorrow . . . Idiaquez, God's work has begun.

(*He rises painfully and goes down on his knees in
prayer. A beat, and the others join him. Mix to:*)

25

Interior, gallery, royal palace, England. Day. Early August 1588.

Walsingham and Tregannon are approaching camera in haste. Pan them by, to the door of the Queen's privy chamber, at which Walsingham knocks.

26

Interior, Queen's privy chamber, England. Day. Early August 1588.

A lady-in-waiting opening the door to Walsingham and Tregannon. They bow. Elizabeth approaches from the window bay, where she has been standing with Essex.

ELIZABETH: Is this the fellow from Howard?

TREGANNON: John Tregannon, noble Queen, master of the *Royal Prince* of Falmouth . . .

ELIZABETH: What of my ships?

TREGANNON: God bless them, for they're most worthy! Like hounds about that great beast of Spain. I'd rather kept the *Royal Prince* in the fight, but my Lord told me that bringing word to you was a greater honour than grappling with the Dons. 'S death, said I, then I'll take less honour and more sport if your Lordship so . . .

ELIZABETH: Fellow, fellow . . . Good Master Tregannon, have pity on me.

TREGANNON: God bless you, noble lady, you stand in no need of pity, for I swear I've never . . .

ELIZABETH: Your news, sir!

TREGANNON (*tugging a dispatch from his doublet*):

You'll find it here in Lord Howard's hand. With more from Master Francis and John Hawkins ...

(*Walsingham takes the letters.*)

Now by your leave, madam, I'll return to my ship. (*Begins to back out awkwardly.*)

ELIZABETH: Stay . . . ! Good sir, I pray you, tell me what you can.

TREGANNON: Why, madam, on the twenty-ninth when Thomas Fleming brought the news to Plymouth the tide was against us and the Dons were to windward. But that night we were warped out of harbour, fifty-four sail. By noon, when my mast-top man sighted the first Spaniard, the wind fell away to nigh on calm, and fog came down ...

ELIZABETH: Be brief, Master Tregannon.

TREGANNON: Briefer it'll be in the telling, madam. At moonrise the wind came up on the starboard quarter, yet not light enough, for there was cloud. And Spanish voices coming out of the darkness. High up, for those ships, as we soon saw, are tall, poop castle and fore-castle, high above my truck. But we closed, and their great guns spat clear over us, and you could see the Dons in plate armour leaning down and cursing us ...

WALSINGHAM: Master Tregannon ...

TREGANNON: Aye, be brief. We fired five rounds to their one, and into their great bellies. We had the windward and they the lee shore, and we galled them when we wished. By Dodman Point and by Plymouth, then they rounded Start Point to Tor Bay. We had at them again on the second, west of Portland Bill. We broke their crescent, and as they tacked toward Wight we be-laboured them again by the Needles. God save me, I never thought to hear men scream so. As they lay upon their decks, their blood ran down the sides of those handsome ves . . .

ELIZABETH: Where are they now, sir?

TREGANNON: Such deeds, in your name, noble lady. I saw Drake go aboard a great galleon and take her master's sword, with Hawkins lying off her quarter and shouting that Master Francis was gone a-pirating again.

ELIZABETH: What of Lord Howard?

TREGANNON: There's the miracle of it. The old gentleman proved himself a great captain. He took the *Ark Royal* alongside the Don's chief galleon, and mauled her prettily until she escaped, being to windward now, you understand, where she had been to leeward of my Lord's sh . . .

(*By movements of his hands, Tregannon tries to demonstrate windward and leeward to the uncomprehending stares.*)

WALSINGHAM: Master Tregannon, is the Armada defeated?

TREGANNON: No, sir, it is not.

ELIZABETH: Then a plague on your bosky humour and tell me the truth!

TREGANNON: When I came ashore we'd fought them again off Catherine's Point on Wight. At dawn I saw them as I rode by the Sussex shore, making for Dunkirk, I'd warrant.

WALSINGHAM: Parma . . .

ELIZABETH (*at last*): Master Tregannon, you've brought me sad news.

TREGANNON (*a protest*): Sweet lady, all the world never

saw such a force as theirs. Have no shame for your seamen.

(*But Elizabeth turns away toward the window and looks out, her back to them. A long beat, and she turns:*)

ELIZABETH: I shall go to Tilbury.

ESSEX: Nay, madam! You'll be safer in the . . .

ELIZABETH: Be silent! Walsingham, I'll join the Earl of Leicester and my soldiers at Tilbury. And you, good Tregannon, get you back to your ship . . .

TREGANNON: Aye, madam, that I will!

ELIZABETH: But tell Lord Howard to send you to me again as soon as he has news.

(*Tregannon, his mouth open to protest. He closes it, swallowing his disgust. Mix to:*)

27

Interior / exterior, Leicester's tent, Tilbury. Day. August 1588.

Two soldiers of the Essex trained band, lean on their pikes at the door of the tent and look beyond it. The old soldier gnaws at a heel of bread which he puts inside his doublet after each bite. The air is noisy with voices, hooves, drums-rolls and cheering.

YOUNG SOLDIER: Rye's a slow crop. To ripen, I mean.

(*The old soldier turns to look at him, chewing dead-pan.*)

But hardy. That's rye bread. Well, wheat and rye. Brown as an hazel nut.

OLD SOLDIER: Bread's bread. A soldier should eat what he can when he can.

YOUNG SOLDIER: Rye for bread. Barley for beer.

OLD SOLDIER (*an appreciative jerk of his head*): Beer . . .

(*A loud trumpet fanfare* (*off*). *He swallows and straightens.*)

There she is, lad.

(*Cut to:*)

28

Exterior, camp by Tilbury Fort. Day. August 1588.

Low angle Elizabeth as she turns her horse to camera. She is dressed in white velvet and wears a silver cuirass. She raises a gold-chased truncheon, and when the fanfare stops:

ELIZABETH: My loving people . . . We have been persuaded by some that are careful for our safety, to take heed how we commit ourselves to armed multitudes for fear of treachery . . . Let tyrants fear! Under God. I have placed my chief strength and safeguard in the loyal hearts . . .

(*Cut to:*)

29

Interior / exterior, Leicester's tent, Tilbury.

The old soldier takes a bite of bread and chews on as both listen.

ELIZABETH (*off*): . . . and goodwill of my subjects, and therefore I am resolved, in the midst and heat of battle

443

to live or die amongst you all, and to lay down for my God and my kingdom and for my people, my honour and my blood, even in the dust.

OLD SOLDIER: Bravely said! By Heaven I recall her father.

YOUNG SOLDIER: And I my wife. She talks less of dying.

OLD SOLDIER: Why, lad, the Dons will do the dying.

30

Exterior, camp by Tilbury Fort. Day. August 1588.

Low angle Elizabeth as she pulls in a restless horse.

ELIZABETH: I know I have the body of a weak and feeble woman ...

31

Interior/exterior, Leicester's tent, Tilbury. Day. August 1588.

YOUNG SOLDIER: Now she comes to it. Now she cogs the dice.

ELIZABETH: But I have the heart and stomach of a king!

32

Exterior, camp by Tilbury Fort. Day. August 1588.

Low angle Elizabeth.

ELIZABETH: And a king of England too! And I think foul scorn that Parma or Spain, or any prince of Europe should care to invade the borders of my realm.

33

Interior / exterior, Leicester's tent, Tilbury. Day. August 1588.

ELIZABETH (*off*): Rather than any dishonour should grow by me, I myself will take up arms. I myself will be your general, judge and rewarder of every one of your virtues in the field. I know already for your forwardness you deserve rewards and crowns, and we do assure you, in the word of a prince, they shall be duly paid you!

(*Overlay with soldier's dialogue following.*)

OLD SOLDIER: God's death, she breedeth courage in a man!

YOUNG SOLDIER: What I feel in my stomach is not courage.

OLD SOLDIER: Stand as my flankman, boy, and I'll show you how we fought the Dons at Zutphen.

(*As Elizabeth comes to the end—sustained cheering off.*)

There, you have her honest word on't. Fight bravely and she swears you'll get your pay.

YOUNG SOLDIER: I'm glad to hear it. For I've had none since I was dragged from my plough.

OLD SOLDIER: Are you a coward, boy?

YOUNG SOLDIER: I truly believe I am.

OLD SOLDIER: Then you'll be no comrade of mine. May you rot first.

YOUNG SOLDIER: Old man, by your temper and your age, I'd say you'll be rotting long before I.

OLD SOLDIER: She comes!

(*They stand apart, and to attention. Cut to:*)

Interior, Leicester's tent, Tilbury. Day. August 1588.

Lady-in-waiting approaches the Queen as she enters with Leicester and Essex. Queen collapses into a chair.

ELIZABETH: God's death, this fancy corselet is crushing me. Unstrap me, girl, before I die for want of breath.

(*The lady-in-waiting begins to unbuckle the cuirass. Essex drops extravagantly on one knee and kisses the hem of the Queen's skirt. Elizabeth eyes Leicester shrewdly.*)

Get up, my Lord, your aged stepfather is envious of your agility.

ESSEX (*rising*): Madam, today youth triumphs over age. You are eternal spring.

ELIZABETH: God save you, boy, we've done with the play-acting now. I'm all but crushed by that steel doublet, and winded by the effort of shouting against the ears of thirty thousand men.

ESSEX (*persisting*): I thank God I'm alive today, for England will never see anoth . . .

LEICESTER (*interrupting*): Your pardon, my Lord . . . madam, I've fresh news.

(*As Elizabeth turns to him.*)

Two days ago the Armada anchored by Calais. Though it got the worst of the fighting in the Channel, it is still a mighty threat.

ELIZABETH: Parma is not at Calais?

LEICESTER: No, mada. His barges are eight leagues to the east, behind the shoals at Dunkirk. It's Howard's opinion that they'll come out on the next favourable tide, join with the Armada and fall upon Kent and this Essex shore.

ESSEX: God be praised, we'll give them a welcome!

LEICESTER (*a withering glance at Essex*): Madam, your army here is all you may depend upon, for your camp in Kent musters no more than broken seamen. Should the Spaniards land at Margate, I can cross the bridge of boats to Gravesend and engage ...

ESSEX: Your Majesty, return to London. The streets are barred with chains, and th ecitizens say they'll fight like the people of Antwerp.

ELIZABETH: No. (*Looks at Leicester.*)

LEICESTER (*the ghost of a smile*): I'm confident your Majesty will stay with us.

ESSEX: But my soul, she'll not!

ELIZABETH: Go to your tent, sir. (*As Essex hesitates.*) I pray you.

(*A resentful glance at Leicester, and Essex bows and retires.*)

You, too, girl. Leave us.

(*When the lady-in-waiting has gone.*)

It pains me to see you so ill.

LEICESTER: God will preserve me until this work's done.

447

ELIZABETH: And longer still.

LEICESTER: Nay, madam. He must make an end to me soon.

ELIZABETH (*a beat*): What will Howard do?

LEICESTER (*worried*): He has little powder and shot, and less food. But he'll fall upon the Armada if he can, before it meets with Parma's flotilla. And yet, I fear he'll . . .

ELIZABETH: My Lord, my Lord . . . do not put yourself in such a pother. Come, sit by me . . .

(*As she sits, she pours him a cup of wine.*)

Sweet Robin . . . Were we once so young?

(*Then.*) How can you bear to look at me now?

LEICESTER: You are the most sacred and dainty thing I have in this world to love.

ELIZABETH: Bold Robert Dudley. Lusty Robin. The treacherous Earl of Leicester. Drink your wine, old man.

(*Though Elizabeth's words are cruel and contemptuous, her tone is soft, almost regretful, as if she were going through the actions of a game that no longer has meaning.*)

LEICESTER: I've no taste for it.

ELIZABETH: Because you're angry with me.

LEICESTER: I'm your loyal and faith . . .

ELIZABETH: Loyal? Faithful? You scoundrel, you've always betrayed me!

448

LEICESTER (*rising and dropping on his knee before her*): Then take my head, madam, for you've always had my heart.

ELIZABETH: Why do you always provoke me to cruel words? Even when I love you most . . . ? Get up, sir. Sweet Robin . . . get up and sit again . . .

(*As he sits.*)

Are you taking the physic I sent?

(*He bows a brief affirmative.*)

Is it better than the other?

LEICESTER: It will preserve me until God and your Majesty have no further use for me.

ELIZABETH: Then I'm content. For He knows I'll always have need of you. When the kingdom is safe, I shall send you to the country for a cure.

LEICESTER: No diet, madam, I pray you.

ELIZABETH (*sharing his smile*): No diet, I swear. And you'll dine here with me now. We'll sit like two old folk and talk of gay times. Sweet Robin, let us recall the past . . .

LEICESTER: If your Majesty so orders me.

ELIZABETH: Orders? God's death, what kind of dalliance flourishes upon orders?

LEICESTER: I am your Majesty's Lieutenant-General.

ELIZABETH: Have you some paramour in your sergeant's tent?

LEICESTER (*rising*): I have an army, madam. Should I neglect it, I neglect you.

ELIZABETH: I command you to stay.

LEICESTER (*remaining on his feet*): As your Majesty pleases.

ELIZABETH (*a beat, staring at him*): Jesu, how old you look! And sick!

(*He says nothing.*)

Your stepson is a pretty boy, is he not?

(*When he is still silent.*)

There was a time when you would have touched your sword at that, and blustered like a bully.

LEICESTER (*wearily*): Nay madam, I would not. I would have left you.

ELIZABETH: Then go now!

(*Leicester bows, turns and has reached the tent door.*)

Robin!

(*He stops.*)

God love you . . . God keep you, sweet Robin.

(*As he goes, close on Elizabeth and mix to:*)

34

Interior, Leicester's tent, Tilbury. Night. August 1588.

Close shot of guttering candles on the table. Muted notes of a distant trumpet fluting. Elizabeth is sitting by the table, reading dispatches, scrawling a hasty marginal note on one. The lady-in-waiting is crouched

*on the floor, leaning against the Queen's chair asleep.
As the trumpet sounds again the lady-in-waiting stirs,
half awakening. Without taking her eyes from the dispatch, Elizabeth puts out a hand and gently restrains
the girl.*

OLD SOLDIER (*off*): Hold!

(*Elizabeth looks up.*)

Hold, I say, or I'll run my pike into your . . .

LEICESTER (*off*): Stand aside, fellow!

(*Another angle, taking in the tent door, as Leicester
pushes the canvas aside and enters, followed by Essex
and Tregannon. The sea captain is ragged and weary.
All three men bow.*)

ELIZABETH (*rising*): My Lords . . . ? And you, sir,
what new . . .

TREGANNON: Now God bless your Majesty.

(*Drops on one knee.*)

ESSEX: Great news, madam!

ELIZABETH: Is it truly so? Up, Master Tregannon, and
tell me. What has befallen my fleet?

TREGANNON (*rising*): Nothing but good, madam. That's
brevity, I'll warrant. Nothing but good.

ELIZABETH: Thank you, sir. Now I'll have more.

TREGANNON: Well, come Sunday night we had the Dons
between us and the Calais shore, with a west wind behind us and a flowing tide against them. So close were
we, they and us, that our fly-boats worked within gun-
shot of each other, but dursn't fire lest we wasted precious powder. Then we sent in fire-ships.

451

ELIZABETH R

ELIZABETH: Jesu!

TREGANNON: Eight of them at midnight. Dismasted merchantmen, stuffed with tar and cordage, their guns shotted to explode as soon as the flames touched the priming. We took them in under low clouds while the moon was becalmed. Am I too brief for you, madam?

LEICESTER: Get on, sir.

TREGANNON: The Dons were herded like sheep in a pen, close by the shoals. We towed the fire-ships in until the Spaniards could have touched them with a pikehead. Then we lit the fires and left it to God's will and the wind.

ELIZABETH: You burnt them all?

TREGANNON (a grin): Nay, madam, even Hell could not burn them all. We heard their trumpets and drums, their voices calling upon their saints ...

(A beat.)

I'll not lie to you, madam. We burnt none of their ships.

ELIZABETH: God's death, then what was the use of th ...

TREGANNON: True they brushed against a galleon or two, and lit a candle in the canvas, but the real damage was done by the Dons themselves, colliding with each other in their fear, yards and rigging meshed like a maiden's snood. At dawn we saw most of them scattered to the north ...

ELIZABETH: They escaped! Do you tell me they escaped?

TREGANNON: Someone among them knew his seaman-

452

ship. They left the galleasses on the shoals and cut the cables of the galleons. North of Gravelines forty of them turned into the wind and waited for us to come up. God be thanked I saw that fight! Five squadrons of your Majesty's ships, passing and passing again in line ahead, firing broadsides into the Dons as we came, and so close that their foolish boarders swung from their yards into our rigging. We offered them quarters, but none of their commanders would take it, and you could see their priest kneeling in the blood. Brave men, madam, though they are papists.

ELIZABETH: And now you destroyed them?

TREGANNON: No, madam. We all but sank one galleon, and drove two more on to the banks of Flushing. But we were out of powder now, and no water for our wounded, and the weather turning against us.

ELIZABETH: Where are the Spaniards? Are they coming against us here?

TREGANNON: Nay, madam, they're running north-east. Lord Howard's after them, but I'll warrant his empty powder casks will bring him back before long. You can safely leave the rest to God, madam.

ELIZABETH: Master Tregannon, I'd rather you told me that . . .

TREGANNON: Leave it to the Almighty, madam, for he's sending such wind I'll swear, that they can do no more than run before it, north-about these islands. Such wrecks there'll be, and wild Scots and Irish to cut the throats of those who come ashore.

(*From outside there is suddenly a great burst of cheering, the sound of drums and trumpets. All turn to it, and then Leicester holds a hand toward the tent door, his invitation unheard above the noise.*)

453

LEICESTER : Your Majesty . . .

(*A beat, then Elizabeth straightens her back, strides out of the tent, followed by all except Tregannon. As the noise increases, Tregannon scratches his weary body. He walks across to the table, a beat, and then he sits in the Queen's chair. He pulls a plate toward him, tears the leg from a roast fowl and begins to eat hungrily. As he pours himself a cup of wine, close on him. Slow mix to:*)

35

Interior, the King's room, the Escurial. Day. September 1588.

Close shot Medina Sidonia staring into camera with melancholy despair.

MEDINA SIDONIA : Your Majesty . . . ?

(*When he gets no reply, he looks to his right, frowning. Medina Sidonia is standing before Philip and looking at Idiaquez. The King sits hunched in his chair, his eye again bandaged. He is not looking at the Captain-General. When he gets no help from the Idiaquez.*)

Such gales and tempests . . . for a month . . . Your Majesty . . .

(*Philip does not move.*)

I have eleven ships . . . More will come, your Majesty . . . but I fear forty are . . .

(*Still no movement from the King.*)

Don Juan de Recalde has died . . . of grief, your, Majesty, two days ago. And Don Miguel de Oquendo of the Guipuzcoan squadron . . . also of grief.

(*Philip crosses himself, but he does not look up.*)

Your Majesty, I believe that of the thirty thousand men you entrusted to my command, not five thousand will come . . .

(*Now Philip looks up, staring at Medina Sidonia, who drops on one knee, bowing his head.*)

Your Majesty, do not reproach me!

PHILIP (*slowly*): Must I then reproach God?

MEDINA SIDONIA (*rising*): Of sixty members of my own household only two have survived . . . Your Majesty, men cry out for my life!

PHILIP: They will have someone's life. You and Don Diego de Valdez are the only admirals to survive.

MEDINA SIDONIA (*trapped*): If your Majesty wishes, I am ready to . . .

PHILIP: Don Diego has been arrested. Let that be enough. Idiaquez . . .

IDIAQUEZ: Sire?

PHILIP: Send clothes and medicine for the sick and wounded. Let them know that I do not blame them. Every widow and orphan will be paid what is necessary for . . .

IDIAQUEZ: Has your Majesty the funds for such . . .

(*And is silenced when the King looks at him.*)

PHILIP (*turning from both of them*): I sent my ships and my subjects against men, not against winds and hurricanes. It is God's will.

MEDINA SIDONIA: How have we sinned, that he should so punish us?

PHILIP: I relieve you of your commission, Don Alonso.

(*Medina Sidonia bows.*)

Go home to your oranges. Go by night. Go secretly.

(*Philip rises painfully from his chair. For a moment, he holds the palm of his hand gently to his bandaged eye.*)

Idiaquez, send for my confessor.

(*He turns toward the door of the inner room, and then pauses.*)

Since the Enterprise of England was most solemnly dedicated to God and his Church, the result of it must surely be most advantageous to Him. We are nothing. Nothing.

(*Pan him away toward the inner room, where he kneels before the altar table. Close on his bent head and shoulders. Hold for a long beat, and then cut to:*)

36

Interior, Queen's privy chamber, England. Day. September 1588.

Close shot of Howard. He is angry.

HOWARD: Madam, your seamen are dying for want of food and medicine. Will you neglect them?

(*Three shot Elizabeth, Howard and Burghley. Burghley seems preoccupied and uneasy and keeps glancing at the Queen, as if trying to anticipate her mood.*)

ELIZABETH (*impatiently*): I've told you, my Lord. They may depart gloriously for their own homes. I'm no tyrant to hold them in service when their duty's done.

HOWARD: Your Majesty, a hundred . . . little more . . . of your sailors were killed in the fighting that made your kingdom secure. But thousands now die of disease and hunger. Madam, they lie crying most pitiably in the streets of Plymouth and Dov . . .

ELIZABETH: Cousin! Is my purse bottomless? The fleet is to be laid up and the army disbanded. Is that unwisdom, Burghley?

BURGHLEY (*whose thoughts were elsewhere*): Your Majesty?

ELIZABETH: My gentle dotard, grasp hold of your wits. Shall I now spend money on idle seamen and soldiers? Tell Howard. Is it wisdom?

BURGHLEY: To spend in time of need is wisdom, my Lord. To continue spending without that need brings bitter repentance.

HOWARD (*stiffly*): Thank you, my Lord, I'll carry that reassurance to her Majesty's servants.

ELIZABETH: Good cousin, I'll have no long faces about me when all should be rejoicing. Tell your captains to bring their captured banners to Saint Paul's this Sunday. There'll be a Day of Thanksgiving and joy throughout my king . . .

HOWARD: Madam, may I have leave to return to my poor seamen at Plymouth?

ELIZABETH: Burghley, we shall strike a medal.

BURGHLEY: Yes, Madam.

ELIZABETH: And upon it we'll record our thanks to God for the mighty wind that scattered our enemies. What say you, Howard?

HOWARD: That God also gave us better ships and better

guns, madam. Before he sent us a tempest. May I have your leave to . . .

ELIZABETH (*pettishly*): Do as you wish, sir. And I'm glad to be rid of your sour face.

(*She turns her back and looks out of the window. Howard bows and leaves. At the sound of the door closing, Elizabeth turns gaily to Burghley.*)

My Lord, I want an accounting of the booty that . . .

(*She sees his miserable face.*)

Jesu, your face is as sour as vinegar too. What is it?

BURGHLEY: Madam . . .

ELIZABETH: Dear man, what can spoil my joy?

BURGHLEY: Gracious Majesty . . .

ELIZABETH: Madam . . . Gracious Majesty . . . Come to the point, sir.

BURGHLEY: The Earl of Leicester is dead.

(*Elizabeth's face is drained of expression, as she stares at him.*)

ELIZABETH (*in a strangled voice*): You lie.

BURGHLEY: Two days since, madam. At Cornbury. Of a continual fever.

ELIZABETH: Leicester dead . . . ? (*And then.*) Sweet Robin dead . . . ?

BURGHLEY: Aye, madam.

(*Elizabeth turns slowly away from him. A beat. She*

458

walks unsteadily to a chair by a desk at the window. She sits. Burghley leaves quietly. She moves at last, looking at the papers on her desk, touching them with her hand and then parting them quickly, finding one and unfolding it. As she reads, overlay Leicester's voice.)

LEICESTER (*off*): 'I must humbly beseech your Majesty to pardon your poor old servant to be thus bold in thus sending to know how my gracious lady doeth, being the chiefest thing in this world I do pray for, for her to have good health and long life. For my own poor case, I continue still your medicine, and find it amends much better than any other thing that hath been given me . . .'

(*She reads no more, but refolds the letter, laying her hand upon it and looking at it. Then she takes a quill and writes upon it. Cut to high angle, Elizabeth writing the words 'His last letter'. She opens a drawer of the desk and places it inside. She locks the drawer. Hold on her calm face.*)

ESSEX (*off*): Majesty . . .

(*She looks up. Cut to Essex standing inside the doors, which he holds closed behind him.*)

Madam, your Court cannot be gay without you.

(*Elizabeth stares calmly at him.*)

ELIZABETH: Do you know that Leicester is dead?

ESSEX: Aye, madam. So I've been told by my mother his wife.

(*Elizabeth, a calm beat, then she explodes: She takes a book from the desk and hurls it with a scream.*)

ELIZABETH: Ingrate!

(Essex ducks the book, turns and tears open the door. Full shot of Elizabeth. Pan her from the desk, as she staggers clumsily toward the door, reaching it just as Essex is closing it behind him. Elizabeth falls against it, arms outstretched, slamming it shut. She locks it with feverish desperation and then slowly slips down to the floor. Sobbing, she buries her face in her hands.)

SWEET ENGLAND'S PRIDE

by

IAN RODGER

Sweet England's Pride was first shown on BBC Television on March 24 1971, as the sixth play in the series *Elizabeth R*, with the following cast:

ELIZABETH I	*Glenda Jackson*
THE EARL OF ESSEX	*Robin Ellis*
FRANCIS BACON	*John Nettleton*
SIR ROBERT CECIL	*Hugh Dickson*
LORD BURGHLEY	*Ronald Hines*
THE EARL OF SOUTHAMPTON	*Peter Egan*
LORD EGERTON	*Clifford Rose*
SIR WALTER RALEIGH	*Nicholas Selby*
O'NEILL	*Patrick O'Connell*
SIR CHRISTOPHER BLOUNT	*Haydn Jones*
LORD HOWARD	*Peter Howell*
LADY LEICESTER	*Angela Thorne*
ELIZABETH VERNON	*Sonia Fraser*
LADY RICH	*Shirley Dixon*
LADY ESSEX	*Judith South*
HORSEMAN TO O'NEILL	*Kevin Flood*
CONN	*Wesley Murphy*
LORD MAYOR	*Harry Webster*
'KING RICHARD'	*Philip Voss*
'BOLINGBROKE'	*David Hargreaves*
HARPER	*Peter Forest*
GAOLER	*Michael Beint*
HORSEMAN TO CECIL	*Derek Martin*
DANCERS	*Sue Bishop, Jacqui Letherby, Lauretta Kerr, Elizabeth Stevenson, Arthur Sweet, Christopher Beeching, Brian Lofthus, Fernando Monast*

Non-speaking

LADIES-IN-WAITING	*Sonia Petrie, Maureen Nelson, Sue Peters, Ann Plenty*
COURTIERS	*Billy John, Tom Sye, Ralph Tovey, Donald Groves, John Moore, Gregory Scott, Daniel Jones, Tony Chantel*
MUSICIANS	*Stenson Falck, Paul Phillips*

RED GUARDS	{ *Steve Patterson, Peter Jolley, Michael Scott, Carl Bohun.*
BLACK GUARDS	{ *Jonas Kerr, Steve Peters, Terry Leigh, Clinton Morris*
IRISH COURTIERS/ SERVANTS	{ *Trevor Lawrence, Bill Richards, Ricki Lancing, Andrew Dempsey, Bob Raymond, Ivor Owen*
ARCHBISHOP	*Aubrey Danvers Walker*
PRIESTS	*Freddie Wiles, Terry Rendel*
DOCTOR	*Willy Bowman*
EXECUTIONER	*Eric Kent*

Producer and Director Roderick Graham

Designer Richard Henry

CHARACTERS

QUEEN ELIZABETH

ELIZABETH VERNON

SIR ROBERT CECIL, Secretary, hunchback

THE EARL OF ESSEX

THE EARL OF SOUTHAMPTON

LADY LEICESTER

LADY RICH

SIR CHRISTOPHER BLOUNT

SIR FRANCIS BACON

LADY ESSEX

SIR WALTER RALEIGH

LORD HOWARD

LORD BURGHLEY

LORD EGERTON

HORSEMAN TO O'NEILL

CONN

IRISH PEASANT WOMAN

O'NEILL

LORD MAYOR

HARPER

HERALD TO O'NEILL

'BOLINGBROKE'

'KING RICHARD'

GAOLER

EXECUTIONER

SERVANTS, COURTIERS, MEMBERS OF PARLIAMENT, LADIES-
IN-WAITING, MUSICIANS, GUARDS, SOLDIERS

INTERIORS

Royal complex: gallery, presence chamber, privy chamber,
bedroom
Tower complex: cell and passageway
Great Hall (Essex's house, Wanstead)
Dublin Castle, large room
Barn
Stable

EXTERIORS

A river bank in Ireland.
Irish bogs, Irish hedgerows, Irish woods.

1

Interior, bedchamber. Day.

We see the Queen's jewelled red-haired wig from the back. It almost fills the screen moving slightly as if the Queen is speaking. In fact it is being held by the hand of Elizabeth Vernon, lady-in-waiting. As the Queen speaks, we see nothing but this wig from the back.

ELIZABETH: By God's death, they give me bad advice. See you, child, you give me no bad advice. Careful, child, careful. My Lord Essex has imperilled the kingdom. We have lost treasure and good men and all for nothing. I will have an end of it. I will have no more expeditions, no more wars. Are you finished, child?

ELIZABETH VERNON: Yes, Majesty.

(Miss Vernon turns the wig. We see her hand inside it. Then she moves aside and we see the Queen full face. She is old and haggard. Her cheeks hollow, her hair limp and scraggy.)

ELIZABETH *(to Miss Vernon)*: Thank you. Give me the mirror.

(After a pause to admire herself in her copper mirror, the Queen rises, attended by Elizabeth Vernon. She moves towards the door and thence to the council chamber.)

I should never have listened. These proud men lead us to a fall. My Lord Essex fights Sir Walter harder than the Spaniard. They squabble like small boys. I shall give them no more toys of war to play with.

(Sir Robert Cecil is at the door of the privy chamber. He bows.)

2

Interior, privy chamber. Day.

ELIZABETH: Sir Robert, I trust you bring me better news?

CECIL: Your Majesty, Lord Essex has landed ahead of the fleet.

ELIZABETH: Bearing a great cargo of excuses no doubt.

CECIL: The whole court now knows of his failure. But his faction argues further ventures, more expeditions. There is more trouble in Ireland. The Irish rebels take advantage of our distress and Spain pays them.

ELIZABETH: Let the Irish hang themselves, Sir Robert. It troubles me more that I am advised to costly wars which achieve nothing, that my so-called councillors behave as if the policy of the realm were in their personal charge. They advise me for their own ends, seeking their own glory. And when they fail, it is I who must pay.

CECIL: I serve no cause but yours, your Majesty.

ELIZABETH: Oh, there is no one without self-interest. I am tired of sweet words. I grow old.

CECIL: Your Majesty's appearance gives no proof of that.

ELIZABETH: Do I look well, then?

CECIL: Youth . . .

(*Essex bursts in to the room, proud, confident. The Queen confused. She is annoyed Essex is come, yet anxious at her appearance. Touches her hair, her face, flicks at imagined fluff on her dress.*)

15. Sir Walter Raleigh (Nicholas Selby) (*Sweet England's Pride*).

16. The death of
Queen Elizabeth,
attended upon by
Cecil (left) and
Egerton (*Sweet
England's Pride*).

ESSEX (*on his knees*): Your Majesty.

(*Before the Queen can speak.*)

CECIL: Shall I leave?

ELIZABETH (*composed now*): This is state business, Mr Secretary. See you take a good note.

(*Cecil is secretly pleased.*)

We had heard you were still at sea, Robert.

(*Essex looks up from her hand. He rises.*)

ESSEX: In a race to your side no courier travels faster than I.

ELIZABETH: When couriers carry bad news it is best to be first.

ESSEX: I have brought the fleet safe home.

ELIZABETH: And the ships are like sieves and your men dying of disease. No. I will have no more of it. I have been tricked into vain wars, into expeditions I cannot afford.

ESSEX: Aye, and jealous men whisper in your ear.

(*A wave to Cecil.*)

Keep a good account, Mr Secretary. Write how they defame me.

CECIL: My Lord—

ESSEX: Ha. His innocence is wonderful. While we risk our necks, his armies of clerks prepare to stab us in the back.

CECIL: Diplomacy, my Lord, (*Ruffles his papers.*) may achieve what war cannot.

ESSEX: Diplomacy did not take Cadiz or burn the Spanish fleet? Who laid a world's ransom at your feet? Sir Walter? My Lord Howard who argued against me?

ELIZABETH: Lord Howard? I have this week made him Earl of Nottingham. In recognition of his services.

ESSEX: That old man is to walk in front of me? For a victory that was mine?

ELIZABETH: Is no one to share your glory? Must it all be yours?

ESSEX: There is no one fights your cause more valiantly and the world knows it. Yes, the world. The court may trick me but the world speaks well of me.

ELIZABETH: Do you threaten me?

ESSEX: Your Majesty, I—I left England as your good friend and servant. I did all I could. I am sick and have ridden two whole nights. I am greatly wronged.

ELIZABETH: Wronged? Who is more wronged than I who have to pay for these follies?

ESSEX: May I take my leave?

ELIZABETH: As it please you.

(*She holds out her hand for Essex to kiss. Essex shudders, puts hand to his face. She looks at him.*)

(*Softly.*) Robin?

ESSEX: It is the fever. It is nothing.

(*He bows. Kisses her hand. Cecil yawns.*)

You must forgive me. I am overcome by unkindness where once I was conquered by beauty.

(*The Queen retains Essex's hand.*)

ELIZABETH: Beauty?

ESSEX: Beauty. Good day, Sir Robert. Go fight your paper was. (*He goes.*)

ELIZABETH: Sir Robert. We are still resolved.

CECIL (*rising*): Your Majesty. There is no doubt that Lord Essex's view is popular.

ELIZABETH: Do you think I don't know that? He is the sun in splendour, Sir Robert. He is all our pride.

(*We see the confusion in her face. Perhaps a nervous flicker of her fingers.*)

3

Interior, the great hall of Essex's house. Night.

The room is brightly lit, contrasting with the Queen's apartments. Furnishing and decoration is lavish. The company is seated, finishing a meal. Liveried servants enter and leave, clearing table and serving wine, fruit etc., throughout the scene. Candles on table. Gold plate, silver ornaments. Spanish glass, goblets. Essex is huddled in a big chair at the fire, with his feet on a stool. He is shrouded in rugs, skins. At table, Lady Lettice Leicester, his mother, sits at the head and furthest from him. Nearest to him, so that she can turn to attend him, sits his wife, the countess. On her right, the Earl of Southampton. On her left, Sir Christopher Blount. Next to Blount, Lady Rich, Essex's sister. Next to Southampton, Francis Bacon. A musician plays (or is heard playing) on a lute.

SOUTHAMPTON: There's no doubt, she's sorry.

LADY LEICESTER: Sorry is not enough. She has behaved abominably.

SOUTHAMPTON: Well, I think she wants to make it up.

LADY LEICESTER: We are of royal blood, Southampton.

ESSEX: Mother!

(*Waves a hand. Lady Essex turns and takes it, kisses it.*)

LADY LEICESTER: No, my son. We are dealing with the scion of a Welsh butler. She has the manners of a fish-wife.

(*Bacon nervously covers his mouth with his napkin.*)

It is true, Mr Bacon. She's never forgiven me for stealing her lover. She keeps me from court because I would look her in the eye.

(*Bacon is saved reply by a servant offering him drink.*)

LADY RICH: And give her your tongue, Mother.

BLOUNT: Well, I am for holding out. The country's with us and the Queen knows it.

ESSEX: You're a good man, Christopher.

SOUTHAMPTON: My little friend at court—

LADY RICH: You have a little friend, Henry?

SOUTHAMPTON: I have interests in all directions, Lady Rich. She tells me—

LADY RICH: A she? Is it possible?

SOUTHAMPTON: It is not only possible. It is even practical.

ESSEX: What does your little friend say?

SOUTHAMPTON: She says the Queen reads your letters with apparent distaste. But—

(*Reaction from Lady Leicester.*)

No please let me finish, Lady Leicester. When she is alone, she takes them out again and reads them with more pleasure.

ESSEX: Francis writes a good letter.

LADY ESSEX: Yes. You say nothing, Mr Bacon.

BACON: It is not my place, my Lady.

LADY ESSEX: But we ask you.

LADY LEICESTER: It is a waste of time. She listens to no one but his damned cousin Cecil. She has given Howard precedence and she dotes on that peacock Raleigh.

SOUTHAMPTON: No. She changes, you know.

ESSEX: Was there ever a time when she didn't? Women are weathervanes, Henry.

SOUTHAMPTON: And very vain, too. (*He laughs at his joke.*) I think she knows she's gone too far. I think you should be generous and return to court.

LADY LEICESTER: Generous? My son has been publicly insulted, my Lord. He must be totally restored to favour. Raleigh and Howard must be put in their place.

BLOUNT: Raleigh takes what he can get, madam. He's no danger. It's these damned clerks and lawyers. It's Cecil who holds the inner keep. Get rid of him.

LADY LEICESTER: Well, Mr Bacon. What do you say to that?

BACON: My cousin Robert serves the Queen as well as any.

BLOUNT: Serves himself, you mean.

BACON: We all serve ourselves, sir. We live in a time when each man goes his own way.

ESSEX: And what way do you advise, Francis?

BACON: Her Majesty mellows towards you. She is sorry you have been so ill. She misses your company. I say, go to her.

BLOUNT: No.

BACON: The Queen must not be forced into a corner. If you force a challenge from her, she has the last word. It is not safe to be too proud.

LADY LEICESTER (*rising from chair*): Not safe to be proud. I have heard enough. Come ladies, we will leave you. Robert, good night.

(*Lady Rich rises. The rest follow suit. Servants draw chairs, light tapers.*)

We shall leave you, Robert.

(*Essex puts a hand over his face. Company moves towards the door. Lady Essex leaves Essex. We see the company leaving.*)

ESSEX: Christopher?

BLOUNT: Yes.

ESSEX: Stay, man.

(*Blount shrugs, returns to Essex. He takes a chair nearer to Essex.*)

Some more wine.

(*Blount takes a flagon from the table. A servant offers help.*)

Leave us.

(*Servants go out. The room is darker now. They drop their voice.*)

BLOUNT: Well?

ESSEX: I must go back to her.

(*Reaction from Blount.*)

I have no choice.

BLOUNT: You could go to Plymouth. Raise the men of the fleet. March on London. Save the Queen from her enemies.

ESSEX: Treason, Chris. Treason.

BLOUNT: Those who win are not called traitors.

BLOUNT: Call out your men of the Fleet.

ESSEX: No.

BLOUNT: But why?

ESSEX: Because I couldn't even pay for their breakfast.

BLOUNT: But you've got control of the Horse. Estates. The wine tax.

ESSEX: I am a poor man with rich tastes, Christopher. If the Azores had gone well . . . (*Raises hands.*) Hm. But I am nearly bankrupt. All I have is a name.

BLOUNT: But we live like Kings.

475

ESSEX: Like Kings. Yes. And Mr Bacon advises me to eat humble pie. No. Don't mock him, Chris. He is leaving my service. I cannot pay him.

BLOUNT: So you must go back to her.

ESSEX: Yes. Like a small boy needing pocket money, I must say please and thank you and wash my face and comb my hair. And what is worse . . . (*Looks at ring.*) I also love her.

BLOUNT: So you are trapped.

4

Interior, gallery. Day.

Cecil and Bacon.

CECIL: Is he coming?

(*Bacon shakes his head.*)

BACON: She must give more proof.

CECIL: Does he think he's God?

BACON (*pauses*): Yes. I think he does. Sometimes.

(*They exchange a smile.*)

CECIL: You'd do better elsewhere, cousin.

BACON: I shall have to. He needs money.

CECIL: How much?

BACON: A great deal.

CECIL: Then I must see he gets it. Oh, yes. Poor men with rich ideas are dangerous. This business . . .

(*Indicates papers*.) now may take me to France. I am grateful to you, cousin.

(*Bacon accepts the compliment. Turns to go*.)

One moment, Francis. Touching upon poor men with rich ideas, we should find you new employment.

5

Interior, great hall. Essex's home. Day.

Brightly lit. We see only Essex's face at first.

SOUTHAMPTON: And she's thinking of sending Cecil to France.

ESSEX: Better and better. Nothing but total power for me, Henry. The world's at our feet.

SOUTHAMPTON: I prefer it in our grasp.

ESSEX: The Lord of her Court. We do not crawl. We command. We are Tamburlaine.

(*Throws a chair across the room. Southampton looks worried*.)

SOUTHAMPTON: Yes.

ESSEX: What's the matter?

SOUTHAMPTON: You are so swiftly changed, Robert.

ESSEX: Changed? I am the same as ever.

SOUTHAMPTON: But only last week.

ESSEX: I know nothing of last week. I was ill. Do not speak of it again.

(*Pauses, then he is gay again. Jumps a chair*.)

She needs us again. Henry. The hunchback shall be outwitted.

SOUTHAMPTON: Raleigh's not going to like your coming back.

ESSEX: No. We bear no grudges, Henry. We are generous. Open-hearted. Gay. We are the sun shining on a dark court. (*Laughs.*) She must have had such a miserable time.

6

Interior, gallery. Day.

We see (from overhead) a coloured football and a page racing after it. He picks it up and tosses it to his companion, a second page. They skip ahead. A couple of musicians, their instruments slung or held, eating an apple. Lady Rich and Lady Essex. Servants. Christopher Blount, Essex with Southampton. They pass some distance along the corridor and stop. We see them looking ahead. We see the Queen and her courtiers at the far end of the cloister. The Queen is standing without anyone behind her. We approach her. Her company is markedly older than that of the Essex party. Cecil is on the inside alone. On the outside, the garden side, Raleigh, Lord Howard, the Lord Keeper, who may both be seated either on chairs or on stone seats. Behind them Elizabeth Vernon and others. We see the Essex party cool it a little. Still grinning etc., but they look back to Essex. Essex catches Southampton's eye. Winks or pulls a face, then nonchalantly moves forward through his party. Lady Essex turns to take his arm. Essex slightly surprised. (If she wants to be in on this, okay.) They move forward, at a few feet, Essex bows and Lady Essex curtseys. The Queen is delighted and is trying not to show it.

ELIZABETH: Welcome, my Lord.

ESSEX: Your Majesty.

ELIZABETH: You look well. (*To Lady Essex*.) Is he well?

LADY ESSEX: I have been your Majesty's good nurse.

ELIZABETH: Hm. Fit and well for any service?

ESSEX: If service is what your Majesty—demands.

(*He could have said requests.*)

ELIZABETH: We have an arduous office in mind.

(*Essex exchanges glance with Lady Essex. The Queen sees this, enjoys it.*)

It has been vacant many years and we think it time to fill it. We are still threatened by Spain. The defence of the realm must be placed in strong hands. We have decided to appoint you Earl Marshal, my Lord.

ESSEX: Your Majesty!

ELIZABETH: It is good to see you all. I have danced these poor creatures (*Her company whom she refers to.*) off their feet. Come, my Lord Nottingham. Let us see you show the love we have for both of you.

(*Essex shakes hands with Lord Howard, Earl of Nottingham.*)

ESSEX: My Lord. Your servant.

HOWARD: And I yours, my Lord.

ELIZABETH: Sir Walter?

RALEIGH: It is good to see you, my Lord.

ESSEX: It is good to be back at Court.

479

(The Queen turns to accept honours from the rest of the Essex retinue, Southampton first.)

ELIZABETH: Come, my good people.

(Sees Elizabeth Vernon with Southampton. Elizabeth Vernon goes out along cloister regretfully.)

I bid you all be merry. *(To Lord Howard.)* Come, my Lord. Age must lead the way.

(Essex frowns. Raleigh shakes his head. Let it go, he is saying. Cecil moves towards Essex. The party is beginning to move slowly along the cloister.)

CECIL: My Lord.

ESSEX: I hear you go to France, Sir Robert.

CECIL: Yes.

ESSEX: And who is to mind England while you're away?

CECIL *(smiles)*: The Earl Marshal, of course.

ESSEX *(laughs)*: But you put the beggar in charge of the bank.

CECIL: Yes. There is a cargo of cochineal newly arrived and at the Queen's disposal. She has agreed my proposal that you should have it for £50,000. That's eighteen shillings a pound.

ESSEX: It's worth twice that.

CECIL: Well, say thirty-eight shillings a pound. I also suggested you should have £7,000 worth as a gift.

ESSEX: That's extraordinarily kind, Robert. Frances, do you hear, my love? *(To Lady Essex.)*

LADY ESSEX: Yes. I trust the country will want to dye itself red for our advantage.

CECIL: Better dye than blood, my Lady.

(*They laugh but Cecil doesn't. They stop when they see he doesn't.*)

ESSEX: I am much indebted to you.

CECIL: I am glad for that. I have been much maligned. In a high place one has few friends.

ESSEX: Friends? Friends are always few.

(*They move off. The company follows. Only Sir Walter Raleigh and Southampton are left.*)

RALEIGH: If she ever finds out, she'll stick both of you in the Tower.

(*Southampton laughs.*)

Her ladies-in-waiting are very precious. Besides, Elizabeth Vernon is cousin to my Lord Essex.

SOUTHAMPTON: Do you think I don't know that?

RALEIGH: You're a fool, my lad.

SOUTHAMPTON: Perhaps. (*Nonchalant.*)

RALEIGH: I have seen bigger men than you go down.

(*Southampton shrugs. Raleigh turns to follow the others. They walk together.*)

Has he really forgiven me?

(*Laughter. Essex laughing ahead.*)

SOUTHAMPTON: He's a man of bright morning. He forgets the black nights as quickly as he can.

RALEIGH: And you?

SOUTHAMPTON: I take things as they come.

RALEIGH: Be careful how they come.

SOUTHAMPTON: Thank you. But now I think we feast and make merry.

RALEIGH: Oh, yes, my Lord. For a week, perhaps; for a month. In the shade of the axe, my Lord.

(Flicks hand. We follow the hand movement upwards to the ceiling of the cloister. A gargoyle grins at the vaulted centre. We hold it.)

7

Interior, the presence chamber. Night.

A ball with evidence of a consumed feast. Servants passing with swan carcasses etc. Music. Sellingers round or the like. Not a pavan. Something fairly fast. The Queen dancing with Essex. Lady Essex with Raleigh. Lady Rich with Mountjoy. Southampton with Elizabeth Vernon. Bacon with anonymous lady. We see the dancers fairly close. Essex has eyes for women not dancing. Southampton and Elizabeth Vernon demonstrably in love. Bacon not a very good dancer. Burghley is sitting watching.

(Note: The dance need not be one which requires dancers to join at the onset. Southampton and Raleigh with their partners may join in their own time.

The dancers are seen from many angles. Superimposed shots etc. The object here to dwell on the sense of gaiety and occasion. When music stops, applause of a genteel kind. We see the minstrels at rest exchanging glances of approval. The Queen nods in their direction. They bow from the waist.)

482

ELIZABETH (*to Essex*): We dance as well as ever.

ESSEX: In step with the time.

(*The Queen is nevertheless tired.*)

ELIZABETH: Time? We must sit.

(*The dance starts again. A pavan. Essex pauses.*)

ESSEX: It is a pavan.

ELIZABETH: Slow or fast I am tired.

(*She goes to her chair. Essex follows.*)

I am not the athlete I once was.

(*Servant gives her silver goblet. She drinks.*)

ESSEX: You dance superbly.

ELIZABETH: You had little time to notice. (*Looks towards ladies at side.*)

ESSEX: Beauty is looked away that is looked on too often.

(*Elizabeth smiles then looking past Essex, looks concerned. Essex turns. We see Burghley slumped in a chair.*)

ELIZABETH: I must go to Burghley.

(*Essex shrugs. Elizabeth crosses to Burghley. Essex starts dancing with some relief.*)

BURGHLEY: Your Majesty.

ELIZABETH (*sitting beside him, fussing over him*): My spirit. It is brave of you to come. You are in much pain?

483

BURGHLEY: It is always less in your good company.

ELIZABETH: Yes. We have been good company. It is good to see the young dance.

BURGHLEY: Yes. We may watch but we cannot own what they enjoy.

(*Elizabeth looks at Burghley.*)

—He has too much promise, my Lady.

(*Essex dancing.*)

ELIZABETH: He has ambition.

BURGHLEY: Ambition is a fierce stallion. It can throw those who ride it.

ELIZABETH: I can still ride, my spirit.

BURGHLEY: Yes. But you will need the curbed bit and a strong snaffle. I have seen many proud men.

ELIZABETH: And will see many more.

BURGHLEY: No, my dance is nearly over. There is only one partner awaits me now.

ELIZABETH: No. No. I have need of you.

BURGHLEY: My lady. You can command much but not that. Besides, you have my son. I have trained him well.

ELIZABETH: You. You have no drink.

BURGHLEY: No. The good time they keep is my drink. And my meat. I pray God you have their measure.

ELIZABETH: I have their measure, my Lord.

(*Elizabeth smiles. The two of them survey the dance. Music and voices up.*)

Exterior, courtyard.

We see Cecil dismount from a horse. Muddy. Tired. Guard takes reins etc. helps him down. It is a cloudy day. Rain? Cecil walks the colonnaded cloister. A couple chasing each other, with laughter, stop as he approaches. He notices a ribbon, a hat perhaps, on the ground. Picks it up. Shows distaste. He is the hard-working bureaucrat. These people are foolish spend-thrifts etc. Essex trendies.

8

Interior, gallery. Day.

Cecil in palace corridor. Guards acknowledge, then exchange knowing looks. Trouble is on the way.

9

Interior, presence chamber. Day.

The Queen seated on low throne. Essex, Cecil, Lord Keeper Egerton, Raleigh are present. Essex on corner of table. We start close to the Queen.

ELIZABETH: Has the King of France no gratitude? I have spent nearly a million pounds on his behalf. I have sold land to meet the cost of armies. Englishmen have died for his cause. A Protestant cause he has already rejected. Paris is worth a mass, he said. Tcha.

Interior privy chamber. Day.

CECIL: O'Neill of Tyrone has risen. He is backed by Spanish money. If we sign peace with Spain that money will cease.

485

ESSEX: The Irish will fight whether they have Spanish gold or not.

CECIL: You propose another war?

ELIZABETH: Sir Robert you make too much of it. War or no war we have no Lord Deputy in Ireland. I have given this matter some thought. I have a mind to send Lord Mountjoy.

(*Pause. Essex reacts negatively.*)

What is wrong with Lord Mountjoy? I thought he was your friend.

ESSEX: He has little experience.

CECIL: Friends are best at court.

ELIZABETH: I will have no more of this sniping. There must be a Lord Deputy in Ireland. Sir William Knollys.

ESSEX: My uncle.

ELIZABETH: Yes. Your uncle. Is he not old enough?

ESSEX: Your Majesty. My uncle does good service here.

ELIZABETH: To whom? To you or to me? Every name you reject.

ESSEX (*tired*): I have told you. I favour Sir George Carew.

RALEIGH: Sir George cannot be spared.

EGERTON: Somebody will have to go.

ELIZABETH: Thank you, my Lord Keeper, as you so rightly say someone must be sent. Nobody wishes their friends to take this high office. I am no fool. I know the reason.

(*Cecil and Essex now stand facing her.*)

But I have decided. The new Lord Deputy of Ireland shall be—Sir William Knollys.

(*Essex deliberately turns his back on the Queen. The Queen pauses. Then enraged, steps forward and boxes his ears.*)

Go to the devil!

(*Essex wheels round. His hand on his sword.*)

ESSEX: This is an outrage that I will not put up with.

(*Egerton restrains him.*)

I would not have put up with that from your father.

(*They stare at each other. Hold gaze. Then Essex turns and rushes from the room. Everyone is frightened. They look at the Queen. Her face gives away nothing.*)

10

Interior, gallery. Day.

Southampton and Elizabeth Vernon, frightened.

VERNON: Please go.

SOUTHAMPTON: But she does nothing. You must know what is in her mind?

VERNON: I don't know. Please.

SOUTHAMPTON: Elizabeth. Essex waits any sign.

(Elizabeth Vernon looks nervously down the corridor.)

VERNON: Lord Burghley is dying. She is pitiful. My spirit, she calls him. My poor spirit. If you could see her. She goes to *feed* that old man.

SOUTHAMPTON: Touching.

VERNON: She has had more from that old man than she ever had from my Lord Essex.

SOUTHAMPTON: I see.

VERNON: Oh. Henry, no. He has been a long time at her side. When he dies, the old will feel a great gap as if an age was over. She can think of nothing.

SOUTHAMPTON: Does she not spare any thought for— for our friend?

VERNON: Yours. Not mine. Never whisper he's a friend of mine. *(Pause to look round.)* All she has said. He has played me long enough. Now I shall play with him. And—I value myself as high as he.

SOUTHAMPTON: Hm. She could not say less. Tell me more.

VERNON: I must go. He is dying and she will be with him. *(She leaves him.)*

SOUTHAMPTON: Elizabeth.

(Vernon turns.)

I love you.

(Guard appears. Coughs. Elizabeth Vernon goes confused.)

11

Interior, Essex's house. Night.

We see close up the Lord Keeper Egerton.

EGERTON: There is only one thing you can do. You must beg her forgiveness.

ESSEX: But I have given no cause.

EGERTON: My Lord. Duty, policy, religion, compel you to yield. Between you and your sovereign there can be no proportion of duty.

ESSEX: I owe her Majesty allegiance. In *that* I do not fail. But I have no duty to attend the court.

EGERTON: My Lord. Your pride has driven you to great things. Suppress it now and her Majesty will be gracious. Your friends will do well and you yourself reap further honour.

ESSEX: I do my friends no harm. It is she who has done the harm.

EGERTON: That is not for you to say.

ESSEX: Why? Does God say it? Cannot princes be wrong? Is earthly power infinite?

EGERTON: You ask frightening questions.

ESSEX: That is as maybe. But I have had a wrong done to me. She struck me, my Lord.

EGERTON: She is the Queen.

ESSEX: Aye and should behave so. I am of the blood of kings, my Lord. Kings.

EGERTON: I can offer nothing?

ESSEX: Princes are best served by those who do not hide their injuries.

EGERTON: You chart a dangerous course.

ESSEX: Does the country say so? The City of London is with me. The university of Cambridge makes me their Chancellor. Tell the Queen I am a Devereux. We are not mocked without cost.

(*Essex turns away. We see Egerton realize he has failed.*)

12

Interior, Queen's bedroom. Night.

We see Egerton close up first. The Queen is seated. She avoids looking straight at Egerton.

EGERTON: He is adamant.

ELIZABETH: I know. I stand more from him than any man.

EGERTON: It cannot go on, your Majesty.

ELIZABETH: I have not sent Knollys to Ireland. I have not answered the Dutch. I have not. Since he left, nothing.

EGERTON: Sir Robert Cecil says—er . . .

ELIZABETH: No. Sir Robert plays with paper houses. We must play with fire. The wind is out there in the streets and it whispers Essex.

EGERTON: Majesty?

ELIZABETH: Princes rule best by seeming to surrender.

I know. I have said he must come to me on his knees.
But we do not train thoroughbreds to pull draycarts.

EGERTON: But to capitulate.

ELIZABETH: Capitulate? I do not think you understand
me, sir. I give nothing but for the peace of the kingdom. (*Looks away.*) He must be seen to be forgiven.

(*Egerton looks wonderingly.*)

I am not Gloriana without the magic of his mirror.

EGERTON: It needs a pretext.

ELIZABETH: Tyrone has taken a fort on the Black-
water. This action is the Earl Marshal's business. See
to it, word is sent to him.

(*She inclines her head. Egerton bows out. We do not
see him leave the room.*)

13

Interior, privy chamber. Day.

Cecil is at a desk, writing, Raleigh standing.

RALEIGH: Then who is to go to Ireland?

CECIL (*back to his writing*): That is why we meet.

RALEIGH: Whoever goes is lost.

CECIL: You stayed there some time on your estates
and survived.

RALEIGH: I had not the management of the country.
No one who has that survives.

CECIL: With a sufficient army a Lord Deputy could
win a great victory.

(*Raleigh strokes his beard thoughtfully.*)

RALEIGH: How big an army?

CECIL: Fifteen. Twenty thousand.

RALEIGH: That is big bait for a Commander. Will Mountjoy take it?

(*Cecil goes to table.*)

CECIL: He is proposed. But he is also opposed.

(*Noise of approach of Elizabeth and retinue. Cecil looks up. Orders his papers. The Queen enters. Essex at her side. She with sceptre. He with Earl Marshal's staff. Following them are the Lord Keeper, Lord Howard, Earl of Nottingham, Francis Bacon.*)

ESSEX: The office must be taken, I think, by a man of stature and of military reputation.

(*Elizabeth waves a hand gently.*)

ELIZABETH (*equable*): You start before we begin my Lord. (*Cecil bows.*) Sir Robert.

(*She looks around. Takes chair at head of table.*)

My Lord.

(*Indicates Essex to sit at her right hand. Cecil has his papers on her left. The others seat themselves at will. We look along the table to the Queen.*)

Sit, my Lords. The Lord Deputy. This appointment can wait no longer. My Lord Essex, you had already begun. Will you say again?

ESSEX (*moving in his chair*): Your Majesty, the Lord Deputy must speak with authority and presence. He must be a Commander of known reputation so that the very news of his appointment shall make the Irish shudder. But military prowess alone is not enough. He must have nobility.

ELIZABETH: Very well. Then who, my Lord?

ESSEX: I have defined the attributes required.

ELIZABETH: Yes. Leaving us with only one name. We see that you, who write the qualifications, are the only one who fulfils them.

ESSEX: I am sorry. You confuse me with this great honour. I have been so keen to have the post—properly filled, I've never thought of it for myself. Never.

ELIZABETH: Then.

(*Rising. They all rise. She turns to Essex.*)

We appoint the Earl of Essex, (*Essex kneels.*) Lord Deputy of Ireland.

ESSEX: I am honoured and most grateful. (*He rises.*)

ELIZABETH: The matter is settled, my Lords. (*She goes.*)

(*Essex struts round. Scans the company. Stops at Cecil who gives an urbane smile.*)

ESSEX: Ireland!

RALEIGH: I wish you luck, my Lord.

(*Essex goes with great flourish.*)

(*To Cecil.*) I would have gone myself.

CECIL: And chain yourself to his destiny.

RALEIGH: You're a sly fellow, Robert.

14

Interior, gallery. Day.

We see Essex striding out. Southampton waiting.

ESSEX: It's mine, Henry

(*Pause. Southampton looks blank.*)

I am Lord Deputy.

SOUTHAMPTON: Good God.

ESSEX: I can make you a general. Ireland is at our feet.

SOUTHAMPTON: But you said the Court was the centre of all.

ESSEX: I am better with soldiers than with courtiers. This kind of world is for small hunchback creatures, for scratchy clerks. We have a campaign, my boy. Oh, God, you should have seen their faces.

SOUTHAMPTON: Yes. What did Cecil say?

ESSEX: Nothing. Absolutely nothing. Looked as if he'd swallowed a sour apple.

SOUTHAMPTON (*smiles*): Success.

(*As Essex goes, his face full of concern. To himself aloud. Elizabeth Vernon from behind.*)

VERNON: Henry?

SOUTHAMPTON: My love. Essex goes to Ireland.

VERNON: No?

SOUTHAMPTON: He wants me to go.

VERNON: And will you?

494

SOUTHAMPTON: Well the war could be fun but I gather Ireland's rather dull. No theatres, my love. (*Mock horror*.)

(*She takes him by the hand, leads him to an alcove. He immediately makes to kiss her. She turns her head away.*)

VERNON: I am pregnant.

SOUTHAMPTON: What?

VERNON: I am certain.

SOUTHAMPTON: Then . . . then we must marry.

VERNON: But she. She might. Oh Henry.

SOUTHAMPTON: We must marry in secret.

VERNON: Oh, yes. And then the child is born and you're safe in Ireland.

SOUTHAMPTON: No. Look. We are safe now. Essex will see to it. But first we must marry.

VERNON: Oh. Henry. I'm so afraid when the Queen finds out—

SOUTHAMPTON: She is a woman, too.

VERNON: Aye. One that never had a child and never will and maybe never could. (*She leaves up corridor*.)

SOUTHAMPTON: I'll talk to you soon. (*To himself*.) God give me a good actor for a priest.

15

Interior, the privy chamber. Day.

Cecil at desk. Bacon standing.

BACON: What is she doing all these months? Essex has not yet left for Ireland. Has he got his commission?

CECIL: On one day, yes. The next, no. A book has come into her hands.

BACON: Why does she want to see me?

CECIL: It's a history of Henry the Fourth. It is dedicated to my Lord Essex.

BACON: But I know nothing of this.

CECIL: You are a scholar, Francis. She wants an expert opinion. Oh. She's translating *Ars Poetica*. She's been at it for weeks. It's very good.

(*Bacon walks to Queen's door.*)

ELIZABETH (*from within*): Come in.

16

Interior, Queen's bedroom. Day.

Door opens. Queen at a writing desk. Paper. Books, dictionaries etc. Desk in a window bay. Bright day. Queen does not rise. She turns in her chair.

ELIZABETH: Ah, Mr Bacon.

(*Indicates a chair. Bacon sits uneasily.*)

My work goes well.

BACON: Sir Robert told me.

ELIZABETH: My Latin has never left me. I find it a great relaxation. (*Leans to pick up book.*) This book.

(*Gets up and hands it to Bacon. Then sits again. While she does this, she speaks fast.*)

History of Henry the Fourth. Printer John Hayward. Dedication My Lord Essex.

(*Bacon takes book. Opens it.*)

The book contains a detailed account of the disposition of Richard II, look at the preface. Bottom of the page.

BACON: 'Most illustrious Earl, with your name adorning the front of our Henry, he may go forth to the public happier and safer.'

ELIZABETH: Meaning, Mr Bacon?

BACON: That the book, may be well received.

ELIZABETH: Yes. It could also mean that if Henry IV had had the names and titles of my Lord Essex, his right to the throne would have been better recognized. This book is treason.

BACON: It is history, your Majesty. King Richard was deposed.

ELIZABETH: Of all the history in England, they choose this one incident. The idea behind it is treason.

BACON: It would be hard to prove.

ELIZABETH: Then it must be forced from him. He must be charged with treason.

BACON: He? (*Thinks she means Essex.*)

ELIZABETH: The printer, Hayward.

BACON: Try him for theft. Not treason, your Majesty.

ELIZABETH: Theft?

BACON: He has stolen so much from other authors.

497

(*Elizabeth laughs.*)

ELIZABETH: Pretty. All writers are thieves. (*Stops the joke.*)

(*Elizabeth Vernon opens door. Stops.*)

VERNON: I'm sorry, your Majesty. I thought—

ELIZABETH: Thought! Done should be your word, my lady tart!

VERNON: Your Majesty—

ELIZABETH: Get out of my sight, girl. She has used these rooms for a brothel, Mr Bacon.

(*Vernon stands terrified.*)

See how she swells with the profit of her fornication. By God's death, get out.

(*Vernon goes out and closes door.*)

I want this book suppressed. You must find me a legal reason.

BACON: Your Majesty.

ELIZABETH: Good day, Mr Bacon.

17

Interior, privy chamber. Day.

Cecil facing Essex.

ESSEX: But when man? When?

(*Cecil indicates a scroll on the desk.*)

CECIL: It is here now.

(*Essex picks it up. Looks at it.*)

ESSEX: It is not signed. Until I have it signed I am Lord Deputy of nothing.

CECIL: She will sign it, my Lord.

ESSEX: Today, next month, next year?—It has taken five months already.

CECIL: It is not well to rush these things.

ESSEX: I can arrange nothing until it is settled. I must appoint a council and officers. Until I have it—

(*Elizabeth enters.*)

ELIZABETH: You will have it now.

(*Essex turns. Bows.*)

ELIZABETH: Give me the commission. A pen, man. (*She signs and hands it to Essex.*) There is your commission, my Lord.

ESSEX: Your humble servant, your Majesty.

ELIZABETH: Ireland was never easy, my Lord. She has buried many reputations, but these rebellions must be utterly crushed. You will take O'Neill and I will see his head on London bridge. You will see to it that the Irish know who is their queen.

(*Essex reacts as if she has finished.*)

But read it well, my Lord. There is more. I will not have Sir Christopher Blount on your council.

ESSEX: Your Majesty—

ELIZABETH: Nor will you appoint the Earl of Southampton. He is a lecher, my Lord.

499

ELIZABETH R

ESSEX: But these are good men.

ELIZABETH: Good?

ESSEX: I trust them.

ELIZABETH: It is my trust that matters.

ESSEX: I thought I had that trust.

ELIZABETH: I look on you as myself.

ESSEX: I have not changed.

ELIZABETH: My Lord. There is something more.

(*Looks towards the scroll. He holds it up, enquiringly.*)

You must not return unless we order it.

ESSEX: You tie me hand and foot. Am I your servant or your slave?

ELIZABETH: My slave. It is the time, my Lord, and it is only duty that we must serve. If I could choose, my Lord, it could be other.

(*Essex pauses, stares at Cecil, who smiles blandly. Then bows to take the Queen's hand. Kisses it.*)

I see you wear the ring. (*Smiles.*)

ESSEX: Always. (*Tears in his eyes.*) Sweet lady. (*Turns quickly and goes.*)

CECIL: He took it well.

ELIZABETH: Took? He always takes. They say he is the world's wide wonder. They are right, Mr Secretary. Right.

(*She cries.*)

500

Exterior, a road in Ireland.

We see a man on a horse riding towards a woman at the side of the road. She has a cow or a goat. He stops and leans towards her.

HORSEMAN: O'Neill ata ann? (*The O'Neill?*)

WOMAN: O'Neill? (*She is suspicious.*)

HORSEMAN: Ja Essex ag teacht. (*Essex is coming.*)

WOMAN: Essex?

HORSEMAN: Na sasanaig, mile saighduiri. (*The English, thousands of soldiers.*)

WOMAN: Saighduiri? (*Soldiers.*)

(*Woman crossing herself.*)

Dia le O'Neill.

(*Moves out to show him the way.*)

San treo sin ata se imithe. (*He is that way.*)

HORSEMAN: Guibh maith agat. (*Thanks.*)

WOMAN: Dia leat. (*God be with you.*)

(*Horseman rides on.*)

18

Interior, O'Neill's room. Night.

The room has rough walls. Fire in the middle of the floor. Rough table, one good high-back chair. Stools.

R

*O'Neill is seated in the chair. Foot on a stool. Cups,
plate, etc., are gold, silver. His harper, sits near him.
All others at table (men only) are armed but 'at ease'.
A horseman stands. Harper plucks idly. All look to the
horseman.*

HORSEMAN: Thousands there were. A week and they'd
still be passing.

O'NEILL: And Achilles himself? The world's wide
wonder.

HORSEMAN: Ah now. I never saw the Earl. He was
sick, they said.

O'NEILL: He'll be sicker yet.

(Chuckles of agreement.)

CONN: We could take them easy. Jesus, so we could.

O'NEILL: Easy, you say. *(To the harper.)* The battle of
Down, Giolla Brighde. How does it go? Unequal . . .

HARPER: 'Unequal they engaged in battle. Foreigners
and the Gael of Tara
fine linen shirts on the race of Conn
the English in one mass of iron'.

O'NEILL: Them in iron, my boy, and us in linen. So we'll
have no gay abandoned frontal attacks. We'll play it
our good way.

CONN: Could we not tickle them a bit?

O'NEILL: We could so. They think us all here in Lein-
ster. Let e'm think it. There's enough here to give them
sport.

CONN: Sport, you say.

O'NEILL: Yes. That's how they see us. So much good

game to be hunted down. Till Ireland fights war her own way, she will not be free. *Their* way is to make a killing ground and lead us to it. So we avoid all grand battles and pray the rain rusts their mass of iron. We parley and know it wastes another of their days. And we pray for rain. Rain, boys. God's gift to Ireland.

19

Interior, Dublin castle: council chamber. Night.

Remnants of a dinner on the table. Lord Mayor of Dublin on Essex's right. On his left, Blount. Next to Blount, Southampton. We see the horseman from the previous scene conspicuous as a servant listening while handing out food, etc. Essex is standing; goblet held high.

ESSEX: Gentlemen. Her sovereign Lady, Queen of England, France and Ireland.

(*The guests rise.*)

RESPONSE: The Queen.

(*Essex turns. Foot on his chair.*)

ESSEX: And now gentlemen, Henry, Chris—to matters of state. My good mayor (*Nods to Lord Mayor.*) has not been idle, gentlemen. The strategic issues are clear to me. The south is full of rebels. Small isolated bands. To the west, rebellion is poorly organized. Tyrone hides away somewhere in the north. I want your opinions. My Lord Mayor?

MAYOR: We—that is to say my colleagues in office—we feel you should go south.

BLOUNT: Why south?

MAYOR: If you go north first striking his main force,

you will have these smaller forces at your back. Troops will have to be left here to defend Dublin.

SOUTHAMPTON: And why will O'Neill do nothing if we attack the south?

LORD MAYOR: If he fights, he fights on his own ground. You have good towns in the south. Towns now threatened which are loyal.

SOUTHAMPTON: But O'Neill; O'Neill's in the north; O'Neill's what we're here for.

ESSEX: Henry, these people live here. Our task is to pacify the country.

BLOUNT: Yes. My Lord Mayor, you say the forces in the south are small.

LORD MAYOR: Yes. I'm not a military man but I would say it wouldn't take more than a week or two.

BLOUNT: It takes time to move twenty thousand men.

LORD MAYOR: I think you have only to march and the rebellion will be crushed. These country people are easily frightened.

ESSEX: A parade of our strength. A progress. They are right, Chris. We march south.

(*Horseman taking good notice.*)

Exterior series of images in montage.

Dominant themes. Essex riding sometimes alone, sometimes with Southampton and/or Blount. At first confident. Gradually dejected. Outline of sequence of shots.

Essex proud, smiling on open road. Turns to Southampton, laughs.

(*Sound: Drums in good march time. Trumpets? March sound.*)

O'Neill drinking, laughing with his head back.

Green dark woods, wild hedges.

(*Harp.*)

Essex on a forest track or road beside a wood. Blount points. Nobody to be seen. Gesture from Essex—forget it.

(*War cries in Irish.*)

Beggars at side of road. Half-naked. Looking up at the horsemen.

Some English soldiers tired. Their feet in rags. Rain.

(*Ragged drum.*)

Essex facing front. Rain.

O'Neill's harper in good clothes singing.

The green dark woods of Ireland.

(*Harping continues under.*)

Essex sitting on a grass bank. Opening a letter with seals. Starts to read:

(*Elizabeth reads the letter over. See following page.*)

Cut to:

Essex on horseback reading the letter.

Cut to:

Beggars, tinkers on road.

505

Cut to:

Shots fired in a wood. Smoke.

Cut to:

Rain on sacks of wheat.

Cut to:

O'Neill laughing.

Queen reads letter over.

This reading is against the series of montage shots which begin with Essex opening the letter.

ELIZABETH (*over*): We pay you a thousand pounds a day to go on progress, my Lord. You send nothing but complaint. You give us no victories, wander the roads of Ireland. You march south while Tyrone is in the north. Why, my Lord, why? You have made knights against my orders. You harbour the Earl of Southampton against my express command. My armies are wasted and achieve nothing. I command you, return to Dublin. You shall not come to England without my express warrant. You have only one duty. To crush the rebellion. Send me no more complaints; no more tales of your hurt pride.

20

Interior, room in Dublin castle. Day.

Essex is slunk in a chair. Sick again, he is covered by skins. Blount straddles a chair. Southampton is standing, reading another letter from the Queen.

SOUTHAMPTON: 'With three-quarters of your men in garrisons, you have no power to take Tyrone.' How does she know?

BLOUNT: We have been spied upon from the first.

ESSEX: The truth is worse. I have not more than four thousand.

SOUTHAMPTON: We are done for then. (*Strokes his neck.*)

BLOUNT: No, she will not live forever.

(*Essex looks up at Southampton. Blount not looking at either, continues.*)

We cannot take Tyrone but we could take England. King James in Scotland, would favour it.

ESSEX: We are in Dublin, Chris, and I am sick.

(*Blount looks up or gets up.*)

BLOUNT: We are all sick, Robin. But we do not whimper in a corner. You have only to stand up and give the word and England will come running.

ESSEX: There still remains Tyrone.

BLOUNT: Parley with him.

ESSEX: Parley?

BLOUNT: As Lord Deputy, you can pardon treason. You have done it.

ESSEX: And who pardons me?

BLOUNT: No one. You will not need a pardon. Not then.

ESSEX: She sends me nothing but abuse and rancour. She rings me with spies. She—(*Stops.*)

BLOUNT: Well then? Send word to Tyrone.

507

ESSEX: No. She must see she does me wrong. I must go straight to England.

SOUTHAMPTON: Hm. I should have liked to have seen Tyrone. Just once before I faced the gallows.

(*Essex looks up, smiles wanly at Southampton.*)

ESSEX: Why then, you shall.

BLOUNT: You'll parley?

ESSEX: Yes.

BLOUNT: And then to England?

ESSEX: We'll see what bargain can be struck. Whatever I do, I'll get that hunchback off the Queen's back.

Exterior, a river bank.

Essex in full parade armour. Ribbons, plumes etc. Blount and Southampton likewise. Nothing visible on the far bank.

ESSEX: Nothing.

BLOUNT: Is it a trick?

SOUTHAMPTON: No, wait. Look.

(*Two men appear. Naked to the waist. One carries O'Neill's standard. They enter the water.*)

BLOUNT: Hm. That is all the armour they ever wear.

(*The standard bearer stops in the middle of the river. The other man, a herald, comes across. He stops while still in the water.*)

HERALD: Lord Essex. (*Pause.*) The high Lord Hugh O'Neill is waiting.

508

ESSEX: Tell him that I wait too.

HERALD: He bids me say you are to meet him by the standard. Alone. No man with you.

BLOUNT: I don't like it.

ESSEX: I risk nothing. (*To herald.*) I agree to that.

HERALD: No arms. No swords or small daggers.

(*Essex takes out sword. Kisses it. Hands it to Southampton. The herald watches—turns, raises his hand to the standard bearer. The standard bearer gives a similar sign. O'Neill appears on horseback. He is dressed as for a ball. He rides into the river.*)

SOUTHAMPTON: He is like a Prince.

ESSEX: He *is* a prince. (*Rides forward slowly.*)

BLOUNT: She called him her most famous rebel.

SOUTHAMPTON: Which one?

BLOUNT: Steady, Henry.

(*We come close now to the two men on horseback in the river. We come in after formalities of greeting.*)

O'NEILL: It is ungracious but I feared a trap. It is better we talk here.

ESSEX: We can speak more freely, too.

O'NEILL: That doesn't sound like a man who would have my neck.

ESSEX: I need peace only.

O'NEILL: Ah! don't we all? And don't the English

s   509 always want peace? Their kind of peace. They can never see they would have it if they left us alone.

ESSEX: And you have no cause with Spain? (*Tut tut.*)

O'NEILL: A war is a great inconvenience. It costs money. I would take money from the Emperor of China if he had it to give. You don't think a grown man enjoys this kind of thing? It's putting years on me. I have seven—eight thousand men back there—

ESSEX: Eight thousand?

O'NEILL: Oh! Did you not know I had that many? Ha. Well now. The year creeps on. You've a mind to go to England, I hear. Some deal with King James.

ESSEX: You hear strange tales.

O'NEILL: Well never mind. Supposing I do. You'd need an assurance of my good behaviour. I'm sorry I can't oblige with my head on a platter.

ESSEX: For me, that was never sought.

O'NEILL: Good so. If I could have Ireland and yourself —er—the other place, that'd be a brave condition.

ESSEX: I am the Queen's Lord Deputy.

O'NEILL: Aye. You must forgive me dreaming. To be practical though, I'll give you this for nothing. A six week truce.

ESSEX: Six weeks.

O'NEILL: Renewable though. Indefinitely. No trouble for six weeks, another truce. As far as you're concerned it would be indefinite. To you, in England, in good stead, indefinite.

ESSEX: The Queen would not accept it.

O'NEILL: The Queen? Who's talking about the Queen, man? She's as good as dead.

ESSEX: That is not true.

O'NEILL: So that's the way of it.

ESSEX: What do you mean?

O'NEILL: I thought you were free of her.

(*Starts to turn his horse.*)

ESSEX: No wait. I will take the truce.

O'NEILL: That's better.

ESSEX: Can I have it in writing?

O'NEILL: I'm a terrible lazy man with a pen, my Lord.

ESSEX: Then your hand.

O'NEILL: Indeed. I would give that any day to the conqueror of Cadiz.

(*They shake hands.*)

ESSEX: We should be better known, my Lord.

O'NEILL: Maybe we shall.

ESSEX: You will keep the truce?

O'NEILL: If you remove the army, there's no one to fight.

ESSEX: Renewable.

O'NEILL: Now look. I have a feast prepared. Good beef and salmon. Good wine. Will you not come over?

511

ESSEX: Thank you, no. I have not much time.

O'NEILL: I like you, my Lord. No horseman would leave my camp ahead of yours.

ESSEX: I must get to England.

O'NEILL: So the tales I heard were not so strange.

ESSEX: Good day, my Lord.

O'NEILL: Good day to you. As we say in Irish, may the path be straight that's in front of you.

(*Essex turns. Walks the horse slowly back. O'Neill sits watching. He waves. A great shout goes up from the trees.*)

21

Interior, palace corridor. Queen's apartments. Morning.

We see Essex exhausted, dirty, travel-stained, making his way to the Queen's room. We see him, perhaps, pause for breath. We see a guard, amazed to see him, attempt to block his way. He pushes him aside. Finally, he bursts open the door. Pauses. The Queen is facing us, no wig. She is half-dressed, none of her normal make-up. Lady-in-waiting (not Elizabeth Vernon) astonished.

ELIZABETH: My Lord.

ESSEX: Your Majesty, I had forgot the time. I—

ELIZABETH: I see you learn Irish manners. (*Laughs.*) You are so cold, my Lord.

ESSEX: I have won peace. I rushed to tell you. Wanted with my own lips. I am deeply sorry. (*Despairing gesture; he can get nothing right.*)

(*Lady-in-waiting puts a light shawl of silk on Queen's head, and shoulders.*)

ELIZABETH: Make more of it, and you make it worse. When I am dressed I shall hear the rest.

ESSEX: I thank God I find such sweet calm at home.

(*Essex bows out in confusion. The Queen smiles when he has gone.*)

22

Interior, privy chamber. Day.

Cecil and Egerton. Egerton tense, sitting on a chair. Cecil suave and relaxed.

EGERTON: He burst into her room. God knows where the guards were.

CECIL: Taking their ease. I had word he was coming.

EGERTON: You play with such fire. She expressly told him to stay in Ireland. Now this.

CECIL: Now this.

EGERTON: Why hate him so much?

CECIL (*less relaxed*): That man would rule us all. The crowds who hail him as a hero would be the first to suffer. He would be mighty at every man's expense.

EGERTON: She did not send him away. She told him to come back.

CECIL: He has been at some devilment with the Scots.

EGERTON: Does she know?

CECIL: No.

EGERTON: She is unguarded. This is madness.

CECIL: You do not see how weak he is. How father-less, how eager to lay a trophy at her feet.

EGERTON: Supposing she falls for the trophy?

CECIL: No. She is wiser than that. Besides, I have only to whisper Scotland.

EGERTON: But in the end, it must be King James.

CECIL: Perhaps. I say nothing to that. The mention of his name is like a sentence of death. The man who speaks it, points a dagger at her heart.

EGERTON: Pray God, we all survive these times.

CECIL: In a time of heroes and tyrants, the true heroes are the small men. (*Shuffles cards.*)

23

Interior, Queen's bedroom. Night.

The Queen talks with Essex—alone. The Queen plays patience or similar game. Tarot cards? Both are seated. The Queen has a small table of the coffin stool variety. Both are now neatly dressed. We see close the cards being played. Queen is in apparently good and sympathetic mood.

ELIZABETH: These garrisons then, reduced your force?

ESSEX: The loyal towns required them; our men were hostages to their loyalty.

ELIZABETH: But could you not have marched with the full army against O'Neill and brought him down?

ESSEX: No. They don't observe the common rules of war. Ireland is not France or Spain. By day, you'd scarce see them at all. Their main attacks were always at night. And the rain! Oh God, the rain.

ELIZABETH: Yes, but what has been achieved?

ESSEX: Peace.

ELIZABETH: Is O'Neill disarmed then?

ESSEX: He has accepted my conditions of truce.

ELIZABETH: I did not send you for a truce, I sent you to bring down O'Neill.

ESSEX: He assures me of his loyalty.

ELIZABETH: To me, my Lord?

ESSEX: I would not have left if I had any doubt of his word.

ELIZABETH: You have given knighthoods.

ESSEX: They were honours given in the field.

ELIZABETH: I expressly forbade it.

ESSEX: You would have done the same.

ELIZABETH: You and I are not the same, my Lord. I am the Queen.

ESSEX: And I do nothing but serve you, your Majesty.

ELIZABETH: And your return?

ESSEX: I—I admit the fault. But my aim was to report

success. I wanted to be the first to tell you. If you wish me to return to Ireland, I shall leave immediately.

ELIZABETH: No. You are here. You shall stay here.

ESSEX: You are most gracious.

ELIZABETH (*rising. Holding out hand*): We must consider how to treat your achievement. (*Acid in her voice.*)

ESSEX: Your Majesty.

(*Kisses her hand.*)

24

Interior, a wooden door. Day.

Essex in shirt sleeves, beating against it.

EGERTON (*from other side of door*): What is it, my Lord?

ESSEX: Egerton?

EGERTON: My Lord.

ESSEX: Oh, thank God. It's locked, I can't get out.

EGERTON (*from other side*): On her Majesty's orders.

ESSEX: Open this door. Don't play the fool, man.

EGERTON: You are detained, my Lord.

ESSEX: Detained? On what count?

EGERTON: I am sorry. I—have no further orders.

ESSEX (*listens against door*): Egerton, Egerton? (*Pause. No reply.*) He's gone. She can't mean it. Oh God. (*Slumps against the door.*)

25

Interior, bedchamber. Day.

ELIZABETH: What am I to do, Mr Bacon? The mob brays his name. He puts himself above me. Who gave him leave to return so soon. I sent him to Ireland on other business, and I will have him tried for his disobedience.

BACON: By what court?

ELIZABETH: The Star Chamber.

BACON: It would be difficult, your Majesty. The case would be hard to prove unless you commit yourself to a public scrutiny of your policy and he is popular, especially here in London.

ELIZABETH: He has openly disobeyed my orders. He has not crushed the rebellion, but has made some gross intrigue with O'Neill. He can no longer be Lord Deputy. He must leave my Council and the people must know of his insolence and incompetence. Who is the monarch here? He must be cut down.

BACON: A trial would be ill-advised. Besides he is too ill.

ELIZABETH: Ill? he is always ill when he is out of favour. I will not again play the guilty parent to his hurt child. It shall go to the Star Chamber.

BACON: A statement could be read to the Chamber. In his absence. A statement of iniquities. Not a charge. I don't think he would challenge it and the burden of proof would thus be avoided.

ELIZABETH: I take your advice, Mr Bacon. There will be no hearing.

BACON: Simply a statement.

ELIZABETH: I would have made a fine lawyer.

BACON: And a good judge, your Majesty.

26

Interior, gallery. Day.

Sir Walter Raleigh in a fury. Passes guard, dozing.

RALEIGH: Have a care!

(*Guard adopts 'have a care' position. Door opens. Cecil appears.*)

Ah, Sir Robert. What madness is this?

CECIL: Madness? Sir Walter? I see none but yours.

RALEIGH: He goes scot free. You had him pinned to the wall and you've let him go.

CECIL: The Queen has done it. Not I.

RALEIGH: Who tells the Queen?

CECIL: No. It comes from her. And my cousin, Francis.

RALEIGH: I might have known. He worked for Essex.

CECIL: Did.

RALEIGH: Maybe still does.

CECIL: His life has been threatened.

RALEIGH: Aye and more, too, when my Lord high and mighty walks free to his merry band of cut-throats.

CECIL: He is done. He is very sick.

RALEIGH: The malice in that man is constant. No sickness or remedy can purge it. You have all distrusted me, thinking me driven by jealousy. I know enemies long before they show their colours. I had his measure. The Queen is mad to let him go.

CECIL: He has been deprived of all office. He is without any status.

RALEIGH: You think that words will stop him; he needs four thick walls.

CECIL: Sir Walter, I'm obliged for your advice. (*Smiles distantly, bows and walks off.*)

RALEIGH (*shouts*): Clerk.

(*Guard laughs softly.*)

27

Interior, Essex house. Great hall. Night.

Essex, Southampton, Blount, seated by the fire.

ESSEX: It's no use. It's all no use.

BLOUNT: But Mountjoy has agreed to send the army from Ireland.

ESSEX: What Mountjoy said before he took Ireland is neither here nor there. He has Ireland now.

SOUTHAMPTON: King James still believes us. He's convinced that Cecil plots against him.

ESSEX: So then?

BLOUNT: So we still invite his support. We can manage without the army from Ireland. Men gather by the hundred every day.

519

SOUTHAMPTON: And all say that Cecil has sold the succession to the Spaniards.

ESSEX: They say that?

SOUTHAMPTON: Since I whispered it abroad. Yes.

ESSEX: We talk, Chris. We talk but we haven't the means to action.

SOUTHAMPTON: We have great support.

ESSEX: But no money. Damn it, Henry, will you never understand? I have but one source of income and I stand to lose it. The monopoly on the sale of wines. It's the last thing.

BLOUNT: Afterwards, you can have anything you want.

ESSEX: But I need it now.

SOUTHAMPTON: So he has once again written one of his sweet pleading letters. 'Haste paper to that happy presence, whence only unhappy I am banished.' I trust she pays you by the line.

ESSEX (to Blount, who rises): Let me write.

SOUTHAMPTON: Another sweet piece of invective?

ESSEX: No. Scotland. We must work out a concerted plan. (Breaks from reason to rage.) Oh! Damn. Damn her! I rode in triumph before her. I laid the ashes of Cadiz at her feet. I pumped new blood into her old veins. She said nothing then. I have created all and she takes all.

BLOUNT (handing quill): Write man.

ESSEX: What? Oh, yes. (Reaches for pen.) To our Sovereign Lord King James of Scotland, the Sixth . . .

(Fade on last speech.)

520

28

Interior, privy chamber. Day.

Cecil is seated. Egerton, Bacon, standing. Raleigh standing by the door. The Queen sits.

EGERTON: They grow stronger every day.

BACON: He must be contained. For his own good.

RALEIGH: For the country's good, man. I tell you, if I could have ten men, I'd kill him with my own hands.

CECIL: He is strong in men and weak in money. Without his monopolies, the income from his sweet wines he is nothing.

RALEIGH: What does that matter if he has the city at his feet? We are lost if he is not taken.

CECIL: Taken?

RALEIGH: Disarmed and under close escort, lodged in the Tower.

CECIL: We cannot risk it we ...

EGERTON: We cannot act in haste, Sir Walter.

RALEIGH: If we do not act we are lost.

ELIZABETH: We? We? But who is for me? We revoke his monopolies. All.

RALEIGH: And arrest? (*Draws sword.*)

ELIZABETH: No!

CECIL: I fear it will provoke him to raise the city.

ELIZABETH: For his sake, Sir Robert, I pray God it will not. I play no Richard the Second to his Bolingbroke.

29

Interior, Essex house. Night.

Essex's companions are ranged in chairs with Essex in the middle. They are watching a performance of Richard II. Staging is ad hoc, like a charade. We come in towards the end of Act IV, Scene I. We start close to the crown which has the hands of Bolingbroke and Richard on it. Richard has just spoken 'the golden crown like a deep well' speech. As we see the crown, we hear Bolingbroke. Later as the play within the play proceeds we leave the two actors on the stage to study the knowing looks and appreciative smiles of Essex's coterie.

RICHARD:
Give me thy crown.
Here, cousin, seize the crown.
Here cousin.
On this side my hand, and on that side thine.
Now is this golden crown like a deep well.
That owes two buckets, filling one another.
The emptier ever dancing in the air,
The other down, unseen, and full of water,
That bucket down and full of tears am I,
Drinking my griefs, whilst you mount up on high.

ESSEX: Is this it now?

SOUTHAMPTON: Listen to King Richard.

BOLINGBROKE: I thought you had been willing to resign.

RICHARD:
My crown, I am; but still my griefs are mine
You may my glories and my state depose
But not my griefs; still am I king of those.

BOLINGBROKE: Part of your cares you give me with your crown.

RICHARD:
Your cares set up, do not pluck my cares down,
My care is, loss of my care, by old care done.
Your care is, gain of care, by new care won.

(*Essex catches the eye of Blount, nods.*)

The cares I give, I have though given away,
They tend the crown, yet still with me they stay.

BOLINGBROKE:
Are you contented to resign the crown?

RICHARD:
Ay, no. No ay. For I must nothing be.
Therefore no, no for I resign to thee.
Now mark me how I will undo myself.
I give this heavy weight from off my head
And this unwieldy sceptre from my hand
The pride of kingly sway from out my heart.

(*Reaction here. Either Essex stands up and starts to applaud, going into following speech, or Richard begins to muff his lines and is prompted. Southampton interjects that they haven't done the play for a long time.*)

ESSEX: Well done. Well done.

(*Blount objects.*)

BLOUNT: No, let them . . .

ESSEX: No. We have seen the best. We have seen how it was done, my friends. Thank you, my noble kings.

BOLINGBROKE: You must forgive us, my Lord, it has not been done for a long time.

ESSEX: Fashions change, my good Henry.

BLOUNT: Can't we go on to the death?

523

ESSEX: No, my friends. No. We have much to do. She has cut me off from her exchequer. All she sends me are conditions. Conditions, my friends. Her conditions are as crooked as her carcase. Come, my friends, we have much to do.

(*Laughs from friends.*)

30

Interior, privy chamber. Light fading.

ELIZABETH: As crooked as her carcase.

Queen: fingers crooked drumming the table. Drum roll of execution behind them. The axe striking. Cheers. Queen eventually looks up. We see Cecil patient, inquiring. Queen makes as if to speak. Then gestures him away. The hands start drumming again. She stops. We see the hands clenched together, thumping the table violently. Two or three times. She stops. We see her listening. Shouts in the distance. Shots, sounds of riot. Servant brings in candles. Cecil waiting, looking at her. She looks up. Egerton standing in the gloom. Bacon too.

ELIZABETH: It was like this, my Lords, when my brother died. Waiting for the knock on the door.

(*Door opens. Confused shouts louder. Candles blown by the wind. Raleigh in full armour.*)

RALEIGH: He has lost, ma'am. He tried to raise the city but no one would answer his call.

ELIZABETH: Where is he now?

RALEIGH: At his house. About three hundred of 'em entered the city. My Lord Essex shouting we were sold to the Spanish Infanta. But the men of the city had no faith in him. When he turned and they planned to come here, he was stopped at Ludgate. Blount was wounded. They scurried back to his house.

EGERTON: It is over then.

RALEIGH: Shall I take him?

ELIZABETH: No. Sir Walter, your place is here. (*Turns to Lord Keeper*.) My Lord Keeper, take with you some men of the guard and the Lord Chief Justice. Take Knollys, too. His own kin must arrest him.

EGERTON: Where shall we take him?

ELIZABETH (*pause*): The Tower, my Lord. The Tower.

31

Interior, gallery. Day.

We see Cecil walking down the gallery towards the Queen's bedroom.

32

Interior, Queen's bedroom. Day.

Cecil enters.

ELIZABETH: Is there any news from the Tower?

CECIL: No.

ELIZABETH: No special plea. No supplication? I cannot pardon him. He would become the focus of starving, discontented beggars. A ragged robin inspiring some ill-starred revolt. I cannot pardon him. It is not mercy to keep mad dogs in kennels. It must be done.

525

But the axe is enough. No quarterings. They shall not butcher that body. (*She turns away.*) Tell me when it is done.

(*Cecil turns to go. She turns back.*)

Stay. The Earl of Southampton is a young fool. He has a fondness for the theatre, but he has no place in this (*Pause.*) dramatic spectacle. We pardon him to life imprisonment.

CECIL: Your Majesty shows great mercy.

ELIZABETH: He has a child by that silly girl, Elizabeth. Go tell him of his fortune. And as to my Lord— No. No. Nothing, Sir Robert. Nothing.

CECIL: He is much changed, your Majesty.

ELIZABETH: Changed? We are all changed. (*Trembles.*) Tell him; nothing.

(*She turns away. Cecil slips out.*)

33

Interior, the Tower. Cell. Day.

Gaoler followed by Cecil and Egerton. Door opens, Cecil and Egerton apprehensive. Essex on a low bench. Turns and throws himself at their feet. Clutches at Egerton, whimpering.

ESSEX: My Lords, I have more confession. Others are as guilty. You have not arrested them. They are greater traitors. They deceived me and lured me into this.

EGERTON: Your own guilt is enough.

ESSEX: No. They must all go with me. Sir Charles

Davers and Cuffe. Henry Cuffe, Sir Robert. Write them down. They mustn't escape. Cuffe is more guilty than all. Mountjoy, too—he was in it. And my sister.

(*Cecil looks up from writing.*)

Yes. She is guilty. She too has a proud spirit. Take my sister. She has been false to me as to the Queen. Southampton will tell you.

CECIL: The Earl does not go to the scaffold.

ESSEX: I am to be alone? The only victim? My Lords, I beg you. It cannot be public. I shall not be—able. (*He breaks down.*)

EGERTON: It is to be done here, at the Tower.

ESSEX: Then I thank God my confessions have not been in vain. I seemed far off like a great elm tree, taller than any oak. Elms grow a rotten centre. They fall, suddenly. I am frightened, my Lords, I am frightened.

CECIL: I will send a priest to console you.

(*They turn to go.*)

ESSEX: Take my sister. Don't let her get away.

(*They shake their heads and leave. The door shuts. Essex looks at his ring, takes it off.*)

Gaoler!

GAOLER: Yes, my Lord.

ESSEX: This ring is all I have. Take it and see it reaches the Queen.

GAOLER: Oh, I don't know about that.

ESSEX: It is hers. She gave it to me.

527

GAOLER: It's getting late.

ESSEX: Late? Aye. Very late. Find any way you can. Please, man, I beg you.

GAOLER: I'll do what I can.

ESSEX: Good. Good. I am still her servant. I have been misled. She must see that. She is to blame, too. She . . .

GAOLER: My Lord, you must compose yourself.

ESSEX: Compose? How? I had so little hand in my own making. I was shaped by—by the time. Yes. By the time. There is nothing of me to compose. I am in pieces.

GAOLER: I'll do what I can about the ring.

(*Door closes. Essex collapses.*)

34

Exterior, Tower (courtyard.) Day.

Scaffold with block: snow or frost on the ground: (February 25) courtiers and others gathering for the execution. Raleigh conspicuous. Cecil approaches.

CECIL: Sir Walter.

RALEIGH: Sir Robert.

CECIL: Will you stand so close?

RALEIGH: I am Captain of the Guard, Sir Robert. Besides, he may wish to speak to me.

CECIL: It looks to some as if you gloat.

RALEIGH: Surely we are passed that?

CECIL: But, it would look better if you were not so prominent.

RALEIGH: As you please. My guard knows what to do.

(*Raleigh bows, walks off. Some turn to see him go. Raised eyebrows. Drums.*)

35

Interior, corridor. Tower. Day.

Essex in long black cloak, hatless. His gaoler ahead of him in the gaoler passage.

ESSEX: No word?

GAOLER: None, my Lord.

ESSEX: She has forsaken me.

GAOLER: It seems so, my Lord. It is not far.

(*Drums.*)

36

Exterior, Tower. Courtyard. Day.

Shot of the ravens on the ground. Drums. Raleigh looking out from a window. Silence. Essex looks up. He is on the scaffold.

ESSEX: I have spent thirty-three years on this earth. I have spent my time in lust and wantonness and unclean acts. I have been puffed up with pride and vanity and the love of this world's pleasure. My sins are numberless, more in number than the hairs on my head. I beseech my saviour to pardon these my sins and especially this last most heinous sin which has offended my sovereign and the world. And pray still for the welfare of her Majesty whose death I protest I did not seek. I die neither Atheist nor Papist and in that faith to which I was born I bid you all to pray for me.

(He kneels. Then rises. Takes off the cloak. He is wearing a scarlet waistcoat with long sleeves, his hair about his shoulders, we get brilliant light here. Turns to executioner.)

I shall be ready when I stretch my arms.

(Puts his head on the block.)

Lord, into thy hands I commend my spirit.

(Flings out his arms. The axe falls. Drums. Shot of Raleigh in tears.)

37

Interior, bedchamber corridor. Day.

Sound over of a ballad singer.

BALLAD SINGER:
All you that cry ochone, ochone,
Come now and sing O Lord! with me
For why? Our Jewel is from us gone
The valiant Knight of Chivalry.

38

Interior, gallery. Day.

Raleigh strutting. Cecil approaches with Bacon in tow. They carry briefs.

RALEIGH: What have you there?

(*Cecil clutches papers.*)

CECIL: You would not find them good reading.

RALEIGH: Oh?

CECIL: No. They petition against the giving of favours. Against the monopolies at the Queen's disposal.

RALEIGH: They are hers by right.

BACON: The petitions come from Parliament.

RALEIGH: Parliament? Are shopkeepers to tell the Queen what to do?

BACON: It is feared that the favours enjoyed by the late Lord Essex will soon fall to others.

RALEIGH: It is the Queen's right to bestow favours on those who are loyal.

CECIL: On those who are loyal, yes. You must excuse us. Her Majesty awaits.

RALEIGH: She will do more than wait when she knows your errand. I wish you well of it.

39

Interior, privy chamber. Day.

ELIZABETH: The fault has been mine.

CECIL: It's your Majesty's right—

ELIZABETH: No, Sir Robert. This is not my father's time. I have nourished proud men at the expense of my people. They are right to ask for an end to the giving of monopolies.

531

CECIL: I think Parliament fears that the honours of Lord Essex may fall directly to Sir Walter.

ELIZABETH: We can afford no more hollow heroes.

BACON: The Commons will be much relieved.

ELIZABETH: We have gone beyond the time of great princes. When we sit, we are nearer the ground.

CECIL: I will send a letter to Mr Speaker.

ELIZABETH: No, Sir Robert. I will speak to the Parliament.

40

Interior, presence chamber. Day.

The Queen, and a small number of MP's in background. Cecil, Bacon and Raleigh in attendance. We fade in:

ELIZABETH: We perceive your coming is to present thanks to us. Know I accept them with no less joy than your loves can have desire to offer such a present, and do more esteem it than any treasure or riches; for those we know how to prize, but loyalty love and thanks I count them invaluable. And though God has raised me high, yet this I account the glory of my crown, that I have reigned with your loves. Stand up. I have more to say. Touching upon monopolies, Mr Speaker, you must tell the House from me that I take it exceeding grateful that the knowledge of these things has come unto me from them. Of myself, I must say this, I was never a greedy scraping grasper, nor a strict fast holding prince. Nor yet a waster.
To be a King and wear a crown is a thing more glorious to them that see it than it is pleasant to them that bear it. And for my own part I would be willing to resign

the place I hold to any other, glad to be free of the glory with the labours. For it is not my desire to live nor reign longer than my life and reign shall be for your good. And, though you have had and may have many mightier and wiser princes sitting in this seat, yet you never had nor shall have any who love you better.

(*Members come forward to kiss the Queen's hand.*)

BACON: She is magnificent.

CECIL: Before it goes out, the candle always flares.

BACON: Has she spoken of the succession?

CECIL: *Video et taceo*. Her motto. I see but say nothing.

(*The Queen goes out.*)

BACON: She must have an heir.

CECIL: *We* must have an heir, Francis. He is prepared.

BACON: You have written to Scotland?

CECIL: The horsemen are ready. On her last breath they will ride.

BACON: We shall have to hold our breath, cousin.

41

Interior, the gallery. Night.

Then the other rooms. Candles low. Torches low. The guards moving about impatiently. As we see and move along the corridor and into the empty state rooms, we hear whisperings as of many past voices. As we see the empty throne, we hear the sound of a flock of starlings. Then the whispering. In the corridor, a lady-in-waiting runs towards us shaking her head, clutching her hands. We go past her.

42

Interior, the Queen's bedroom. Night.

Dark candle lit. The Queen sitting in a low chair. Cecil, Egerton, servants.

ELIZABETH: No doctors. I wish to die in peace.

(Cecil leans towards her. She stares.)

I am not well.

CECIL: Your Majesty, to content the people, you must go to bed.

ELIZABETH: Little man. The word *must* is not used to princes. I will stand. Help me.

(They get her to stand. She sways on her feet, then gains control.)

All the fabric of my reign, little by little is beginning to fall.

(Someone hands her the sword. She grips it to her. Reaches her full height.)

—None loved you better. *(To Cecil.)* Leave us, my little snail.

43

Interior, Queen's bedroom. Day.

The Queen is standing with her back to the door. We see Raleigh approaching on tip toe. He signals to Cecil who moves over. Low voices. Cecil dashes past him. Raleigh turns. We see him walk down the corridor. Shakes his head.

44

Interior, presence chamber. Day.

Raleigh pushes open the door of the presence chamber with his foot. Stands at the doorway. We see Raleigh's face. We see him turn his face to look down the corridor.

45

Interior, Queen's bedroom. Day.

We see the Queen still standing.

46

Interior, gallery. Day.

RALEIGH: Hm. Imagination, death. It is all the same.

(*Musicians approach. Passing Raleigh.*)

A wake, my boys? You come too soon.

(*Musicians look surprised.*)

Yes. (*That figures, etc.*) She always liked the music more than the mass.

47

Interior, stabling. Day.

Horseman attending to his horse's girth. He turns.

CECIL: I told you. Speak to no one.

535

HORSEMAN: Is she dead?

CECIL: No.

HORSEMAN: What keeps her so long?

CECIL: Keep your voice down.

HORSEMAN: She's hardly likely to recover now, is she?

CECIL: While she lives, you can be sure of nothing. She's been standing fourteen hours.

(*Cecil walks off. The horseman watches.*)

48

Interior, Queen's bedroom. Night.

We see ladies-in-waiting wilting beside the Queen, still standing. One collapses and is carried out.

ELIZABETH: I am tied. I am tied, and the case is altered with me.

49

Interior, bedchamber. Night.

The musicians are playing. The Queen is sitting. Everybody has their eyes on her. She taps her lips to the music. Her fingers stop. Egerton goes forward to take her wrist. Her eyes open. Stares at him.

ELIZABETH: Not so fast, my Lord. How long is it now?

EGERTON: Four days, your Majesty.

ELIZABETH: I take good time. (*Pause.*) Do the people love me?

EGERTON: Yes, your Majesty.

ELIZABETH: They have been good company.

(*Cecil approaches.*)

CECIL: Your Majesty. The succession.

(*Music stops (or earlier). The Queen closes her eyes, leans back.*)

If it tires you to speak. Will you give a sign? Is it—to be the King of Scotland?

(*Raises her hand. Slight, very slight, shake of the head. Contradicting. They look at each other. The Queen shudders and dies. Egerton takes her finger from her mouth and places her hand on her lap. Cecil and others kneel. One by one they stare into her face. Slip away. We see them moving fast down the corridor, one or two looking back. Raleigh stands in the corridor biting his nails. When they are gone, he looks down the corridor. We see the Queen in her chair. Cecil moves nervously to take the sword still clasped in the dead Queen's hand. He wrenches it from her. Lays it on the table.*)